PILLAR OF FIRE
DUNKIRK 1940

RONALD ATKIN

Birlinn

This edition published in 2000 by
Birlinn Limited
8 Canongate Venture
5 New Street
Edinburgh
EH8 8BH

www.birlinn.co.uk

First published in Great Britain in 1990 by
Sidgwick & Jackson Limited, London

ISBN 1 84158 078 3

British Library Cataloguing-in-Publication Data
A catalogue record for this book is available
from the British Library

Printed and bound by
Creative Print and Design, Ebbw Vale

And the Lord went before them by day in a pillar
of cloud to lead them the way; and by night in
a pillar of fire, to give them light.

Exodus, Chapter 13, verse 21.

Acknowledgements

With grateful thanks to Roderick Suddaby, Keeper of the Department of Documents at the Imperial War Museum, and his deputy, Phil Reed; Mme Jacqueline Tréca of the Dunkirk Chamber of Commerce; the Sally Line ferry company; and all those who served at Dunkirk in 1940 and were so helpful in the preparation of this book.

Contents

The German drive to the sea

Foreword to the Birlinn Edition

Only ten months after the Second World War begun, the armed forces of Nazi Germany were close to winning the conflict, with the BEF driven back to the very sands of the Channel. The averting of that catastrophe became known as 'the miracle of Dunkirk'.

In June 2000 the Little Ships set off for Dunkirk again. Sixty years on from the Dunkirk evacuation, the remaining vessels of that motley flotilla, which achieved a miracle by helping to lift the bulk of the British Expeditionary Force to safety in 1940, were paying a final, moving tribute on the anniversary of one of the Second World War's seminal incidents. Aboard the ships were survivors of those terrifying days, members of the Dunkirk Veterans' Association, also paying homage for the last time before the DVA was officially disbanded at the end of the month because of dwindling numbers.

Ronald Atkin
August 2000

1

The Routed Heroes

How the British savour their disasters!

John Terraine

The British Expeditionary Force came home from Dunkirk exhausted, defeated and, to their utter astonishment, heroes. As its routed army straggled on to the quays of Kent's Channel ports at the end of May and beginning of June 1940 the British government hastily concocted stories of pomp and patriotism, larded with propaganda and occasionally plain lies, to cushion the public against the shock of disaster.

The war leaders need not have bothered. The soldiers were welcomed, hugged and cossetted as if *they* had won the battle or, at worst, returned bearing some major sporting trophy. Much of it, of course, was an outpouring of relief at miraculous deliverance from Dunkirk's beaches, a deliverance following swiftly on the long-suppressed news that the Allies had been overwhelmed by German armour, air power and infantry in northern France; plus the sober realization that every man who got back would be available to bear arms for the imminent defence of the island and further prosecution of the war. As the *East Kent Times* put it: 'Each man another potential nail in the coffin of the Beast.'

Brian Horrocks, then a brigadier (and later to become a general, a knight and a TV personality), sailed apprehensively into Ramsgate aboard a small Dutch cargo boat. 'I wasn't looking forward to our arrival,' he admitted. 'We couldn't be said to have covered ourselves with glory in our first encounter with the Germans. So I was astonished to see the waving, cheering crowds. . . . We might have been the heroes of some great victory instead of a beaten army returning home having lost most of its equipment.'

Amazement was the common reaction among the survivors of

1

Flanders and Dunkirk. 'If anybody had even smiled at us when we got home we would have called that a raging welcome,' recalled George Griffin of the Welsh Guards. 'Yet there were voluntary workers, mugs of tea as you moved along, cakes, cigarettes. We were offered every help.' Major John Matthew of the Royal Army Service Corps was 'more moved than I can say by the reception and I had my work cut out not to break down completely'. Others did find the occasion too much for the holding back of tears. When the destroyer *Winchelsea* brought Laurie Whitmarsh of the Royal Artillery into Dover he and his companions knelt and kissed the dockside. 'And we cried, I'll tell you.'

Tom Bristow of Burton remembers being overwhelmed by the welcome from, of all people, the military police. 'I had always understood they were born sadists whose parents had not been married. It was a complete lie; the compassion with which they shepherded the troops to the waiting trains was kindness itself.' As he waited to come ashore at Ramsgate Captain Alan Gilbert of the Intelligence Corps 'felt ashamed to be in the BEF. I was certain the impression was that we had run away.' On landing, Gilbert found things were not as bad as he had feared. He was handed an orange, some sandwiches and a mug of tea.

Things were also not quite as bad as had been feared when, on 28 May, Major General Frank Mason-Macfarlane, the BEF's flamboyant Director of Military Intelligence, called a press conference at the Berkeley Hotel in London and told war correspondents off the record: 'I am afraid there is going to be a considerable shock for the British public. It is your duty to act as shock absorbers.' After warning the reporters, many of whom had only recently returned from France, that the chance of extricating any of the BEF was remote, Mason-Macfarlane added, 'This is no time for mincing matters.' True, but it was not yet time for owning up, either. The stories that came out of that momentous press conference were heavily censored, and indeed the following day's *London Evening News* carried the ultimate double-speak item on the state of the war: 'Authoritative circles in Paris stated this afternoon that the situation on the Northern front was not clear.' Yet Dynamo, the operation to rescue the BEF from Dunkirk, was by then in its third day and thousands of troops had already been brought home.

Two days later, 31 May, the story of the evacuation was officially released. 'Ships Are Coming Home Packed With Troops' announced the *London Evening News*, and the *Daily Express* page one splash read: 'Tired, Dirty, Hungry They Came Back – Unbeatable'. Beneath that stirring headline Hilde Marchant described the BEF's survivors as 'an army that has been shelled and bombed from three sides and had to stagger backward into the sea to survive, an army that has been betrayed but never defeated or dispirited'. Calling the return 'the greatest and most glorious sight I have ever seen', Marchant wrote:

I saw them tramping along a pier, still in formation, still with their rifles. For this army still had a grin on oily, bearded faces. . . . Many tramped off in their stockinged feet. Others were in their shirtsleeves. Many had wounds. Many had torn uniforms and tin hats blasted open like a metal cabbage. They saluted their officers, who stood with ragged mackintoshes and battered caps, and said 'Thank you, sir.' Then they left to sleep.

Hyperbole was rampant as every Fleet Street publication, and many South Coast provincial newspapers, carried an I-saw-them-return yarn. Hilde Marchant again: 'One young lad I saw stagger out of the ship, rather dazed, said "So this is it! So this is England! God bless it!".'

Although, as General Mason-Macfarlane had told the press on 28 May, the need for security about the BEF and Dunkirk was past, newspapers continued to be secretive over details. From an unnamed South Coast port Douglas Williams of the *Daily Telegraph* watched men 'from a famous Guards regiment' disembark: 'They looked clean and smart, many had shaved, some had even found time to polish their boots. They carried their heads high and it was plain that events of the past week had in no way diminished their fighting spirit.'

However, such stirring examples tended to be the exception. Warrant Officer Harold Foster of the Grenadier Guards, who had been forced to swim for it off Dunkirk, removed his saturated uniform aboard the rescuing minesweeper, fell asleep and was shaken awake on arrival at Margate:

Getting dressed I was aware that my feet were in a bad way and it was very painful to walk. My battledress had shrunk and was filthy and I had no boots. Hobbling painfully ashore I called all Guardsmen, no matter what regiment, to form up in three ranks. What a motley collection they were. Some had just a towel over their pants, some a gas cape . . . but all had a weapon of some sort. I marched them off but for the life of me I could not keep up with them because of the state of my feet and it was not long before I was hobbling along on my own.

Many came home wearing items of loaned, and in some cases purloined, naval or seamen's gear, while others made do with clothing picked up on the retreat to Dunkirk. Peter Pring of the 1/6th South Staffordshires landed at Folkestone alongside a soldier kitted out in a French farmer's Sunday-best pinstripe trousers and a sack with holes cut for neck and arms. Lined up at Dover in his damp uniform and suffering from foot and knee injuries, Staff Sergeant Frank Hurrell of the Royal Army Ordnance Corps had a fur coat draped round his shoulders by a woman worried at his condition. At Margate one onlooker took off the shirt he was wearing and handed it to a half-naked French soldier. Another Margate resident sent to the docks a parcel containing his old Army uniform, with a note for the recipient: 'Relic of 1915–18. Good luck, old man.' At Ramsgate a poorly clad small boy delivered a bundle containing his father's spare pair of shoes.

Whenever heavy demand threatened a shortage of refreshments the people and business houses of the ports came to the rescue. Curtain material from a Ramsgate drapery store was cut up to provide facecloths; when cups and mugs ran out, tea was served in jam jars; volunteers toured the streets with wheelbarrows appealing for supplies, and in one case collected a cake made for a wedding due to take place the following week.

Though many, particularly the regular soldiers, had retained their personal arms, most had abandoned or lost belongings and the goods they had looted either during the retreat to Dunkirk or on the beaches. There were those, however, who had clung doggedly to a prized item – a favourite golf club or walking stick, a musical instrument, an engraved shaving kit. Bill Hersey, a private in the 1st East Surreys, brought back his bride, Augusta, the daughter of a French café proprietor, poorly but passably disguised in battledress. Driver Roy Davidge of Taunton carried back from Belgium a cloth doll which he had picked up from the ruins of a bombed toy shop. The doll, a gift for his daughter, was stained with his own blood, reported the *News Chronicle*.

One man came ashore playing a piano accordion; another nursed a dartboard. And, Britain being a nation of animal lovers, there were hundreds who had insisted on departing France with newly acquired pets, usually stray or abandoned dogs. The sudden arrival of these animals in rabies-conscious Britain, with its strict quarantine rules, created what the Royal Society for the Prevention of Cruelty to Animals' chairman, Sir Robert Gower MP, called 'a serious wartime problem'. At Dover alone, 170 dogs were registered on arrival and Sir Robert told the Association's annual general meeting, 'It is certainly a tribute to the humanity of our soldiers that these homeless animals should instinctively turn to our men for protection. However, many were in a distressed condition and a number were wounded and the kindest course in these circumstances was to have them humanely put down, but we were able to arrange for some to be quarantined.'

Despite the vigilance some dogs slipped through. Captain Joe Patterson, a Cumberland GP who detested the Army, found life in the Royal Army Medical Corps more bearable after rescuing a spaniel which he named Splinter and successfully smuggled ashore at Dover wrapped in an army blanket. There were, inevitably, heartbreak tales too. 'I was standing at a gangway when a French soldier came along,' wrote one RSPCA inspector. 'As he stepped ashore another officer and myself heard the whine of a dog. Under his cape we found a small fox terrier. The soldier begged us with tears in his eyes not to take the dog from him, saying "He has been my friend through terrible days." Finally he handed it over and begged me to be merciful.'

In addition to the generally accepted Admiralty statistics of 338,226 soldiers (just over 215,000 British, the remainder French or other Allies)* who got safely to England, various groups and individuals swept up in the chaos of May's events were disgorged along with them. There were thirty Spaniards who had been driven from their homeland by the Civil War and had found apparently safe employment with the French labour corps, various English employees of the War Graves Commission resident in France as caretakers of First World War cemeteries, and nineteen female telephone operators from French Army headquarters in Lille. Before heading off to London to buy a new dress, explaining that, even in wartime, 'appearances do matter' one of them, Mme Madeleine Morel, was full of praise for the BEF's conduct at Dunkirk: 'Ah, la discipline anglaise, que c'est merveilleuse.'

A mixture of shame and grief reduced many of the French military personnel to tears as, often reluctantly, they boarded rescue craft. One soldier was so upset that he committed suicide by leaping overboard from HMS Bideford in mid-Channel wearing greatcoat and full pack. But the wine with which many had filled their water bottles ensured that a good number reached England in jolly mood, and the Sheerness Times recorded how 'the French were subjected to a hot attack from small boys who wanted to get all their foreign coins. The soldiers turned out their pockets and allowed the children to don their helmets for a minute or two. The French were grateful to the women who gave them cigarettes and soon little flirtations and conversations were in full swing.'

*The addition of 27,936 men rescued by 26 May, before the official commencement of Operation Dynamo, lifts the total to 366,162. The War Museum in Dunkirk gives the total as 342,618 (215,587 British and 127,031 French).

The arrangements to receive the survivors were in the hands, both professional and amateur, of an army of welcomers. 'From the moment we stepped ashore at Ramsgate we were cared for with wonderful organization,' said Bill Brodie, a sergeant in the Royal Corps of Signals. Sometimes, however, the enthusiasm of the reception became dangerously excessive. Tom Peck, a private in the Royal Norfolks, was carried ashore at Dover suffering from a chest wound. 'Most of us came off on stretchers because not only were we wounded but we were physically knackered as well. First thing they did was stick a cigarette in my gob. Any catastrophe, it's a mug of tea and a cigarette. As soon as I started to smoke, I was coughing and spluttering. A nurse took it away.'

Corporal John Hammond of the 6th Lancashire Fusiliers was another stretcher case at Dover: 'Two chaps, Local Defence Volunteers I think, picked me up and carried me to a hospital train, which prompted an industrial dispute about them doing railwaymen's work. I was very definitely back in England.'

Bill Brodie, the Signals sergeant, headed for dockside treatment with a pal, Gerry Fisher:

Gerry had an alarming-looking infection round his mouth, probably some form of herpes caused by the trauma of the occasion. I was wearing only one boot and my foot was giving me considerable pain. We were directed to a Medical Aid Post on the quayside and, holding on to Gerry's shoulder, I hobbled through the door. A doctor wearing a once-white apron now covered in bloodstains looked up as we entered and a smile lit up his face. 'Sister,' he exclaimed, 'ring the Ministry – foot and mouth disease.' It was probably the only joke he had made that day.

The task of getting the BEF back to barracks and camps inland was organized smoothly and efficiently by the four major railway companies – Southern; Great Western; London, Midland and Scottish; and London North-Eastern. For the duration of Operation Dynamo (27 May to 4 June) a total of 186 trains were earmarked for the ports of disembarkation – 55 from Southern, 47 from the LNER, 44 from LMS and 40 from Great Western. In those nine days they made 565 journeys, and in one period of forty-eight hours alone more than two hundred crowded trains pulled away from the Channel ports. Nowhere were the railways' organizational skills more stretched than at Folkestone on Sunday 2 June, a day when some 3,000 of the town's children were also being evacuated by train to Wales. If there had been a demarcation dispute about whose job it was to load John Hammond's stretcher onto a hospital train there was never any question of working to rule among the train and station personnel at a time of national emergency. Nor was there, again, any shortage of volunteers to assist. The platform of Kentish wayside halts such as Headcorn and Paddock Wood became makeshift buffets, serving round the clock. Under the headline, 'Village Feeding An Army', a *Times* reporter described a typical scene:

Day and night for a week now this little station has been as busy as a main line terminus. Trainload upon trainload have been given food, tea and cigarettes and a rousing greeting. . . . Separated by a field from the station is a large barn. Inside this barn between 30 and 40 women of the village, working in relays, have been cutting sandwiches. One woman said she had cut so many she never wanted to eat again. Yesterday there was to have been a cricket match in the village but it was postponed and the teams were brought along to the barn to lend a hand. . . . Everything is counted in thousands at this station. Thousands of hard-boiled eggs were eaten yesterday. Last night 5000 hot pies were delivered; 5000 hot sausages . . . tired though they are, the troops wake up when their trains pull up and their comments and reactions after some hot tea and food are convincing proof of their good heart.

'Food, fruit and chocolates were showered upon us,' recalled the Royal Army Medical Corps colonel, John McDonald. 'Women waved and cheered all along the line, bless their hearts. It was perhaps the most soul-stirring sight I have ever witnessed.' Blank telegram forms and ready-written postcards containing the message 'Am Safe' and requiring only the address of next-of-kin were issued and collected at the next halt up the line. When the postcards ran out, railway luggage labels were used.

Then there were the flags. Joe Catt, a signaller with the Royal Sussex Regiment, said, 'All the way up to London there were Union Jacks hanging out of the windows, people cheering. You would never think we had just had our backsides kicked. It really was remarkable. At every window and every door there was somebody waving. And we did look a bunch of scarecrows, too.'

Sheet and banners bearing messages like 'Well Done BEF' hung from walls and embankments or were scrawled on bridges, and the soldiers responded by chalking slogans on their carriages: 'Back to Blighty – but not for long' and 'Look out Hitler, we haven't started on you yet.'

But it was the quiet moments that one Green Howards officer remembered best: 'With the suddenness of turning over a page life was normal once more and utterly peaceful – that was the greatest difference.' The most vivid memory of his train journey for Tom

Collins of the Royal Artillery was of one of those in his compartment –
all strangers to each other – calling for a minute's silence for comrades
left behind in France.

The French troops continued to carry their popularity up the line.
When asked to pay for refreshments at a London suburban station
they could offer only their own currency, but waiting passengers came
to the rescue. One man 'opened his weekly wage packet and cheerfully parted with eight shillings', reported the *London Evening News*
under the headline 'What's Yours, *Poilu*?'

For those wounded considered well enough to withstand them, the
train journeys were not so carefree. Irene Phillips of the Women's
Voluntary Service called the conditions 'a nightmare', adding,

It was terribly hot and the coaches were stifling . . . how the men survived
the long journey I do not know. It was even worse for those who were
lying on the bottom layer of racks as they had the misfortune to have two
stretchers over them, so no air could circulate to them at all. The lovely
crisp white caps of the nurses began to wilt long before the journey started.

The consequences of such travel were witnessed by June Cole, a Red
Cross worker at Tring in Hertfordshire, who assisted the wounded off
the trains and into Green Line coaches converted into makeshift
ambulances by stripping out their seats to make room for stretchers.
'The heat, added to the sweat and dust of France, made their faces
look like masks. Several died *en route* to the hospital and many were
hysterical.'

Those who were able to leave the trains unaided were sometimes in
only marginally better shape. Sapper Jack Toomey and his colleagues
of the 42nd Division Postal Unit got off their train at Reading: 'It was
about 8 a.m. and people just going to work stopped and stared. We
must have looked a mob, none of us shaved or washed for a week, our
uniforms ripped and torn, with blood and oil stains . . . one or two old
dears took one look at us and burst into tears. I don't blame them – I
frightened myself when I looked into a mirror.' The postal unit
gratefully accepted a bus ride to barracks, where breakfast was offered
with the apology that it was nothing better than tinned salmon and
mashed potatoes. Commented Toomey, 'We, who had been on half or
no rations for three weeks, were too busy eating.' At Warwick the
Welsh Guards got off with other units, which accepted lorry transport. 'But not the Guards, oh no,' said Sergeant George Griffin. 'We
had to march to camp to show the discipline expected of us. We could
have done without that at the time, but in retrospect it was the thing to
do.'

The most senior-ranking survivor, the BEF's Commander-in-Chief, General Lord Gort, arrived at Dover by motor torpedo boat early on 1 June. Gort had insisted on staying with his embattled army until he was personally ordered home by the Prime Minister, Winston Churchill, lest his capture provide the Germans with a propaganda coup. Before leaving for London and an audience with King George VI, at which he was invested with the GCB, the Knight Grand Cross of the Order of the Bath, a downcast Gort reacted irritably when told that everyone would be glad to hear of his safe return. 'It is not the arrival of myself that matters,' he answered, 'it is the arrival of my army.'

After Lieutenant General Alan Brooke, commander of the BEF's 2nd Corps, had called in at the War Office on his return he set off, exhausted by the strain of the previous three weeks, for his home in Hartley Wintney, Hampshire, but was so afraid of falling asleep and overshooting his station that he walked up and down the compartment to keep awake. Once home, Brooke enjoyed a nursery tea with the two young children of his second marriage, 'after which I retired to bed and to one of the very deepest sleeps I have ever had'.

The naval rescuers were just as weary by the end of Operation Dynamo. Commander Greville Worthington, the officer in charge of unloading at Dover, nodded off over breakfast and woke up with his beard in the eggs and bacon, while a charge of drunken driving against Lieutenant Commander Cyril Williams was dismissed because of evidence that he was suffering more from exhaustion than alcohol. After driving his car across the pavement and into some railings at Ramsgate, Williams was found fast asleep at the wheel.

The genteel South Coast resort of Bournemouth was swamped by thousands of French soldiers sent there for rest and reorganization before returning to their homeland to prosecute the war in the as-yet unoccupied areas of France. The first trainloads arrived on 1 June and the *Bournemouth Times* was there:

The men were obviously tired but that did not deter them from exchanging jokes and giving the thumbs-up sign to people lining the streets. Intermingled with them were many sons of France's vast African empire, including dusky, turbanned warriors from Morocco and cheery, grinning Singalese [*sic*]. One local resident said he had not seen so many smiling faces in the town for years.

Hundreds were taken into private homes or out into town for that English speciality, Sunday tea. One café waitress estimated that at least half her customers that day were accompanied by French soldiers. Two and a half thousand were accommodated at the Bourne-mouth School for Boys, where teachers and pupils had set up beds in classrooms hung with tricolours and *'Vive la France'* banners. Bourne-mouth's bookshops were stripped of French dictionaries, and appeals for clothing and soap met an overwhelming response. Masses of volunteers flocked to the French billets with clothing and bedding. One girl got home to find a note from her mother: 'Shall be a bit late. Down at the church hall washing French feet.'

British or French, soldier or sailor, it made no difference to the warmth of the welcome that sunny June in 1940. Driver Tom Bristow of the RASC was inundated with free drinks in a Coventry pub, and at closing time the contents of a Forces Fund collecting box were emptied into the top pocket of his tunic. In Bristol an elderly woman stood in Corn Street handing out ten shilling notes to every passing BEF soldier. When Commander Thomas Kerr, a naval beachmaster at Dunkirk, arrived at London's Victoria Station still wearing the steel helmet, haversack, revolver and bedroom slippers in which he had done his work of organizing the lifting of troops from the shore, there were cries from the waiting crowds of 'Good old Navy!' A woman planted a kiss on Kerr's cheek and a man led him to a taxi, rode with him to the Admiralty and insisted on paying the fare.

The heroes of the fight to come, the Battle of Britain, were not so popular then, at least with the returning troops who had suffered incessant air attack in France and blamed the RAF's lack of cover for that suffering. When the troop train carrying Captain Joe Patterson of the RAMC and his smuggled dog Splinter moved slowly past another train full of RAF personnel the soldiers hurled abuse at the boys in blue, yelling: 'Where have you been?' The airmen, not understanding, cheered back.

Many Army heads were turned by the enthusiasm of the welcome home, and there was soon a ready market for unofficial BEF shoulder flashes in the rehabilitation camps. At his barracks in Devizes Alfred Baldwin noted: 'Some enterprising Herbert was making and selling the flashes as souvenirs and there were plenty of people buying them.' Major General Bernard Montgomery, whose 3rd Division had performed particularly efficiently in France, was irritated by the appearance of the unauthorized insignia. In ordering them banned, Montgomery stressed that Dunkirk had been a humiliating reverse which placed Britain in danger of defeat and occupation. Winston Churchill was quick to make the point, too. Announcing the BEF's safe return to the House of Commons on 4 June he said, 'We must be very careful not to assign to this deliverance the attributes of a victory. Wars are not won by evacuations.'

Obviously Churchill shared the nation's joy at the rescue of what he called 'the spinal column' of the British Army, and later termed it 'a milestone in our pilgrimage through years of defeat'. That speech on 4 June closed with his best-remembered rallying cry of the war:

Even though large tracts of Europe and many old and famous States have fallen or may fall into the grip of the Gestapo and all the odious apparatus of Nazi rule, we shall not flag or fail. We shall go on to the end . . . we shall fight in the seas and oceans, we shall fight with growing confidence and growing strength in the air; we shall defend our Island, whatever the cost may be. We shall fight on the beaches, we shall fight on the landing-grounds, we shall fight in the fields and in the streets, we shall fight in the hills; we shall never surrender.

When Ed Murrow of the Columbia Broadcasting System persuaded the Prime Minister to repeat that speech from Broadcasting House in London for the benefit of American listeners, Churchill obliged, then clapped his hand over the live microphone before telling Murrow, 'And if they do come we shall hit them on the head with beer bottles, for that is all we shall have to fight them with.'

Most people embraced the outlook of the *Evening News* editorial, which told the people of London: 'Never has any generation of Britons lived in days as great as these, in days when the dangers were more threatening and the glories to be achieved more splendid. These are times of terrible grandeur. The curtain has gone up on the most majestic and the most enthralling drama ever unfolded on the human stage; and as yet we have seen only the prologue.'

There was a rush, of women as well as men, to volunteer for the defence of the country – and a distinct hardening of attitude towards Germany. The few prisoners whom the army had succeeded in bringing back were reviled and threatened. Able Seaman Ray Cole saw a small boat pull alongside at Ramsgate with many British dead and wounded on the upper deck following air attack. Cole asked why they hadn't taken shelter below and was told that German prisoners had been locked up there. When these prisoners were led ashore they had to be protected from angry soldiers by an officer with a drawn revolver. 'I think they would have been pushed in the sea if the troops had had their own way,' Cole recalled. As the Germans made their way out of the dock area they were attacked again, this time by women wielding brooms and shovels. Les Boyce, a driver in the RASC, was aboard a hospital train which had to make a special stop to unload a captured German. 'There were some Guards in our carriage,' said Boyce, 'and they had threatened to throw him through the window.'

In Germany on 5 June Hitler officially proclaimed victory in 'the greatest battle of all time', and ordered the flying of flags for eight days and the ringing of church bells for three. However William Shirer, Berlin correspondent for the Columbia Broadcasting System, reported,

There is no real elation over the victory discernible in the people here, no emotion of any kind. . . . Despite the lack of popular enthusiasm for this colossal victory quite a few Germans are beginning to feel that the deprivations which Hitler has forced on them for five years have not been without reason. Said my room-waiter this morning 'Perhaps the English and French now wish they had less butter and more cannon.'

Perhaps, but in Britain there was somehow satisfaction, a strange elation even, that we were now alone. It started at the very top. The King wrote to his mother, 'Personally, I feel happier now that we have no allies to be polite to and to pamper.' Major General Sir Hastings Ismay, Churchill's military adviser, recalled how he had shared His Majesty's pleasure: 'So far from being alarmed we were relieved, nay exhilarated. Henceforward everything would be simpler. We were masters of our own fate.' Air Chief Marshal Sir Hugh Dowding, Chief of Fighter Command, told the Foreign Secretary, Lord Halifax, 'Thank God we're now alone', and the thriller writer Margery Allingham noted 'genuine satisfaction at getting the boys back in the country and taking the job on ourselves'. And the historian Peter Fleming recorded: 'The British, when their last ally was poleaxed on their doorstep, became both gayer and more serene.'

2

The Day War Broke Out . . .

'If we lose this war then God have mercy upon us.'

Hermann Göring

Like most of the people whose lives were to be changed for ever by Dunkirk, Shaun Slinn remembered exactly what he was doing when Neville Chamberlain quaveringly informed the world on Sunday, 3 September 1939 that Britain was at war with Germany. Slinn, a private in the East Surrey Regiment, was undergoing six months' training at Kingston Barracks. On that Sunday morning, he recalled, 'I was sitting quietly in the NAAFI, reading some of Siegfried Sassoon's war poems, a pint to hand, when the Chamberlain man said we were at war. He seemed upset about it, as well he might have been. I said to a companion that our six-month stint was likely to go on a bit longer: it did, by seven years.'

Harry Dennis, also with the East Surreys, was peeved to have his call-up papers delivered on 1 September while he was putting up shelving in the new house he and his wife had just moved into at Ashford, Middlesex. Ordered to report to Kingston by midnight, Dennis set off to join some pals for a farewell drink. 'I got pissed at a pub called the Airmen in Hanworth and ended up on Feltham station being helped aboard a train with half a bottle of whisky to keep me company on the ride to Kingston.' The following morning a forage cap was provided for Dennis's aching head and he picked up the rest of his uniform; a day later, while Chamberlain addressed the nation, Private Harry Dennis was marching through Kingston *en route* to Colchester and a job as a colonel's chauffeur.

Don Ellingworth, who had joined the Army in 1938 to train as a despatch rider, 'thinking it was a glamorous job', was posted to the 1st Guards Brigade.

That Sunday, just before eleven, all D/Rs were called into Command HQ at Aldershot and handed mobilization letters to deliver. Riding out in Aldershot it was a very strange feeling because the people were shouting and waving, something they'd never done before. A lot of the citizens of Aldershot regarded the Army presence as a bit of a canker. If they could deride us they did. Before the war the Army was not much thought of but after eleven o'clock on the third of September 1939 the Army was something wonderful.

Colonel Palmer Cook, who had fought in the First World War, crowded with his officers of a Territorial Royal Engineers field company into a cookhouse at Rowley Regis, just outside Birmingham, where a fatigue party were peeling potatoes while listening to the radio. No. 1 Company of the Royal Corps of Signals was drawn up on parade in summer camp at Scarborough to hear its colonel announce the news. 'After the first shock some started cheering,' said Lawrence Vollans. 'Then the band struck up the national anthem and we all joined in.'

Alfred Baldwin's most vivid memory was of the riotous afternoon in the NAAFI at Bulford, where the 1st Royal Horse Artillery were in camp. 'The beer flowed and there were songs. People were very excited. There was a great upsurge of patriotic feeling, probably the same as the Falklands. It was a great big game.' Joe Catt forever associated the historic broadcast with the anxious discussion his family were having at home in Hastings about the heart attack his mother had suffered earlier that morning. When Chamberlain, previously always so polite in his references to, and dealings with, Hitler dropped the prefix 'Herr', Lieutenant Gregory Blaxland of the Royal East Kent Regiment felt 'this did more to bring home the reality of the situation than anything he said'. To Anthony Eden, soon to be Secretary of State for War, the speech sounded more like the lament of a man deploring his own failure than the call of a nation to arms.

Only minutes after Britain officially went to war, the air raid sirens wailed. Not knowing what else to do, Lance Corporal Alf Hewitt affixed bayonet to rifle as he stood on guard at the gates of his regiment's barracks in Dover. A bunch of MPs, drawn by herd instinct to the House of Commons, gathered on the terrace listening for danger until Edward Spears, a war-wise major general and Tory member for Carlisle, told them if there was a bomb aimed at them they would not hear it. 'My audience thinned out noticeably after this,' said Spears. At their London home Mrs Churchill heard the sirens and commented favourably on German punctuality and precision. Her husband, pausing only to collect a bottle of brandy 'and other appropriate medical comforts', escorted her to a shelter.

The warning was a false alarm, triggered by the approach of an aircraft carrying a French military attaché from Paris. Two of the fighters scrambled to engage the 'enemy' collided over London, and one of the pilots was killed. He was the first British casualty of a war scarcely half an hour old.

A public opinion survey published in Britain on 2 September showed that only 2 per cent of those canvassed had said they would be glad to go to war. Half were resigned to the inevitable, while 34 per cent felt anything was better than war.

The reaction in Germany, whose leaders had provoked the conflict, was similarly low-key. The CBS Berlin correspondent, William Shirer, was in the Wilhelmplatz when a loudspeaker announced the news: 'Some 250 people were standing there in the sun. They listened attentively to the announcement. When it finished, there was not a murmur. They just stood there as they were before. Stunned. The people cannot realize yet that Hitler has led them into a world war. . . . I walked in the streets. On the faces of the people astonishment, depression.' Shirer then made his way to the Hotel Adlon with other foreign correspondents for drinks with some of the British Embassy staff 'who seemed completely unmoved by events. They talked about *dogs* and such stuff.' The Nazi leaders were as stunned as their subjects. Hitler is reported to have 'sat immobile, gazing before him' while his portly acolyte, Hermann Göring, blurted: 'If we lose this war, then God have mercy upon us.'

Public reaction in France was much the same as that in Britain and Germany. After listening to Chamberlain's speech on the BBC ('I broke down and wept') Henry Greenwall, journalist, author and long-time resident in France, drove from his Chantilly home to Paris:

I clung to the thought that some eleventh-hour miracle might emerge from the fact that France was not yet at war. . . . Paris railway stations were still full of men called up and going away, and women standing about crying. On the streets people stood looking up at the empty blue sky. There was a crowd outside the Foreign Office on the Quai d'Orsay. Four hours had passed since Britain went to war, and France had said no word. I went and had a drink; several drinks. At 5.30 I heard the news. For half an hour France had been at war. The streets were dull now. People came back from the races at Longchamp, bought the papers and sat down on the still sunny café terraces and read the news. There was no excitement.

3

The Cardboard Army

I have a hunch that the war will be over before the spring.

Neville Chamberlain

The BEF was sent off to war with the assurance that it was 'as well, if not better, equipped than any similar army'. That assurance, given to the House of Commons by the Secretary of State for War, Leslie Hore-Belisha, was at best wishful thinking and at worst wilful deceit. Major General Bernard Montgomery read Hore-Belisha's comments with astonishment. 'In September 1939 the British Army was totally unfit to fight a first-class war on the continent of Europe. We sent our Army into that most modern war with weapons and equipment which were quite inadequate and we had only ourselves to blame for the disaster which overtook us in 1940.'

Lieutenant General Alan Brooke was even more scathing: Britain's Army was far less ready for a continental war than in 1914, he felt. Its artillery had little more than half the range of the German guns, it was without any but the lightest armour, and pre-war training had to be undertaken with flags and dummies instead of batteries and tanks. In the Southern Command manoeuvres of 1939 most of the Bren gun-carriers (low, open-topped, tracked vehicles designed for rapid move-ment across country) bore an inscription on their sides: 'Not to be used in action. Mild steel only.' On other manoeuvres in that summer of 1939, witnessed by an incredulous German military attaché, infantry-men carried lengths of gas piping stuck into pieces of wood to represent anti-tank rifles and blue flags denoting the lorries in which they were supposed to be riding. Ronnie Noble, a cameraman with Universal News, watched one exercise involving a river crossing. 'They were using collapsible boats. The troops ran up to the water, opened up the boats, got in and they all sank. And this was the stuff we were going to tackle the Germans with.'

Things were so bad that Lieutenant Richard Camrass of the West Yorkshire Regiment went to war wearing a glossy new revolver holster stuffed with paper because he had not yet been issued with a weapon. In the opinion of Second Lieutenant Toby Taylor of the East Surrey Regiment, 'The British Army was geared, if anything, for small colonial wars and imperial policing, but the idea of actually going to war in Europe was never mentioned when I was a young subaltern.'

New equipment like the 25-pounder guns and the Bren light machine gun (named for its Czech place of origin, Brno, and place of manufacture, Enfield) was in steady supply by the outbreak of war, but many divisions were so short of transport that lorries and vans belonging to removal companies, coalmen, butchers and bakers were commandeered. Montgomery complained that, when his 3rd Division crossed the Channel, 'the countryside of France was strewn with broken-down vehicles'.

The uniforms were, according to one BEF officer, 'the old khaki service dress that had been in use, with little alteration, since soon after the start of the Boer War'. Even such antiquated dress was not always readily available. Les Cannon joined the Royal Artillery in April 1939 but had to do without a uniform until the end of July.

Such embarrassments did not deter would-be soldiers from flocking to the colours. Derek Ramsdale felt it was wrong to be conscripted to do something he believed was his duty. So on the morning of his nineteenth birthday he set off for the local recruiting office in Hull, where there were so many anxious to sign up that they were sworn in ten at a time, with the Bible being passed around. Les Boyce, a Norfolk farmer's son keen to get away from a broken marriage and into the war, drove his milk float to the local station, caught the train to Norwich and sent his family a telegram saying he was off to be a soldier. At his medical it was pointed out that he was in a reserved occupation, but when Boyce insisted he wanted to enlist the doctor crossed out the word 'farmer' on the enrolment form and substituted 'independent means'.

Tom Willy joined the Territorial Army as a despatch rider because he loved motorcycles. Tom Peck saw a recruiting poster and decided the Army looked better than his hated job as a tunneller on the London Underground. Alf Hewitt, also a Londoner, joined the 1st Battalion South Lancashire Regiment because he had a girlfriend in Dover which was where the battalion was stationed (by the time Hewitt finished recruit training in Warrington and was posted to Dover the romance had collapsed). Joe Catt signed up for the Territorials because the £4 annual bounty, paid every December, bought his Christmas presents and the two-week camp gave him a break from a demanding employer at the greengrocer's shop where he worked in Hastings.

On 1 September Frank Southall reported to his Birmingham Territorial drill hall, where he was told to go home, get into uniform and pack. Having heard nothing by the next morning he went shopping with his wife. On their return there was a registered letter ordering him to report for duty immediately. 'I had to go by bus and even paid my own fare. It was a good job it was Saturday – any other day I might not have had the cash.'

Albert Gaskin, a bugler with the King's Shropshire Light Infantry, was swift to suffer one of the Army's early morale-crushers, the military haircut. 'We looked like convicts. When I asked one of our officers why our hair had to be mutilated like that he replied that during the Great War the medics had difficulty treating shrapnel head wounds because of the hair – but we noted that officers, warrant officers and certain NCOs managed to escape.'

Hair shorn and, in some cases, their conviction that they were doing the right thing already undermined, the recruits frequently suffered another Army speciality – the driving of square pegs into round holes. Len Wilson, a butcher from Stoke, was put into the Royal Army Medical Corps and told, 'Well, at least you'll know about anatomy.' Alfred Baldwin requested training as a driver and was posted instead to a horse unit, the Royal Horse Artillery. There he took a written test to become a signaller: 'It was like a school examination. The super brains became specialists, the not-so-dumb became signallers, the next in line were made drivers and the dunderheads, for some unknown reason, became gunners.' When Laurie Whitmarsh applied for ordnance he was put into the Royal Artillery. 'We had to take a gunnery examination. I came out in the top three. The sergeant instructor said one of us would have to be a driver and the other two gunners. We spun for it and I was the odd one out so I was told "Right, you'll be a driver." I had never driven in my life.'

Alfred Baldwin, the signaller, spent the last summer of peace training for his new job at a holiday camp in Rhyl. 'It was ideal: we had a contingent of fifty ATS girls to run the camp for us and absolutely no equipment. I spent most of the time teaching people to swim, which was as good an introduction to the war as one could want.' When Baldwin joined the 65th Field Regiment only two of the thirteen men in his troop were issued with rifles. No wonder he went to France with the firm opinion that 'we were very poorly trained and extremely badly armed'.

The general nominated to command the BEF was John Standish Surtees Prendergast Vereker, the 6th Viscount Gort. It was a surprise appointment, even to Gort, who first learned of it by reading a newspaper. He had not displayed noticeable genius as a leader, but had reached the top with some speed. In November 1937, at the early age of fifty-one, he was appointed Britain's top soldier, Chief of the Imperial General Staff, by the War Minister, Hore-Belisha, who saw mileage in Gort's heroic record (he had won the VC, MC and DSO with two bars in the First World War). At the War Cabinet's first meeting on 3 September Hore-Belisha secured Gort's installation as C-in-C of the BEF and replaced him as CIGS with Sir Edmund Ironside, the Army's senior general, who was bitterly upset not to be leading the BEF to France. Gort, who had not expected the job, was thrilled. 'He was simply beaming and kept saying "Isn't it *grand* to be going to the war"', according to one War Office official.

There were others in addition to Ironside who were miffed by the appointment. Gort's immediate subordinates as commanders of the BEF's two corps, Lieutenant General Sir John Dill and Lieutenant General Brooke, had both been senior to Gort until Hore-Belisha began to push him. They were also older: Dill was fifty-eight and Brooke fifty-six. Brooke described his chief as possessing 'one of those cheerful dispositions, full of vitality, energy and joie de vivre and the most wonderful charm. . . . But I had no confidence in his leadership when it came to handling a large force.' Montgomery considered Gort's appointment a mistake because 'the job was above his ceiling', while Major General Spears, the Tory MP and Britain's special emissary to the French government, thought Gort 'a simple, straightforward but not very clever man'.

Though the Royal Navy carried advance parties of the BEF across the Channel on 4 September and both 1 Corps and 2 Corps were in France within a month of the outbreak of war, the British contribution was inevitably no more than symbolic. The Allies would have needed to launch an offensive within a week to expose Germany to conflict on two fronts, but that sort of urgency was nowhere apparent as Poland struggled on alone to stem the offensive unleashed against it on 1 September.

The Allies, in fact, had written off Poland. While assuring (and misleading) the Cabinet on 11 September that Poland was putting up a good fight and that its main army was still intact, the CIGS, Ironside, noted in his diary: 'Nothing can save the Poles.' Hitler's threat to 'cook the Allies in a stew they'll choke on' because of their support for Poland had no need of early enforcement as the BEF trundled into

France by roundabout routes to minimize the possibility of attack from air or sea on troopships and transport vessels. The closest ports, such as Calais, Boulogne and Dunkirk, were avoided for this reason. Instead, most of the men were landed in Cherbourg or Le Havre, their vehicles were put ashore through Brest and St Nazaire, and all were assembled at the towns of Laval and Le Mans, hundreds of miles from the frontier of an enemy far too busy with a campaign of conquest to consider disruptive action against the BEF.

Most of the soldiers sailed from Southampton on ferries converted into troop carriers. As Albert Gaskin's vessel nosed out into the Channel he recalled that one of his fellow buglers in the King's Shropshire Light Infantry 'stood at the bows of the ship with his fair hair blowing in the wind and played "Auld Lang Syne"; like me, many were gulping and some weeping'.

Nursing a hangover from the previous night's farewell party, Lieutenant H C F Harwood of the Royal East Kent Regiment, thought the dockside scene a dismal one. 'None of the Noël Coward stuff here. All I saw was the quay glistening sadly in the rain and deserted but for the long line of khaki-clad figures slowly passing up the gangway. It was a grim procession that moved silently towards the open sea on that cheerless, misty evening; in no way similar to my exuberant cross-Channel journeys of previous years.'

As Les Shorrock's 91st Field Regiment of the Royal Artillery boarded each man was handed an apple, a pork pie and a bar of chocolate. Others fared even worse. Robert Holding of the Royal Sussex Regiment was issued tinned rations to eat *en route* 'but cold stew, thickly encased in solidified fat, is not to be recommended on a sea voyage'. Bernard Gray, war correspondent of the *Daily Mirror* and *Sunday Pictorial*, found cabins had been provided for officers and journalists on his ship, as well as decent food for those who could afford to pay for it. 'We ate, and glanced in wonder at a party of army chaplains who will certainly go to heaven if their souls are half as big and well-sustained as their stomachs. They ate prodigiously.'

As Lance Bombardier Eric Manley's artillery regiment docked in Le Havre a Salvation Army officer played 'We'll Meet Again' on his cornet. 'We hope he is right,' he wrote, 'though we are a little unconvinced.' Tom Willy arrived in France to a cheerful scene: 'The lads were all singing "Lambeth Walk" and the locals were throwing fruit up to us. One of the apples hit me right in the eye.' That was not the only blow for this despatch rider on arrival – he found that somebody had stolen the waterproofs strapped to the carrier of his motorcycle. 'So for three weeks, until I could be issued with new ones, I got soaking wet whenever it rained.'

For many, the initial sight of their allies was a depressing one. 'My first shock of the war was seeing a French soldier on guard duty in Cherbourg, rifle leaning against the sentry box, hands deep in pockets, cigarette hanging from his mouth,' said Geoffrey Rothband, a second lieutenant with the Lancashire Fusiliers. The signals sergeant, Bill Brodie, recalled that his group's arrival in Cherbourg 'was watched by a solitary Negro sailor on sentry go who occasionally took a bite from an apple skewered on his bayonet'.

The truth was that there was even less appetite for the new war in France than in Britain – or Germany. Denis Barlone, a lieutenant in command of a horse transport company of the 2nd North African Division, recalled in his diary that the reservists reported 'without the enthusiasm of 1914 . . . and annoyed at not being able to complete the harvest. No one has the least desire to fight for Poland, of which ninety-five Frenchmen out of every hundred are completely ignorant.'

France's reluctance to go to war again was understandable. Her dead in the 1914–18 conflict totalled 1,315,000 or 27 per cent of all men between the ages of eighteen and twenty-seven, compared with British losses of just under a million. At the end of that war the population of France was 39 million, compared to Germany's 59 million. A dozen years later she had still barely made good those casualties, while Germany enjoyed a healthy birth rate. So the French took up arms with no great keenness, and the damage to morale and the war effort was enormous.

After a few days in France General Brooke began to entertain 'most unpleasant apprehensions as to the fighting qualities of the French in this new war', and that opinion was reinforced when he attended a parade in November to mark the anniversary of the 1918 armistice:

Seldom have I seen anything more slovenly and badly turned out. Men unshaven, horses ungroomed, clothes and saddlery that did not fit, vehicles dirty and complete lack of pride in themselves and their units. What shook me most, however, was the look in the men's faces, disgruntled and insubordinate looks, and, although ordered to give 'Eyes left', hardly a man bothered to do so.

Gregory Blaxland, then a twenty-one-year-old platoon commander with the East Kents, considered France's Army 'clumsy, still beladen with much equipment from 1918 . . . and desperately vulnerable to air attack'. Its transport was heavily reliant on an efficient railway system, a system that would prove an early target for Hitler's Luftwaffe. The ability to move columns by road was embarrassingly poor. One reconnaissance group – the first troops to be needed in action – manned entirely by reservists, assembled near Orleans on 27 August but was unable to set off for the German frontier until a week later because it was entirely lacking in clothing. So desperate was the shortage that berets had to be purchased from a department store to ensure uniform headgear. One regiment, the 21st Foreign Volunteers, was equipped with rifles made in 1891 and iron rations date-stamped 1920. When Denis Barlone's transport division moved off he thought it resembled a tribe of gypsies. 'These convoys remind me of the last war – I've been on leave for twenty years.'

Yet for a decade the French Army had been regarded as the world's finest by Britain's politicians and generals, unable to spot the brittle reality beneath the glitter manifested by its officers. 'Thank God for the French Army,' Winston Churchill told the Commons in 1933, two months after Hitler came to power. The German Field Marshal Wilhelm Keitel did not share Churchill's opinion: he considered each division of the BEF the equivalent of three or four French ones as far as fighting merit was concerned.

Gastronomy was the one area where the French commanders excelled without question. Most of the ones whom General Brooke met struck him as excellent company, amusing conversationalists – and thoroughly unreliable. Soon after his arrival in France he noted 'a wasted day as far as work was concerned . . . champagne lunch consisting of oysters, lobsters, chicken, pheasant, cheese and fruit, coffee, liqueurs etc. We sat down at 1 p.m. and got up about 3 p.m.'

All this despite the fact that a French captain was paid the equivalent of about £11 a month and a major £16, compared with £38 and £53 for their British equivalents. As for the ordinary private, the *poilu*, his pay had changed so little since 1918 that it even compared unfavourably with the wretchedly low money paid to his British counterpart. Alexander Werth, the *Manchester Guardian*'s Paris correspondent, noted understandable envy among France's serving personnel that a private's pay was at most 70 francs (about eight shillings) a week while the British collected the equivalent of 200 francs, though the French did receive complimentary cigarettes and rail travel concessions, and their families back home lived rent-free.

One reason why France paid its soldiers so poorly, and also why it lagged fatally in the provision of modern weapons, was that all the money had been spent on the Maginot Line. French military thinking had turned, soon after 1918, to the construction of a massive defence rampart to keep the Germans at bay in any future war. In January 1930 a vast majority in both chambers of France's National Assembly voted to implement long-debated plans for the Great Wall, and work began at once. The project was named after the War Minister at that time, André Maginot, a politician whose enduring popularity had much to do with his record in a war from which he emerged badly crippled and still bearing the rank of sergeant rather than that of a commissioned officer.

The Maginot Line was to run, not from the North Sea to the Mediterranean as forecast in the British press, but only from Basle, just inside the border with Switzerland, to Longwy, where the French, Belgian and Luxembourg frontiers met. Plans to extend the Line along the Belgian border to Dunkirk were never implemented, partly because of the cost of building through the rich industrial areas of northern France but mainly because Belgium, a close and valued ally in 1914, would be abandoned on the wrong side of the fortifications.

Marshal Henri Philippe Pétain, the hero of Verdun and Maginot's successor as Minister of War when Maginot died in 1932 aged fifty-five, dismissed the obvious perils of Germany's invasion route of 1914 over the Belgian plains. He stressed French ability to move swiftly into Belgium in case of German aggression and thus fight the battle on someone else's soil, while he considered the Ardennes forests, at the northern end of the Line, 'impenetrable and therefore not dangerous'.

When Churchill visited the Maginot Line in 1937 its offensive possibilities were explained to him. Winston was unimpressed. He felt the fortifications 'exercised an enervating effect' on France's military strategy and national vigilance, an attitude which became known as the Maginot Mentality. A British officer, Anthony Rhodes, thought the Maginot Line had become, in the eyes of the French, 'a veritable Rock of Ages . . . being the best that money could buy it was believed, American fashion, to be as invincible as it was fabulous'. A French major showing Rhodes round some of the defences told him the Maginot was as valuable to France as the Grand Fleet to Britain. But Rhodes was no more convinced than Churchill had been.

That it stopped short halfway up the frontier should perhaps have given us some cause for suspicion but, encouraged by the constant avowals of the French that they not only wanted, but even invited, an attack to the north of the Line we remained as duped as we were fascinated. Nothing, they cheerily said, could suit them better than a German attack through the Low Countries.

An example of Maginot Mentality was provided by the comment of France's ageing Army chief, General Maurice Gamelin, that 'whoever is the first to leave his shell in this war is going to get badly hurt'. For someone who considered himself an intellectual, Gamelin's comments were often memorable only for their foolishness and arrogance. Towards the end of August 1939 he forecast that Hitler would collapse the day France declared war on Germany. 'Instead of defending the frontiers of the Reich, the German Army will be forced to march on Berlin to suppress the trouble that will immediately break out. . . . We shall go through Germany like a knife through butter.'

In 1939 Gamelin was sixty-seven and on the brink of retirement. A competent divisional commander in the 1914–18 war, he was a small, plump man in high-laced boots much given to clasping his hands in front óf him as if in benediction when he talked. General Edward Spears, the British emissary to the French government, admired Gamelin's self-possessed dignity; others were less complimentary. General Edmund Ironside, Britain's 6 ft 4 in. CIGS, patronized him as 'a small, dapper man with dyed hair and well-cut breeches', and Sir John Slessor, destined to become the Royal Air Force's top officer, felt Gamelin was 'a nice old gentleman, not remotely equal to his enormous job'.

Gamelin sat, without benefit of radio communications and surrounded by a small and sycophantic group of junior officers, in a convent-like atmosphere at his headquarters on the eastern outskirts of Paris, the gloomy château of Vincennes where Henry V of England had died and many of France's enemies, such as the spy Mata Hari, were executed. His office, bright with Moroccan furnishings, and his breast, gleaming with an enormous detachable metal plaque of multi-coloured medal ribbons, were a colourful contrast to the bleak backdrop of Vincennes. After a visit to Gamelin's headquarters the tank commander Charles De Gaulle considered his Commander-in-Chief 'completely insulated from current events'.

An expert on French military history, Gamelin lacked the ability to inspire those under his command although he was highly rated by, of all people, the German Field Marshal Gerd von Rundstedt. They had got to know each other while in London to attend the funeral of King George V in 1936, and von Rundstedt said of the Frenchman, 'My little Gamelin certainly knows what he is doing.'

Gamelin tended to be less complimentary towards his rivals in the Wehrmacht, considering the German Army handicapped because very few of its generals in 1939 had served in responsible positions in the First World War. Unlike Gamelin, however, the Germans were not planning a replay of 1914.

In order to guarantee as far as possible its security from further German aggression, France had insisted on harsh terms in the peace treaty drawn up at Versailles at the conclusion of the First World War. In addition to payment of reparations, the losers were required to disband that most revered of German military institutions, the General Staff, and their army strength was slashed to one hundred thousand militia forbidden to possess tanks, heavy artillery or aircraft.

The severity of these terms ensured that in due course Germany was forced to rebuild its forces virtually from scratch, which turned out to be no bad thing. What emerged was an efficient army with a high level of pride and ability. Versailles also ensured instant popularity for the first German leader openly to oppose the treaty. That man was Adolf Hitler.

A corporal who had been wounded and gassed in the 1914–18 war, Hitler became Germany's Chancellor in 1933 and then Head of State the following year on the death of Field Marshal von Hindenburg. Hitler rapidly went about carrying out his pledge to remove the humiliating restrictions of Versailles by ignoring them and pushing for a strongly armed Germany. His success in lifting the country from depression, reducing unemployment and restoring national pride was the foundation for the uncritical adulation bestowed on him by so many in his country.

By the end of his first year in power Hitler had secretly ordered the Army to treble its permitted strength and in March 1935 he announced the birth of his new air force, the Luftwaffe. Having got away with that, the Führer promptly issued a decree creating a German Army based on compulsory military service.

Even before Hitler's rise Germany had battled, with some success, to frustrate the Versailles Treaty. At one stage, of its permitted army of one hundred thousand men, forty thousand were NCOs, all of them regarded as potential officer material. In the early days those struggling to re-establish a German Army needed all their dedication, as well as a vivid imagination and a keen sense of humour. On exercises in 1929 small motor cars were draped in canvas to resemble tanks and their red-faced crews had to suffer the jeers of infantrymen who 'wounded' the vehicles by sticking bayonets through the canvas.

From the beginning, however, Germany possessed soldiers of vision who, unlike those in France, recognized that static warfare was a thing of the past. Such a man was Heinz Guderian, a Prussian who, according to his biographer, 'was bent on innovation on a scale which would leave . . . the world breathless'.

Guderian had been an intelligence officer in the First World War, and his experiences in the senseless carnage and static warfare at Verdun, from which he had emerged unscathed in mind and body, convinced him that an alternative had to be found to the trench mentality. He became interested in tanks as early as 1922 when he was in the Inspectorate of Motorized Troops, and began to teach tank tactics in 1928. The bulk of what he knew had been picked up, incredibly, from the British, who in 1923 had become the first of the world's armies to establish a Tank Corps detached from the infantry, artillery and cavalry branches yet who then left the full development of armour to another country.

The inspiration behind the Tank Corps was a British officer, J F C Fuller, who foresaw the ability of armoured columns, with air and artillery support, to breach a fortified line and then achieve a deep enough penetration of enemy territory to bring about a collapse of morale and resistance – the very tactics which would be employed by Germany's Panzer divisions against the French in May 1940. A document by Fuller, *Provisional Instructions for Tank and Armoured Car Training*, was freely available from His Majesty's Stationery Office, price ninepence. Guderian had the booklet translated, at his own expense, and on the basis (as he said in his autobiography) that 'in the country of the blind the one-eyed man is king' he set out to lecture his fellow Germans on the new mobile method of warfare.

By 1929, convinced that tanks working alone or supported only by infantry could never achieve victories of decisive importance, Guderian pushed for the creation of armoured divisions possessing all the support needed to allow the tanks to operate with maximum effect. As he fought for the establishment of such divisions Guderian's temper was not always equal to the delays imposed by the old guard among German commanders, and he became involved in too many arguments for the good, at that time, of his own career. Nevertheless when, in October 1935, the first three Panzer divisions were formed as part of Hitler's new, provocative expansion of his armed forces, Guderian was made commander of the 2nd, although he was then still only a colonel. So enthusiastic was he about pushing the merits of armoured warfare that he continued to spend his own money on providing copies of foreign books and periodicals on the subject, and in the winter of 1936 he published *Achtung! Panzer!*, a collection of his lectures and articles in which he wrote, prophetically, 'The goddess of battle will crown only the most daring with laurels.'

In March 1936, shrugging off the caution of his generals, Hitler began the moves which were eventually to engulf Europe in war by reoccupying the demilitarized Rhineland, admitting later that the subsequent forty-eight hours were the most nerve-racking of his life. France, preoccupied with a general election, merely blustered. Exactly two years later, in March 1938, in pursuit of the policy of *Lebensraum*, more space for Germany's burgeoning population, Hitler annexed his native land, Austria. France and Britain did nothing. Within twelve months Czechoslovakia, with its important arms-producing factories, had passed into Nazi rule, too, without a shot being fired.

Hitler next turned his attention to Poland, well aware that the consequences this time could be war with Britain and recognizing that such a war would be a long one. On 23 May he gathered his top generals and advisers in Berlin and told them: 'The idea that we can get off cheaply is dangerous: there is no such possibility. We must burn our boats. It is no longer a question of right or wrong but of life or death for 80 million human beings.'

So the army of a nation which a few years earlier had been playing war games with cardboard cut-outs was able to muster close to 2 million trained men in ninety-eight divisions, fifty-six of which were assigned for the invasion of Poland. It was a raw force in many respects and General Walter Warlimont, Deputy Chief of Operations on Hitler's staff, complained that no German Army had ever gone to war so ill-prepared. Yet it was a confident Army, eager to put to the test the new theories of such as Guderian and to assess the strength of the Luftwaffe's support power. As Germany's armies swept into Poland on 1 September Wilhelm Prüller, a diary-keeping infantry-man, noted: 'We've crossed the border! We're in Poland! *Deutschland, Deutschland, uber alles!*'

4

'Queer Kind of War'

We called the first part of the war 'funny'. In America they called it 'phoney'.

Margery Allingham

Having overcome the sort of panic which persuaded the British government to stockpile papier maché coffins in expectation of devastation from the air, and which brought a run on chewing gum in Paris because it could be used to plug bullet holes in petrol tanks and also stopped teeth chattering, the Allies settled back to await Germany's intentions. 'We waited patiently to be attacked,' wrote Montgomery. 'If this was war, I did not understand it.'

The Germans were clearly anxious about the possibility of conflict on their western border while they were occupied in Poland, and particularly concerned that any threat against the Siegfried Line, their response to the Maginot, would expose its serious deficiencies. General Alfred Jodl, the Wehrmacht's Chief of Operations, admitted after the war that in 1939 the Siegfried Line was 'little better than a building site'. When Field Marshal von Rundstedt inspected it for the first time he was moved to laughter. The thickness of concrete was inadequate to withstand heavy bombardment, some of the bunkers had no field of fire, barbed wire defences were few and the armament was paltry.

According to von Rundstedt's Chief of Staff, General Erich von Manstein, Germany was able to spare only eleven regular divisions to face the West at that time. 'The risks which German leadership ran were very great indeed. Because of the unexpected brevity of the Polish campaign and, above all, as a result of the complete inaction of Poland's Western allies, these risks have hardly ever been properly appreciated.' At the Nuremberg Trials Hitler's Chief of Staff, Keitel, said this failure to attack 'confirmed our idea that the Western Powers did not desire war against us'.

Gamelin's attitude supported Keitel's point of view. Promising 'I shall be miserly with blood', he announced his intention to 'lean against' the Siegfried Line some time in late September.

The British attitude was no better. The MP Leopold Amery went to see Sir Kingsley Wood, the Air Minister, on 5 September with a suggestion that incendiaries should be dropped on the Black Forest, which cloaked many ammunition dumps. It had been a dry summer and, Amery urged, the area would burn well. To his amazement Wood told him the Black Forest could not be bombed as it was 'private property', nor could military targets such as arms factories at Essen or German lines of communication be attacked. To do so would invite retaliation, he said.

Instead, Britain's first decision, taken at a War Cabinet meeting on 3 September, was to bombard Germany with leaflets, appealing to the people to get rid of their evil leaders. Chamberlain's hope, clearly, was to win the war by convincing Germany of the error of her ways through reasoned argument. To Noël Coward it appeared to be an attempt to bore the German people to death.

The size of Britain's commitment to the Western Front remained an embarrassment. By December Lord Gort had under his command a quarter of a million men, but of this total the fighting force was only six divisions. After he and other British visitors had been given a war-room briefing by Gamelin, Anthony Eden confessed, 'I was not proud of the minute British contribution represented by two small Union Jacks amid a forest of Tricolours.'

The Germans, skilled propagandists since the rise of the Nazi Party, made much capital out of the fact that while one Frenchman in eight was in uniform the proportion in Britain was one in forty-eight. The theme that Britain was proposing to wage war with French blood was pushed hard. Placards along the banks of the Rhine and loudspeakers aimed at the Maginot garrison stressed that war between France and Germany was unnecessary. 'Let us not kill one another on England's orders,' they said. 'We won't shoot first.' Skilful use was also made of the pay differentials between French and British troops. One loud-speaker asked the French how many times they had seen British troops inside bars or restaurants that they themselves could not afford to enter. The sexual theme was exploited, too. Second Lieutenant Toby Taylor of the East Surrey Regiment collected an air-dropped pamphlet showing a pretty French girl sitting up in bed wearing a bonnet. Beside her, smoking a pipe and wearing nothing except a monocle, was the Germans' idea of a typical British officer. The caption read, 'This is what the English officers are up to while you're in the Maginot Line.'

Fortunately, the messages were not always taken seriously. The Germans put up one enormous board on which was written: 'Soldiers of the Northern Provinces, beware of the English. They are destroying your properties, eating your food, sleeping with your wives, raping your daughters.' The French regiment opposite, which hailed from Gascony, immediately erected the reply: *'On s'en fout, on est du Midi'* ('We don't give a damn, we're from the south').

On 10 October William Shirer, the CBS Berlin correspondent, went by train to visit his wife in Geneva:

Coming up the Rhine from Karlsruhe to Basel we skirted the French border for a hundred miles. No sign of war and the train crew told me not a shot had been fired on this front since the war began. Where the train ran along the Rhine we could see the French bunkers and at many places great mats behind which the French were building fortifications. Identical picture on the German side. The troops seemed to be observing an armistice. They went about their business in full sight and range of each other . . . the Germans were hauling up guns and supplies on the railroad line, but the French did not disturb them. Queer kind of war.

In Britain, via the United States, it became known as the phoney war. The French called it *la drôle de guerre*. The Germans, too, had a word for it: *Sitzkrieg*. As Anthony Rhodes, a second lieutenant in the Royal Horse Artillery, moved into billets near Lille, he wrote, 'We settled down to wait and see what Hitler had in store for us; it seemed from the very start that we had nothing in particular in store for *him*.'

The frontage allotted to the BEF was a forty-five-mile stretch of the French–Belgian border in flat, dull country west of Lille and many miles from the nearest German. The 'fortifications' behind which they assembled and the conditions they endured were a grim joke. An officer with the Green Howards Regiment recalled: 'Some of the ditches on the frontier proper were so caved in as scarcely to present difficulty to a handcart, never mind a tank.' Because Belgium was regarded as a prospective ally little had been done by the French to strengthen that section of her borders.

Anthony Rhodes noted, 'When we arrived on the Belgian frontier there were a handful of pill boxes, a few French soldiers equipped with 1914 rifles and a strand or two of wire to keep French cattle from straying over into Belgium.' So, with no immediate prospect of action, the BEF was unleashed on the construction of what became known as the Gort Line. As a soggy late autumn turned into the coldest winter for forty-five years Britain's army laboured to prepare pill boxes and defensive posts, connecting trenches and barbed wire entanglements. They built forty miles of anti-tank obstacles and some four hundred concrete pill boxes, often excavating equipment and skeletons of the earlier war as they did so.

It was dour work. Tom Bristow, a lorry driver, took a digging party up to the trenches and joined in with them in an effort to keep warm:

I selected a piece of virgin soil and, raising the pick above my head, brought it down with great force. Instead of penetrating the iron-hard ground it bounced back and narrowly missed smashing into my face. Before leaving I looked at the very small amount of earth I had taken all day to excavate; still, the exertions had prevented me from becoming a frozen carcass.

In wet weather it was worse. Alf Hewitt of the South Lancashire Regiment, said,

As had been proved at the time of Passchendaele, that area is a swamp. At the end of the day we would be smothered in yellow clay. When it dried you looked like a banana. We had no change of clothing, so when we wanted to go out in the evening we would have to clean it all off beforehand. That mud used to dry like a shell, especially on our boots, which had to be polished before we were allowed out.

If the working conditions were grim, living conditions invariably gave more cause for complaint, at least for the other ranks. Though the *Times* reported that Britain's soldiers 'have plenty of warm straw and the barns are solidly built and free from draughts', the reality was much different.

Tom Bristow's first billet in France was a disused lace factory,

a dreadful place, a relic of grimmer days, the industrial revolution and child labour. Now it was to be home for eight hundred British soldiers. We were given a straw-filled palliasse and two blankets, one underneath to keep out the cold from the tiled floor and one on top to keep out the cold from above, neither being very effective. It reminded me of a picture I'd seen of a slave ship, with the slaves lying head to head on the decks with a narrow gangway between all the feet. The Medical Officer, who of course did not have to live in the place himself, inspected the ruin and declared it unfit to house so many men without more ventilation, so half a dozen holes eight feet wide were knocked out of the walls. This certainly solved the fresh air problem but also let in the rain, the freezing winds and later, when the snow fell, drifts of the stuff which piled up inside the walls.

Derek Ramsdale's field ambulance unit in the 50th Northumbrian Division was billeted in pig-pens ('fortunately clean' he noted) at Carvin. 'We were in a long brick building with a passageway down the middle and pens, each with its little gate, at the sides. We slept four to a pen. The floors were brick and for once we had palliasses. Reveille was sounded by a sergeant kicking a petrol tin along the brick floor.'

Private Chris Cardy's RAOC unit was quartered in a sugar beet factory. 'It had been occupied by the French Cavalry and declared unfit for human occupation. But not for the British Army! I remember men placing their groundsheet capes on the floor and being unable to pick them up in the morning because they were stuck to the floor by the congealed sugar beet.'

A Lancashire Fusilier, John Hammond, decided France was still in the Dark Ages after being obliged to sleep in a pig-sty. 'This village was only the second we had seen and neither of them had made-up roads, piped water or sewers. We washed and shaved in a nearby stream.'

Arnold Johnson's troop-carrying company was based in the hamlet of Hattenville:

We stepped back a hundred years. The inhabitants were peasants who scratched a meagre living from the soil and their ill-kempt and run-down homes testified to their low standard of life. Housing was a simple matter. We were marched into a farmyard, shown a barn and told to climb the ladder to the hay-loft above. We shared the barn with the animals, pigs and cows. We could see them through the cracks in the floorboards and smell their animal odours that drifted up to us. From my father's account of life in France during the Great War nothing had changed one iota.

Gunner Alfred Baldwin was not alone in thinking the British Army operated on a them-and-us basis:

If there was a barn, that was good enough for the ordinary ranks. The officers, of course, enjoyed châteaux or large houses, they looked after their own comfort very well indeed. There seemed to be, in my experience, very little concern for the comfort of the troops. As long as I was in France I never slept in anything but barns. But there was no discontent. You could look back and say our officers treated us not very caringly but we automatically accepted it as our lot. It came back to our upbringing.

The sort of set-up enjoyed by Lieutenant H C F Harwood of the Royal East Kent Regiment was what Baldwin was referring to. Harwood's 5th Battalion was in billets at Fleury-sur-Andelle and he remembered,

Oh yes, the days passed pleasantly. I climbed out of the enormous wooden structure which was my bed at 7.15 in the morning. A quick shave in cold water was the height of discomfort. Little did I know about real discomfort in those days [he was later taken prisoner]. Then over to the mess for breakfast. Parade with my company and the rest of the morning spent in training the men. Back at the mess for lunch at 1.30. Administrative jobs in the afternoon until five o'clock or thereabouts and then work was over for the day.

The Café de la Poste was used as the officers' mess. Most of the officers were there by seven o'clock and then a spot of serious drinking would ensue before dinner. Madame would produce superb dishes out of the very mediocre ration meat and there was a particularly good Château Margaux '29 which was very cheap. After dinner we played bridge or dominoes and joined in the conversation with all the old locals who came in every night to drink their Pernods and discuss the war. We went to bed fairly early; drinks could not be obtained after 10.30 and, anyway, we were all quite ready for sleep by then.

What frightfully dull and ordinary days, and yet how enjoyable they seemed at the time.

A Royal Engineers major, Eric Booth, concurred.' I must say that, with a batman to fetch and carry, to produce hot water and cups of tea at the right moment, I felt that for a soldier on active service I was in clover.'

Alfred Baldwin, not surprisingly, considered the food provided for the ordinary soldier 'very poor, very badly cooked and unevenly distributed; I can't recall anything other than stew. The first in the line got a big scoop but if you were on the end of the queue you were lucky to get half a scoop.'

Another gunner, appropriately named Les Cannon, remembered the BEF diet as follows: breakfast – bacon or corned beef; lunch – beef or corned beef stew, potatoes, beans, biscuits, prunes or rice; evening meal – bread and jam. Cannon and his mates supplemented their rations by purchasing fresh produce from the farmer with whom they were billeted, 'to cook ourselves a wholesome tea or supper'. John Hammond, shopping at the local store on behalf of colleagues in the 6th Lancashire Fusiliers, struggled with the language – only to be told, as he paid up, by the woman behind the counter in a strong Lancashire accent: 'You did very well, lad.' She was a lady from Lancashire who had married a French soldier during the First World War.

To Alf Hewitt of the South Lancashires the food in France came as 'a great shock, almost starvation rations', while Arnold Johnson of the RASC considered the utensils even worse than their contents: 'We ate out of those awful mess tins, two aluminium rectangular cans with wire handles, one fitting inside the other. I considered these mess tins to be the most uncivilized piece of equipment issued to the British soldier. What was wrong with having an enamel plate and a mug?'

Sergeant Bill Brodie's signals section was fortunate to share barracks for a short time with French troops, and enjoyed the fruits of their cook's labours: 'He had obviously been primed on the necessity of maintaining good international relations, and produced every morning as his idea of the typical English breakfast a steak, a bottle of beer and some coconut cakes.' This certainly sounded better than the dinner served night after night at the artillery officers' mess at Visterie, where Colonel Graham Brooks ate: 'Marmite soup, fish cakes (made from tinned salmon), bully beef (stewed, fried or neat, with onions or leeks), tinned apricots, sardine (one) on toast.'

On their free evenings the troops ate – and drank – copiously at cheap bars, bistros and the shabby cafés called *estaminets*. Arnold Johnson claimed he would always remember 'a tumbledown village called Taisnil' for the excellence of its solitary café. 'Despite an interior devoid of all luxurious fittings the proprietor and her two daughters did a roaring trade serving egg and chips. On many occasions we would eat the meal twice over in one evening. Madame had never known such business.'

'It was cheap living in France in those days,' said the despatch rider, Tom Willy. 'So we ate out most of the time.' Gunner Cannon confessed himself 'amazed at the cheapness of wine and spirits'. 'Compared with the French troops we had jolly good wages, so it was a boozing time,' said Alf Hewitt.

We spent every evening in the *estaminets*. There were very few teetotallers around at the time. I didn't know any myself. We used to booze until about eleven at night, then go rolling back to our billets. We would be in a drunken stupor all night and next morning early we would be taken out to the defences and work it all off. I suppose there was an excuse because our living conditions were so miserable we wanted to blot it out. In France that winter all my illusions about the glamour of Army life and my childhood ambitions to be like my Dad and fight the Germans went completely out of the window.

Hewitt retains vivid memories of his social contacts with the locals:

Apart from those who owned the cafés, who were naturally very friendly to us, we didn't come in contact very much with the normal civilians – but I know there was some discontent among them because their soldiers were poorly paid and the wives received a pittance. It was the same sort of thing that went on in later years in Britain with the Americans, who were so well paid. The French women whose husbands were away saw masses of British soldiers going out on the booze every night and throwing their money away.

We also realized it was a bit unfair and in Turcoing we were moved to run a raffle in our favourite *estaminet* to collect money for the poor women of the district. Because this place was also run as a brothel the first prize was a whole Sunday afternoon in bed with a very jolly middle-aged lady. This was quite a prize because lying in her big warm bed was bound to be a big improvement on being on a factory floor with just two blankets over you. Never mind about the sex part of it, the comfort was a big reward. We all bought tickets. I won. Very enjoyable afternoon it was, very comfortable. I slept practically all the time.

'She was a very big-hearted, generous woman,' concluded Hewitt, now an elder of the Mormon Church but at that time as he conceded, 'rather a wild young chap'.

Tom Willy maintains that, because of drunken behaviour, the French in billet centres were frightened of the BEF soldiers.

When I read of the football hooligans now I think of those people. We used to go in a bar near Lens, six of us, educated lads. One of them asked if I was listening to what the French were saying about us, discussing what awful people we were. Two of them were sticking up for us and we got to know those two men and their families. When we ran away after the fighting started I often wondered what those two thought of us. Twice the 30th Field Regiment I was with held identification parades after girls had been raped. The girls picked out the guilty people but their pals gave them alibis and they got away with it.

Elsewhere, naturally, firm friendships were struck; marriages made, even. Len Wilson of the Medical Corps used to visit a Béthune family whose daughter, a hairdresser, was married to a soldier serving in the Maginot Line. 'When he came home on leave we had quite a do,' Wilson recalled. 'We must have had quite a bit to drink because next morning when we woke up both of us found our hair had been permed.'

When Bill Brodie's signals section moved away from the steak-and-beer breakfasts into new billets at Entremmes they found that this time they were sharing with a battalion of the Highland Light Infantry. 'For obscure reasons that date back to service in India it seems impossible for the Signals and HLI to live in harmony,' he said. 'Soon brawls were springing up in the *estaminets*.'

Mainly, however, the French civilian were spared the effects of British misbehaviour. Graham Brooks, the artillery colonel, recalled an occasion when most of the battery headquarters staff helped a signaller to celebrate his twenty-first birthday.

At least twenty were blind drunk, two were found lying unconscious under the trees – one really ill – and the rest were in various stages ranging from pugnacity to girlish giggling.

We discovered the delinquents had been drinking vodka and cognac – drinks to which they were not accustomed and which civilians were forbidden to sell to the troops; so we placed all cafés and *estaminets* in the village out of bounds. Next thing was for the guilty ones to have the alcohol driven out of them in a way which would leave an impression, so they were ordered to parade in full kit, steel helmets, packs and the rest and were led off on a route march at brisk pace on a hilly course. Two hours later, when we got back, they were a chastened lot.

Brooks dismissed the incident as unusual: 'The hefty beer-swiller is so rare as to be almost a freak. Given the chance, Thomas Atkins drinks more tea than beer these days.'

There was support for that point of view among the BEF diary-keepers. Les Shorrock of the 91st Field Regiment RA remembered:

Most of the lads would spend their evenings in *estaminets*, others would visit the houses of ill-repute and take their pleasures. They tried to persuade me to join them but I would have none of that. Not only did I eschew alcohol but I was also fearful of being personally contaminated and reluctant to confess I had no sexual knowledge of the female form, due to the segregated lives we young men lived in peace-time. I was content to write letters home, read books and listen to the popular songs played over our little radio, a prized possession.

Gunner Cyril King of the 92nd Field Regiment also stood aside from the pleasures of the majority.

Because of a moderately good education and the way I spoke I was considered to be something of a snob and I never really grew used to the language and rough jokes. Thus I withdrew into a shell of my own, spending more time with French civilians in Armentières whenever possible and guarding the expectancy that the war deadlock would soon be terminated and I would be released from my predicament.

'How foolish and incorrect I was proved to be,' lamented King, who was taken prisoner a few months later.

Montgomery, a much higher-ranking but similarly correct soldier, was distressed to hear that by mid-November 1939 there had been forty-four reported cases of venereal disease in the 3rd Division which he commanded. He attempted to combat the problem with a confidential memo to his subordinate officers urging the establishment of the sort of early treatment rooms which had existed at his previous posting in Palestine. 'It is no use having one room in the battalion area,' he wrote. 'There should be one room in each company area. The man who has a woman in a beetroot field near his company billet will not walk a mile to the battalion ET room.' He also suggested that since the licensed (and therefore relatively safe) brothels were well known to the military police 'any soldier who is in need of horizontal refreshment would be well advised to ask a policeman for a suitable address'.

This sort of breezy opinion, to become familiar in Montgomery's later utterances, was brought to the shocked attention of the BEF's senior chaplains, who wasted no time complaining to Gort. The C-in-C considered removing his outspoken divisional commander – how *that* might have changed history! – and Monty admitted in his memoirs, 'There was the father-and-mother of a row. They were all after my blood at GHQ. But my Corps Commander [Brooke] saved me by insisting on being allowed to handle the matter himself. This he did in no uncertain manner and I received from him a proper backhander. He said, amongst other things, that he didn't think much of my literary effort.' As usual, however, Montgomery had the last word: 'Anyhow it achieved what I wanted, since the veneral disease ceased.'

The East Surreys signals officer, Toby Taylor, did as Montgomery suggested when he and two other junior officers set off in search of girls.

We asked a policeman where the red light district was, but there was no need because when we got near the whole area was absolutely chock-a-block. One couldn't get within a quarter of a mile of any of the brothels because of parked army vehicles. Later on in the phoney war girls were always available and I suppose armies have been like this since time began.

'Half our unit was down with scabies and the other half had crabs,' said Harry Dennis of the East Surreys. 'We gave each other blue unction treatment.'

VD was not the only concern during that bitter winter. On New Year's Eve 1939 Private Bill Gardner of the 5th Division's Postal Unit wrote home detailing his bleak experiences since arriving in France a couple of weeks earlier:

It was a bit too damn cold for me as we slept in stables, barns, any old place. Finally I caved in and was left in a French convent two days before Christmas. The nuns were very kind – and very poor. Also very dirty. I laid in bed five days and in that time they did not make the bed once, empty the old slash-pot or sweep round even. The bed smelt. For Christmas dinner I had roast horse (honest!), potatoes and three dates. I managed to get out of the place alive and was taken to a British hospital.

An acute form of influenza known as 'blitz flu' swept the BEF, rapidly depleting medical supplies. 'By the middle of January, although our Medical Officer had an adequate supply of shell dressings, he did not possess one aspirin,' said Bill Brodie. 'On occasions we had to carry a despatch rider in from his motorcycle and thaw him out. They were placed on stools, stuck in a sitting position, whilst we rubbed life back into their limbs. One man had his eyelids frozen.'

Like the other despatch riders, Tom Willy found the conditions impossible. Once he was required to accompany a colonel, whose car was fitted with wheel chains, on a visit to some gun pits. 'I fell off about six times, naturally, because you can't ride a motorbike on ice, so he stopped his car and called out to me, "Can't you keep up, DR?" I thought "You stupid bloody fool."'

Those on foot fared little better on the frozen highways. As George Davey of the 1st Border Regiment pointed out, 'Icy roads and studded boots were never good partners.' The RAMC colonel, John McDonald, reported on 27 January, 'The roads are like glass. Tonight, walking from the officers' mess to the orderly room, a distance of a quarter of a mile, I went down twice.'

When Eric Rankin's unit undertook a train journey (in horse boxes bearing the First World War legend; '40 men, 8 horses') it was so cold that a beer bottle burst, leaving the frozen liquid upright and intact. A dixie of boiling tea brought from one end of the same train had become iced tea by the time it reached the other. One soldier wrote home that he was now buying his beer by the pound rather than by the pint.

In such conditions the maintenance of vehicles presented a severe problem, since the availability of anti-freeze was restricted to the armoured sections. Petrol froze in carburettors, while even in those lorries using diesel the fuel turned to a jelly. 'So all drivers had to take it in turn to start up all cars and lorries every hour through the night,' recalled a signals driver, Dave Parry.

Bill Edwards, an RASC driver, ended a night of guard duty on a petrol dump 'smothered in snow and boots frozen to my feet'. In his motorized section the radiators were drained every night for safety, and replenishing them could sometimes present hazards. 'I was filling my lorry up one morning when the can slipped and the water froze on my fingers and split them. It was so painful I sat on the running board and cried. I've never known cold like it.'

Sports, vigorous exercises and work details were undertaken to keep the troops tolerably warm. Alan Johnson, a Royal Engineers major who had served in the First World War, recalled a match in which officers and NCOs played the other ranks and where the frozen field was presumably the setting for working off a grudge or two: 'All the officers played, including me, and there were no rules. A soccer ball was used but handling, pushing, barging or anything else except kicking or scratching your opponent was allowed. With the ground so hard it was surprising no one was hurt.'

At first the weekly outing from billets to Mobile Bath Units or pithead showers in the mining areas was one of the few welcome diversions from the routine, but gradually entertainment was laid on. Touring parties brought film stars and well-known music hall names to France. Gunner Les Cannon recalled he had had 'the good fortune to see Will Hay, supported by a very entertaining cast', and when news of a forthcoming Gracie Fields concert was delivered to the 3rd Division it came by despatch rider in an envelope marked 'SECRET AND URGENT'.

Films, too, began to get through, though they were not always well received. Eric Rankin remembered the showing in a village hall of something called *Mutiny in the Big House*, sent in lieu of a Ginger Rogers film which had been promised and billed.

We were prepared to be entertained by almost anything but it was too much to show us in prolonged detail the interior of some Sing Sing, the miseries of its inmates, their ultimate rebellion, and the heroic salvation wrought for all by the local padre. Whoever had considered its macabre sentimentality the stuff to give the troops slipped up badly. I went to the men in charge of the cinemas in Arras and spared no words, and I believe the thing was jettisoned. Afterwards we had excellent films – George Formby and Ginger Rogers herself.

However, nights on the town – particularly the bigger towns – remained the most popular form of relaxation. When the weather eased the Royal Engineers major, Eric Booth, opted for a night out in Lille with three fellow officers. 'We went by car,' said Booth.

Strictly speaking this was an improper use of Army transport and we were all a little nervous of being stopped by the military police (foolishly so, because all units were abusing their transport in this way). We arrived without hindrance and, with difficulty in the black-out, found first a cocktail bar and then a lively restaurant for dinner. Afterwards we walked round in search of further amusement. The city was crowded with British officers with the same intent as ourselves and had an irresponsible atmosphere of Oxford or Cambridge during term time.

We eventually found a sort of night club where dancing partners and alcohol were provided at exorbitant prices, but military law closed all these establishments at ten o'clock. Thereafter we were reduced to the bar of a private hotel where we drank execrable beer and a highly potent liquor which tasted like raw alcohol and burned with a pale blue flame when a lighted match was applied to it.

As spring edged towards northern Europe, a Field Security captain, Basil Bartlett, mused in his diary, 'The BEF's a grand little fighting force. It has stood up to its long winter of digging and patrolling and manning A/A guns and being bored by ENSA with fortitude. The soldier's needs are few. Give him food, sleep and a football and he seems quite contented. He has enough of all three out here.' Bartlett also listed his own source of contentment: 'In the mess we have a fine collection of wine, including a Corton Charlemagne '29 and a sound Côtes Roties.'

5

Through the Forest

Hitler stays up late and sleeps badly, which I fear is the world's misfortune.'

William Shirer

No sooner had Poland been dismembered than, on 27 September, Hitler issued the order to prepare for an early invasion of western Europe. The instruction disconcerted the German High Command and so alarmed some of its generals that they reactivated an earlier plot to assassinate the Führer.

Their worry was understandable. At that stage of the war the Wehrmacht was numerically inferior. The French had mobilized 110 divisions and the BEF contributed another five (increased to nine by the spring of 1940). Germany had gone to war with ninety-eight divisions, only sixty-two of which were primed for action. The remainder were incompletely equipped reserve units with a heavy content of men over forty. The need to garrison Poland with experienced soldiers in readiness to meet any Russian threat caused Hitler's generals even more concern.

On the same day – 6 October – that he was offering the Allies a negotiated peace (an offer which went unanswered) Hitler issued official orders for their overthrow. His sixth Directive for the Conduct of the War claimed 'lengthy delay leads not only to a removal of Belgian and possibly Dutch neutrality in favour of the Western powers but to an increasing reinforcement of the military strength of our enemy'. He went on to order an attack through Luxembourg, Belgium and Holland as early as possible, the timing to depend on the readiness of armoured units only recently returned from Poland and on prevailing weather conditions so necessary for the implementation of German air superiority.

The first date set for invasion was 25 October, but even Hitler doubted whether that could be met. Any testing of German readiness was rendered unnecessary by unfavourable weather. Next he nominated 12 November, giving his Army exactly a week's notice. Before hastening to confront his leader Walther von Brauchitsch, C-in-C of the Army High Command, paused only long enough to tell the dissident generals that if he could not talk Hitler out of such madness he would join in the assassination plot. Brauchitsch pleaded that the Army's condition and morale would not stand the strain of another major campaign so soon. His plea was cut short by a torrent of Hitlerite abuse directed at the Army in general and the High Command in particular. Next Brauchitsch mentioned the weather as an adverse factor, only to be told by Hitler: 'It rains on the enemy too.'

In sheer frustration Brauchitsch offered his resignation. Hitler also turned that down, telling him to obey orders; but two days later, on 7 November, he postponed the offensive. Weather was the official reason, but Hitler almost certainly took into account the reluctance of his generals. Next day a bomb exploded in a Munich beer hall a few minutes after Hitler's departure.

According to his Chief of Staff, the monocled Wilhelm Keitel, 'Hitler decided to wait for a lengthy period of clear, frosty weather during the winter instead. During the days that followed, Diesing, the Luftwaffe Meteorologist, sweated blood . . . painfully conscious of his responsibility should his forecast prove wrong.' The new date finally settled on was 17 January. The operation was codenamed *Fall Gelb*, Plan Yellow, but it too was to come to nothing. This time a bizarre incident, rather than the weather, was the undoing of Hitler's ambitions.

On the morning of 10 January a Luftwaffe major, Helmut Reinberger, summoned from Münster to a meeting in Cologne eighty miles away, accepted the offer of a lift in a Messerschmitt 108 piloted by a reserve major, Erich Hönmanns. He was carrying, in flagrant breach of the instructions of his C-in-C, Hermann Göring, secret papers concerning Plan Yellow. The plane took off in perfect conditions but soon the weather closed in and Hönmanns, flying the new Me108 for the first time, panicked. Attempting to pinpoint his whereabouts by descending, he cut off the fuel supply accidentally and the plane crash-landed near Mechelen, just inside the Belgian border with Holland.

Reinberger managed to burn some of the documents before border guards arrived to arrest the two Germans. As they awaited interrogation Reinberger snatched the papers back and thrust them into a stove, only for a Belgian officer to pull them out at the cost of a badly scorched hand. Enough remained legible to alarm the Belgians sufficiently. The French were alerted, German Intelligence spotted the heightened state of Allied readiness and, once more, the invasion was postponed, with deteriorating weather again being given as the official reason. Now Hitler determined to wait for the spring. He also decided to change drastically the direction of his attack.

The original intention had been to invade, as in 1914, through the neutral Low Countries. Now plans were laid for the main thrust to come much further south, through the Ardennes forest, just above the Maginot Line's northern terminal point and in an area considered by the French to be impassable to armoured divisions. The idea was conceived by Erich von Manstein, a veteran of the trenches and now an enthusiastic supporter of mobile armoured warfare. Manstein was regarded by the British military historian, Basil Liddell Hart, as the ablest of Germany's generals. He also seems to have been an able salesman of his plan: so enthusiastically did Hitler adopt it that he rapidly got it into his head that the idea had been his own all along.

So Germany applied itself to honing its two deadliest blades, the Panzers and the Luftwaffe, with which to scythe down its enemies. By May 1940 the Wehrmacht had been beefed up to 131 divisions. As Hitler's biographer, Lord Bullock, has pointed out, the Führer owed his success in the Battle of France more than anything else to the long delay in opening the attack, which had so much irked him at the time.

Although German exercises and preparations did not always progress smoothly (a lack of fuel precluded intensive Panzer manoeuvres, and a shortage of ammunition meant that some tank crews had never fired their guns until they went into battle), the Wehrmacht continued comfortably to outstrip the opposition in such matters.

'The BEF wasn't really geared up to war in France,' said Toby Taylor, the East Surreys officer. 'The Blitzkrieg in Poland didn't seem to make much difference to how we went about our preparations. We never did any serious training. All I can say is thank God Chamberlain gave us a year's grace and we hadn't to get involved with Hitler a year earlier, when we had absolutely nothing.' General Brooke agreed: 'What might have happened if the Germans had attacked before the winter makes me shudder to think.' He noted in his diary that some of the units arriving to reinforce the BEF were completely untrained. He considered one machine gun battalion he inspected totally unfit for war in every respect, saying: 'It would be sheer massacre to commit it to action in its present state.'

Other officers experienced similar deep reservations. It fell to the lot of a First World War veteran, Colonel Lionel Westropp, to command a newly raised force, the 8th Battalion King's Own Royal Regiment, which was formed at Denbury camp, near Newton Abbot, in February 1940:

Many of the men were of low standard of intelligence and some were of poor physique. Most of them came from second-line Territorial units who had obviously seized the opportunity of sending us their unwanted men. We also received seventy men from Regular units, mostly reservists and consequently older men. I instantly saw that many of them came under the category 'hard case'. The senior NCOs with some exceptions were also poor specimens. The officers were also a problem. Besides the Adjutant and Quartermaster I had only one Regular officer. The majority of the remainder, though of quite good type, knew little of infantry work.
The men of the battalion knew little of any military matter and many had not fired their rifles. Light machine guns were 'black magic' to them. There was only one thing in which they were quite passable – marching. . . . Being able to march was to prove of value in the later stages of the retreat.
The battalion, entirely untrained, set out to face the German Army . . . even in my worst imaginings I never expected that I should be sent to the front, or near it, with a so-called Pioneer Battalion which, in reality, consisted of a crowd of completely untrained civilians.

An inexperienced second lieutenant, Robert Neave, joining his regiment, the 13/18th Hussars, was put in charge of a draft of fifty reinforcements travelling over to France. His problems began when he attempted to march them out of the customs shed at Le Havre:

The powers-that-be who had formed my first draft had seen fit to include this one NCO, a Lance Jack of the old school. He and about a dozen of the other old soldiers had succeeded in getting royally drunk. . . . There they were, tight as lords, the remainder too young and too dazed by foreign parts to care much what happened.
The party I was leading was something very different from that I had pictured. Here was I, in battle dress for the first time which fitted only where it touched, followed by a very ill-assorted party. Their few hours' sleep on the concrete floor of the Customs shed had completed the disorganization of their clothes and equipment which a night in a darkened cross-Channel steamer had started. To make matters worse, the rear was brought up by the corporal. He, trailing his rifle upside down behind him, tripped along singing loudly to the vast amusement of the few French who bothered to notice us. It was a sad situation and after getting the draft into the train I went to look for him to threaten him with every sort of military inconvenience. When I found him he was fast asleep in the guard's van amid the kit bags and no amount of shaking would stir him.

Sergeant Bill Brodie was much amused to read in the newspapers that the BEF was Britain's best-equipped army ever. 'Our hearts bled for our ill-provided ancestors, for our stores contained glaring deficiencies. Our lorries were uncovered, our Boyes anti-tank gun lacked a vital part, the firing pin, and our main defence against expected air attacks was three ancient Lewis guns marked 1918.' Brodie considered, further, that the Royal Corps of Signals had gone to war with a communications system, an elaborate network of cables, designed for the sort of static warfare which had become out of date in 1918.

The year 1918 was what popped into the mind of Norman Dixon, a junior reporter on the local paper in Barrow, when he was called up and sent to Salisbury with a Royal Engineers chemical warfare company handling gas. 'They had just got this stuff out of the War Office dungeons. You were supposed to advance in front of your own trenches, put up this equipment and set it alight. It would have been suicide.'

The 5th Battalion of the Green Howards possessed, according to one officer, 'only one weapon capable of making a loud bang, a 3 in. mortar. There should have been two of these extremely useful weapons but facts had not caught up with theory.' When Lieutenant Peter Hadley received a 2 in. mortar for his platoon he was also issued with a foolscap cardboard folder in which he was meant to note every occasion when the weapon was used. 'Not that we could have used the thing anyway, since the firing-pin spring was lost before we went abroad and was never replaced in spite of frequent appeals to the authorities.'

The lack of provision extended to the medical arrangements, which were labelled 'scandalous' by Lieutenant Colonel John McDonald, who had raised in Durham and commanded the 2nd Casualty Clearing Station, which found itself operating a hospital under canvas at Rouvroy, near Lens: 'The marquees are all soaking wet and dispersed around a race track which is a sea of mud. To see rows of stretchers on trestles in such miserable conditions and to think that some of them are quite seriously ill is indeed a most pitiable and pathetic sight.'

Montgomery was one of the few to organize regular battle training for his 3rd Division and, as usual, could not resist a flourish of showmanship. He dangled a coloured light from his car during night exercises, briskly telling his critics that he was contravening black-out regulations 'so that the soldiers will know I am there'. The engineer major, Alan Johnson, prudently laid on a number of exercises involving organization during a withdrawal, explaining: 'I did this because history tells us that we British always underestimate the strength of our enemy in any war and have to start by withdrawing.'

Gunner Alfred Baldwin complained that his 65th Field Regiment only went on one training exercise. 'From my lowly position it seemed one hell of a mess. Everyone got lost, the scheme was cancelled and we returned to billets. The only things we learned were how to get wet and tired and achieve nothing. We didn't appreciate just how badly trained we were. We had the feeling we had beaten them the last time and could beat them again.'

To add to his miseries, Baldwin suffered what he called 'the most depressing day of my life' just before the fighting started:

We were very conscious of parachutists at the time. Our parachute patrol was a Lewis gun mounted in a 15 cwt truck. I was the No. 1 gunner on this thing, though I had never fired it, with a Lieutenant Bissell in charge, a whacking great, hulking ex-Oxford rugby blue who was all for getting stuck into people. We heard that somewhere they had picked up a German parachutist, so he leaps into the 15 cwt and we go tearing across the fields. In the course of all this the Lewis gun, which was only screwed on to the floor of the truck, came off and smacked me right across the mouth, knocking out four of my front teeth.

Eventually we found the so-called parachutist dining with the local priest. Bissell joined them in the wine, we were left in the truck, me bleeding at the mouth. Eventually we got back to our billets. I was taken in the truck to a divisional HQ dental surgeon. He tooked out the stumps of the four teeth.

By this time the truck which had brought me had gone back and I was left to walk five miles back to the billet and when I got there I was told I was on Guard that night. It was pouring with rain and I felt nobody loved me. My mouth was hurting and there I was having to guard guns against enemy attack.

Going about their duties on the Belgian border and incurring the wrath of householders and farmers as they dug trenches through gardens and across fields, the BEF found it disconcerting to watch life carrying on as usual all around them. Thousands of factory and agricultural workers crossed and recrossed the frontier daily, offering excellent opportunities for spying on the British defences. 'These were open to examination by the public from many points,' said Lieutenant Gregory Blaxland of the Royal East Kents. 'So it must have been a simple matter for German Intelligence to maintain up-to-date charts of our defences.'

Spy scares were rampant and trigger fingers twitchy. When a cow brushed against a hedge on the 65th Field Regiment's sector one night the sentry shot it because it failed to answer his challenge. Sometimes the alarms verged on the vaudevillian. The 2nd Battalion of the Royal Norfolks ran a check on a suspicious woman described as 'short, thin, darkish, sometimes to be seen wearing trench boots and has a blind husband'. This suspect was reported to be staying at an *estaminet* with a man she variously described as a Dutch officer, a cheese seller and a manufacturer of chemicals. The Norfolks followed up another report of a blonde woman of well-to-do appearance giving cigarettes and razor blades to British troops from her 'prosperous-looking car'.

There was a flurry of excitement when the 1st Battalion Royal Scots had what they were convinced was their first encounter with a German agent:

At 1915 hrs on 18 October a car from Belgium drew up at a café on the Belgian side of the frontier. Two men and a woman, stated to be a blonde with frizzy hair, went into the café. At 2130 hrs a man came out and tried to entice Private Manson into the café by bribes of beer and whisky. He also tried to see the number plate on Manson's rifle but would not come over into French territory. When he found that his efforts had failed he shouted 'England no good. *Heil Hitler.* He will beat you in two months.'

The British press was powerless to report such goings-on because of censorship. The war correspondents, unable even to reveal that the BEF was guarding a neutral border miles from the nearest German soldier, soon found stories getting thin. An article in the *News Chronicle* headlined: 'More Bakers for the BEF' caused much embarrassment to that newspaper's man in France, Philip Jordan, and amusement among his colleagues. Bernard Gray of the *Daily Mirror* complained: 'Writing about a "front" where there was no fighting, no enemy, no activity, became a complicated and boring business.'

So the Allied decision to send British units in rotation for a short spell of 'battle' service in the Maginot Line and the occasional visit of bigwigs from Britain helped the journalists, though even here over-strict censorship frequently succeeded in frustrating them. In November 1939 the correspondents were told, off the record, that the King was coming to France to inspect his army. So hush-hush was this story, it was stressed, that the King's name was not to be mentioned, even in private conversation. The codename allocated to George VI was Harry the Horse, which was hilariously received by American reporters and all Damon Runyon fans.

No matter; the writers were delighted that the royal visit would provide the first decent copy of the campaign – but the censors stepped in again. No story would be released for publication until the

King was safely back in England. Mutterings turned to howls when, on the afternoon of the tour, the BBC broadcast that the monarch was in France. The source was a hand-out from Buckingham Palace.

In Bernard Gray's opinion anyone with the slightest excuse seemed to think the thing to do during the Phoney War was to embark on a sight-seeing tour of the BEF zone. Gort's headquarters at Premesques, near Arras, became, said Gray, 'the Paris Plage of the Winter season', to the annoyance of the C-in-C who disliked the presence of both guests and the media, and the nickname they had bestowed on him – Tiger.

Gort's needs were simple. He slept on a cot at his quarters, a château at Habarq – a building of gaunt austerity. After a visit to Gort's headquarters André Maurois, the French author turned liaison officer, wrote, 'No great commander's office was ever simpler. His table was no more than a bare plank on a couple of trestles; a few maps hung on the wall.' A non-smoker whose greatest enjoyment came from long pre-supper hikes, Gort did not approve of people falling ill, referring to them as 'pansy'. When Major General the Hon. Harold Alexander, commander of the BEF's 1st Division, was laid low with a severe attack of lumbago, his C-in-C announced with glee, 'Alexander has gone pansy.' At dinner Gort permitted the port to circulate once only, a regulation from which there was no exemption, even for his Chief Liaison Officer, the Duke of Gloucester, the King's brother.

On both sides of the Channel early in 1940 animosity tended to be directed at Hitler personally rather than Germany generally. One air raid warden in Chichester filled in idle hours on duty painting a picture of the Führer on the bottom of a chamber pot. Use of the utensil was referred to as 'wetting Hitler's head'. In Paris terracotta models were on sale of dogs raising a hind leg over a copy of *Mein Kampf*, but Alexander Werth, the *Manchester Guardian*'s man in Paris, lamented: 'We don't even hate the Huns properly as we did in the last war. The papers are genteel; and so is the BBC with Herr Hitler this and Herr Hitler that.'

With the war eight months old Werth reflected, 'You would hardly have thought there was a war on at all – except, of course, that nearly all the men you knew had been called up . . . for a lot of people life was nice and simple in Paris all these months. The Front – well, the Front was far away; and even the soldiers had almost forgotten that war was a dangerous game.'

The fact that the barrage over Paris consisted of only half a dozen balloons was indicative of the city's desire to avoid facing facts. On her way through France to join a women's voluntary ambulance unit Josephine Pearce spent a night in the capital, where she had lived most of her life: 'Deep down I knew this was not my Paris. Someone had dropped a tea cosy over the fact that France was at war. Paris was wearing a mask – she did not want to face up to war.'

Anthony Rhodes was one of many British officers who managed to wangle a visit to Paris towards the end of the Phoney War:

The city had never been quite so lovely as during this last visit in the spring of 1940, in an atmosphere of almost peacetime calm and satisfaction; only a few headlines in the Press and a few uniforms in the streets indicated that such a gross thing as war was possible. . . . Wherever one went, in the theatre, in the restaurants, even in the business offices, one found the same attitude, a distaste for war that manifested itself not in hatred (the Parisians were too civilized for that) but simply in humorous indifference; the war was a joke, a lark, a will o' the wisp, something to be amused about, at all events nothing to lose a night's sleep over.

However, those who knew France better were aware of animosity towards its Allies. 'One could sense the hostility to the British,' said Henry Greenwall, a former *Daily Mail* correspondent. 'There were veiled criticisms in the newspapers but it was in the shops and cafés and the French homes that Britain was the target for open attack: blame for pushing France into the war; blame for doing nothing while France was at war.' While the French sneered that Britain's small contribution to the war effort consisted only of 'generals and lorries', the Security and Intelligence captain, Basil Bartlett, noted, 'Part of my job is to see that relations between the French and the British are cordial. It's the most difficult part of my job.'

It was Germany's good fortune that in the early months of the war the Allies were saddled with pusillanimous leadership. The men who happened to be in command when the bell rang were Edouard Daladier and Neville Chamberlain; by the time of the Blitzkrieg both had, in effect, gone. Daladier was the first. A fifty-five-year-old widower from the south of France who stressed his working-class background (a baker's son) while keeping a titled lady, the Marquise de Crussol, as his mistress, he was in 1939 not only Prime Minister of France but also Defence and Foreign Minister – presumably, in the opinion of Major General Edward Spears, 'because he could trust no colleagues to fill those important posts without the risk of their overshadowing him'.

Early in January 1940 Daladier suffered a heavy fall while out riding on a holiday weekend, and the subsequent pain and insomnia loosened his control of government. On 20 March, six weeks after surviving a vote of confidence by 534 votes to nil, Daladier was toppled. His replacement as Premier of the 98th and next-to-last government of the Third Republic was Paul Reynaud, sixty-two, an outsider and loner who had held Cabinet rank in several governments but belonged to no political party and sat as an independent in the Chamber of Deputies. He was a barrister and belonged to a family made wealthy by ownership of a department store in Mexico City. A short (5ft 3in.), darting, sharp-featured figure, Reynaud was known as Mickey Mouse to his many political enemies; like Churchill in Britain, he had warned repeatedly of the dangers of Nazi aggression.

Reynaud shared one characteristic with Daladier, whom he detested. He too kept a titled mistress, Countess Hélène de Portes, a woman of anti-British sentiments who was to exercise a baleful influence on her lover and his decisions while he was in power. Reynaud's dislike of Daladier did not prevent him installing his predecessor – leader of the party which controlled most votes in Parliament, and therefore essential to his survival – as War Minister. The appointment was to cause as much harm to France's cause as did the utterances of the rival mistresses, hampering Reynaud's intention to shunt aside Gamelin, of whom he said, 'It would be criminal to leave this nerveless philosopher at the head of the French Army.'

In Britain, too, the government was unravelling, though at a more sedate pace. Chamberlain had been Prime Minister since succeeding Stanley Baldwin in May 1937. As he approached his third anniversary in power, he was past seventy and, though few knew it, dying of intestinal cancer. He possessed what has been called 'an unassailable belief in his own rectitude' and, as Churchill wrote of him, 'His all-pervading hope was to go down to history as the great Peacemaker . . . unhappily he ran into tides, the force of which he could not measure, and met hurricanes from which he did not flinch but with which he could not cope.'

Though Chamberlain was respected in some Army quarters because he had kept Britain out of the war until a better state of preparedness was reached, many members of the BEF regarded him as little more than a joke. 'We knew he was trying to win the war with slogans such as "Time is on our side" and "Hitler has missed the bus",' recalled Tom Bristow. 'They were two bigger prevarications than anything Goebbels had been able to dream up.'

The opinion that Hitler had missed the bus by not attacking Britain in the first six months of the war helped push Chamberlain over the precipice. The comment was uttered on 4 April; within a week came the German invasion of Denmark and Norway. As the Norwegian campaign went from farce to worse for the British forces despatched there, the demands mounted for his resignation. The Commons debate on the Norwegian fiasco opened on 7 May, and as Chamberlain rose to speak he was greeted with boos and cries of 'He missed the bus' from the Opposition benches. Even his own Conservative Party followers had had enough and Leo Amery, a Privy Councillor and former Cabinet Minister, completed the Prime Minister's humiliation by quoting the words of Cromwell when dismissing the Long Parliament in 1653: 'You have sat here too long for any good you have been doing. Depart, I say – let us have done with you. In the name of God, go.'

Desperately though Chamberlain manoeuvred, he could find little sympathy or support. On the evening of 9 May he was a few hours from resignation and Britain was, in effect, leaderless. With Reynaud also having submitted his resignation that day in frustration at being unable to rid his Army of Gamelin, France was in a similar parlous state at the worst possible moment.

Among the French armies, and almost without exception in the BEF, complacency reigned as the Phoney War moved into its eighth month. The French transport officer, Denis Barlone, was one of many who totally discounted rumours of an impending German violation of Belgium's neutrality. To do so, he felt, 'would arouse the indignation of the whole world. . . . I cannot believe that they will again commit this enormous mistake.' After being assured at a divisional staff meeting that no French offensive was contemplated before July, Barlone sowed radishes, spinach and carrots in the kitchen garden of his billet and on the evening on 9 May he entertained a dozen colleagues from divisional staff in his mess. They dined on lobster and truffled fowl, played bridge until 1 a.m. and planned another rendez-vous for the following week.

On 7 May Lance Bombardier Eric Manley spent a day in the Picardy village of Lihus – 'a lovely summer day, and almost a lovely war. We are slack, as usual, and the day is spent mainly lounging about on the grass amongst the chickens. I write letters home in the cool of the evening, sitting under an old apple tree in the cemetery.'

As he censored letters home from the men under his command, Lieutenant Peter Hadley remembered, 'I was particularly struck by . . . their cheerful courage and their pathetic blind optimism.' That optimism more closely resembled foolhardiness in the opinion of the war correspondent, Bernard Gray. 'Responsible officers of the BEF, who ought to have known better, were saying they wished the Germans would attack. "Then we'll show them who are the masters" they used to boast.' Britain's soldiers sang of their intention, in the words of the popular song, to hang out their washing on the Siegfried Line, prompting the renegade Englishman William Joyce (Lord Haw-Haw), to threaten prophetically: 'The Englishmen's washing will be very dirty before they come anywhere near the Siegfried Line.'

On 9 May Lieutenant R L Clarke, an engineer intelligence officer in the BEF's 4th Division, had received no intelligence of the imminent conflict. His diary for the day reported,

Telephone activity with the usual trivialities. . . . 18 Field Park Company have lost the bulldozer again. . . . 30 Field Regt RA have indented for yet more sandbags . . . a battalion in 10 Brigade has cut up the local dance floor for revetting material and are faced with a bill for £50. . . . Corps want our return of outsize boots by tonight's Despatch Rider Liaison Service . . . a French civilian arrives with a pot of blue paint to say he has instructions to black out the windows.

In Britain the nation was preparing for the Whitsun holiday weekend, to the annoyance of the *Daily Mirror* which quoted Churchill's comment in the Commons: 'At no time in the last war were we in greater peril than we are now.' 'So what?' commented the newspaper's leader article sarcastically. 'So on with the Whitsun holiday. The last trump might sound, the Heavens may be rent asunder, the earth might gape beneath us. Where are you going for Whitsun? We have at last shaken the fumes of opiated complacency but another sure-footed sleepwalker in Germany never rests. Where is Hitler going for Whitsun? To Holland, Belgium, Sweden, Switzerland.'

At the end of April the American William Shirer made another journey along the Rhine war border and was again struck by the quiet:

In one village German children were playing in full sight of some French soldiers loitering on the other side of the river. In an open meadow not 200 yards from the Rhine and in full sight of a French blockhouse some German soldiers were frolicking about, kicking an old football. Trains on both sides of the Rhine chugged along undisturbed. Not a shot was fired. Not a single airplane could be seen in the skies.

Unlike many in Britain and France, however, Shirer knew well enough that a German offensive had to be imminent. 'Hitler wants to finish the war this summer if he can. If he can't, despite all the German victories, he's probably lost.'

About the same time as Shirer was penning those thoughts, Germany's preparations were being finalized. On 7 May Hitler had grudgingly allowed Göring to impose one more postponement because of poor flying weather, but, insisted the Führer, he would not wait one day longer. On the morning of Thursday, 9 May the Luftwaffe's meteorological expert predicted good weather for the morrow (and was awarded a gold watch by the relieved Hitler). The attack was on. Still the Allies slumbered. As early as 1 May the French military attaché in the Swiss city of Berne had forecast a German invasion between 8 and 10 May. There was other intelligence information along similar lines available from neutral sources such as the Vatican, but all were ignored – as was the sighting, by an astonished French pilot returning from a leaflet raid, of a line of armoured vehicles stretching some sixty miles inside Germany almost to the Luxembourg frontier.

Hitler had long determined to oversee the invasion from a forward command post. Orders had been given the previous winter that the group of forts and bunkers comprising this headquarters should be ready for occupation by mid-March. The bunker, at Münstereifel, midway between Bonn and the Belgian Ardennes, was never detected by the Allied air forces.

Hitler's retinue departed quietly from a small railway station near Berlin aboard the Führer Special on the afternoon of 9 May, proceeding north before making a turn to the west after dark. At 2100 hours the codeword Danzig was broadcast, and early next morning an Order of the Day was released from Hitler to all his forward area troops: 'Soldiers of the West Front! The hour of the most decisive battle of the future of the German nation has come. . . . The battle which is beginning will decide the fate of the German nation for the next thousand years. Do your duty!'

6

The Balloon Goes Up

Dear God in heaven, we thank Thee that we are Germans, and still more that we are allowed to live in this gigantic epoch.

Lance Corporal Wilhelm Prüller, 9th Panzer Division

Rather like 3 September, everybody in the BEF remembered where he was and what he was doing early on the morning of 10 May. Just after 6.30 a.m. Staff Sergeant Frank Hurrell, seated on an outside toilet, heard aircraft approaching. 'I looked through the opening at the top of the door and saw a solitary aircraft. Suddenly the morning quiet was broken by the wailing of the air raid siren, quickly followed by shots being fired from or at something very close. Needless to say, my stay in the "little room" ended rather hurriedly.'

Having watched the film *Captains Courageous* the previous evening, Sergeant Bill Brodie was awakened 'by a terrific anti-aircraft barrage and the crump of falling bombs; from my window the sky seemed ablaze'. S L Rhodda of the 3rd Division Signals also awoke to the sound of explosions, punctuated by the screams of the female owner of the café at which he was billeted: 'In the very clear sky over Lille I could see German bombers unloading.' Alf Hewitt was in a group of soldiers straggling back from a late night out in Roubaix when the sirens sounded. 'There were bombers about, ack-ack guns going and we realized something was up. Sure enough, early next morning our commanding officer got us all together and told us the balloon had gone up, as he put it.'

First news of the balloon's ascent was received by many officers with the early morning drink delivered by their orderlies. Lieutenant R L Clarke of the Royal Engineers remembered: 'When my batman Sedgwick, an efficient but incomprehensible Geordie, brings me my morning cup of café cognac he says the Germans have invaded Holland and Belgium.' Captain Basil Bartlett was woken at six by one of the soldiers in his Field Security Police section: 'He was standing saluting at the end of my bed, wearing a tin hat and with a smile on his face. "I told you so, sir," he said.'

When the French Army's Inspector-General of Artillery, General Georges Boris, heard the explosions he asked an aide where the manoeuvres were being held. Brigadier George Sutton, who had served continuously with 125 Brigade of the 42nd (East Lancashire) Division since 1914, slept through it all, despite having had a large lump of wax syringed from his ear the previous day. Sapper Jack Toomey, of that division's postal unit, joined with some mates in emptying a bottle of rum and another of cognac to help drown the constant sounds of alert from a siren 'in a church tower about twenty feet from our window', and he admitted in a letter home 'I was still drunk when I woke up the next day.'

Aroused with the news at 6 a.m., Anthony Rhodes hurried downstairs in his billet:

I found most of the other officers in their dressing-gowns huddled round the wireless in the mess. . . . We stayed and listened till seven o'clock, when all the previous news was corroborated. There was a funny bit in it out of Ribbentrop's speech in which he said that if the Germans had not attacked Belgium the British would have done so. This made us laugh quite a lot because everyone knew that the British Army was incapable of attacking anybody.

James Hill, a staff officer at Gort's headquarters, had a rather earlier start to the day. At 4 a.m. four waves of bombers passed overhead, an event he considered 'rather unusual'. They were followed at 5.30 by a pair of fighters flying so low that Hill could make out the faces of the pilots. 'I then got up and ordered my horse and rode out to the local AA battery on the hill to see if they had secured any hits. About 7.30 I saw my groom chasing after me to say that the war had started and I was wanted back at HQ at once.'

Lieutenant James Langley of the Coldstream Guards was one of those whose lives were changed for ever by the date of the attack. He was due to leave the BEF for a job as instructor at a new school for snipers in England. The posting arrived on 10 May, so Langley stayed on, subsequently to lose an arm and his liberty. At the time, however, Langley was relieved that the test had finally come. It was a feeling shared by many. 'After all the weeks of waiting we received the news of the onslaught with an odd feeling of relief,' said the signaller Lawrence Vollans.

Relief was also the word used by General Brooke, who added, 'The sword had now fallen and I felt action would be preferable to suspense,' though he was still concerned about vital deficiencies: 'It was certainly not comforting to realise that with such an ill-equipped army we were moving forward to engage a force equipped with all the most modern armaments manned by a personnel already war-experienced.'

Some, like Tom Bristow, gave the impression they would cheerfully have marched off to battle bearing a pitchfork:

I was now going to do the job I had left home for and that gave me satisfaction. I had not put on uniform to have my life wasted by being messed about at the whims of foolish men, but that was what it had been during the last eight months. Now that was a thing of the past. I suppose it was bad news really but we welcomed it as if it was the best news we could have. It was the sense of freedom that filled me with elation.

At French headquarters in the château of Vincennes one of the general staff found the C-in-C, Gamelin, striding up and down and humming a martial air as he prepared an Order of the Day: 'The enemy attack, foreseen since last October, was launched this morning. It is now a fight to the death between Germany and ourselves. For all the Allies the order is "Courage, Energy, Confidence". As Marshal Pétain said twenty-four years ago "We'll get them".' The order took two days to reach the defenders of the Maginot Line.

Since Belgium had been such a staunch ally in the 1914–18 war its decision to remain neutral had come as a shock to France. An alliance between the nations had been signed in 1920, but two years after the death of King Albert in a climbing accident in 1934 his son Leopold revoked the treaty as a result of Germany's unopposed reoccupation of the Rhineland, saying he wished to stand apart from the quarrels of his neighbours. This meant that in the event of war France would not be able to move into Belgium until the Germans chose to attack. More importantly, it shredded the Maginot Line strategy. Leopold, by no means the redoubtable king his father had been, clung to the hope that Hitler, if unprovoked, might forget all about Belgium – an extraordinary attitude. The Belgians even refused to allow the Allies any facilities for reconnoitring their country until March 1940. Then an artillery officer, Brigadier Francis Davidson, received tacit consent to make a discreet tour along the proposed lines of Allied defence in case of German aggression. Although he was obliged to wear civilian clothes and remain in his car, Davidson saw enough to confirm his suspicions that those particular defences were ramshackle.

Leopold need not have bothered to assume such a coy stance. In Hitler's opinion the Belgians were neutral neither in mind nor in heart, since all their newer fortifications had been built along Germany's frontier and not France's.

Holland, having managed to remain neutral in the First World War, hoped with crossed fingers and closed eyes to be spared again. It was a vain hope. Hitler's Chief of Staff, Keitel, considered that both Belgium and Holland had, since the outbreak of war, forfeited their claims to neutrality by turning a blind eye to RAF flights over their territories.

In January 1940 Churchill, at that time First Lord of the Admiralty but already in heavy demand as an orator and broadcaster, delivered a scathing blast at would-be neutrals: 'Their plight is lamentable and it will become worse. They bow humbly and in fear to German threats of violence, comforting themselves meanwhile with the thoughts that the Allies will win. . . . Each one hopes that if he feeds the crocodile enough, the crocodile will eat him last. All of them hope that the storm will pass before their turn comes to be devoured.'

Post-war, and in a more considered light, Churchill wrote sympathetically of Belgium's plight:

If British and French policy during the five years preceding the war had been of a manly and resolute character Belgium might have adhered to her old allies. This would have brought immense security and might perhaps have averted the disasters which were to come. . . . No man in Britain and France has a right to blame Belgium. In a period of vacillation and appeasement the Belgians clung to neutrality and vainly comforted themselves with the belief that they could hold the German invader on their fortified frontiers until the British and French armies could come to their aid.

This aid was to be provided under a scheme known as Plan D (for Dyle, the river – or, rather, stream – on which the Allies would base their first line of defence). The Dyle Line ran south from Antwerp until it linked with the main French defences on the Meuse, a river considered the best anti-tank obstacle in Europe. In the middle of the Dyle Line was a thirty-mile plateau between the rivers, known as the Gembloux Gap, and it was here that Gamelin expected the main German armoured thrust to come.

On the extreme left of the Dyle Line, with its flank on the Channel, was General Henri Giraud's 7th Army. Next came the BEF, guarding the area to the north-east of Brussels. It was regarded by the British as a position of honour but by Gamelin as a psychological move to keep Gort's troops at a distance from home waters. To the BEF's right was the crack 1st Army of General Georges Blanchard, charged with holding the Gembloux Gap down to Namur on the Meuse. Stretching southwards, and behind the Meuse, were General André-Georges Corap's 9th Army, and finally the 2nd Army of General Charles Huntziger linking with the northern end of the Maginot Line. Corap and Huntziger held a front of just under a hundred miles facing the 'impenetrable' Ardennes with four light cavalry divisions, in some cases still equipped with horses, and ten low-quality infantry divisions of the sort which General Brooke had described as surly and slovenly when he watched them parade some months earlier. Behind these forces there was no reserve.

The BEF had seventy-five miles to travel to get to the Dyle, the Germans ten miles less from the opposite direction but against defended positions. Gort expected to have two or three weeks to prepare before the enemy got as far as the Dyle. Instead, they were there in four days.

Plan D was put into operation at 6.15 a.m. on 10 May. So the British abandoned the defence works they had spent all winter and spring preparing and moved forward to a new line of which they knew next to nothing. 'We thought it was foolish to leave those positions and go forward into open country,' said Tom Peck of the Royal Norfolks. 'But orders is orders in the British Army.'

As the British columns prepared to move, John Matthew, the RASC major, noted a theatrical feel in the air. 'The infantry were in full kit and writing last letters home and everyone seemed elaborately over-casual about everything.' After an early lunch and overseeing the loading of trucks, Gregory Blaxland had an hour to relax.

I sat on a chair and had my equipment draped over another chair next to me. I cursed the sun. It seemed to be mocking me with its golden rays while the revolver, equipment and steel helmet by my side forecast an outlook of thunder. There was a nasty queasy feeling inside me that made me yawn and yawn again. Like a jockey hoisted into the saddle before a race, I shed my nausea once we were in motion.

There was hasty instruction for the officers of the 5th Battalion Green Howards in the use of the revolver, but since only three of the thirty actually possessed such a weapon most of the others had to go through the motions of firing one. The battalion moved off to war similarly deficient in compasses and binoculars. Rifle practice was ordered for Derek Ramsdale and his colleagues in the 149 Field Ambulance Unit before they left. 'We were taken to a canal bank and all of us used the same rifle, each firing one round at the opposite bank. We were then given ten rounds each to take up the line. We were, of course, covered by the Geneva Convention whilst we were attached to the Field Ambulance. The rule was that we could only shoot if our patients were being attacked.'

Lieutenant James Hill of Gort's HQ staff was one of the first across the frontier at 9.45 a.m. 'We were mobbed by thousands of Belgians as soon as they realized my car was British. My batman and driver had the greatest difficulty in preventing the car being stripped for souvenirs.' Other units received a similarly enthusiastic reception once they had persuaded Belgian customs officers to let them into the country. Tom Bristow's transport unit, part of Montgomery's 3rd Division, set off in mid-morning with the 12th Royal Lancers. 'We were led by our sergeant, a tall, thin man nicknamed the Battling Bootlace, who was singing "Donkey Serenade" and "Umbrella Man".' They were held up when a Belgian customs official refused to let them take their machine guns into his country without the necessary papers. Bristow watched as a Lancers officer ordered an armoured car to punch a hole through the barrier.

At last the war correspondents had something to write about, and they laid it on lavishly. Under the headline 'Gort's Advance Thunders into Belgium at Dawn' O D Gallagher wrote in the *Daily Express,*

Acetylene flames cut away the steel posts on the France–Belgian frontier at dawn today and let through a torrent of British tanks, gun, lorries, armoured cars and despatch riders. At dusk the BEF is still cascading through, mile upon mile of steel, exhilarating in its immensity and speed. It is as fast as any German army has travelled, and that includes the Polish and Norwegian aggressions. For the British Army is the most highly-mechanised in the world. The nine months of waiting has ended suddenly. The BEF is on the move and I have never seen such determined-looking men.

The *Times*, whose man on the spot was Kim Philby, later unmasked as a spy for the Russians, reported 'The British move across Belgium is going forward on oiled wheels.' Philby was perhaps closer to the truth than he realized, since drivers were being plied with wine and beer at every halt. Bernard Gray told *Daily Mirror* readers: 'With flowers, beer and cheers the Belgians greeted the British Army as deliverers come to the aid of their country . . . enthusiastic girls plucked lilac from the wayside and scattered it in the path of the British troops . . . women ran to the armoured vehicles and hung posies of flowers on gun barrels.'

The RAMC captain, Joe Patterson, remembered the move into Belgium as one long celebration, flowers, fruit and wine all along the roads, a journey rather marred for me by a bout of gastro-enteritis. An elderly man ran out from one farm, greeting us with cries of 'Any more for any more.' There his English vocabulary ended but he brewed us up a fearful infusion made from real British soldiers' tea of 1918 vintage. It was terrible but we drank to l'Entente Cordiale right nobly.

As Robert Holding's battalion of the Royal Sussex Regiment marched through one village an old man fell in step alongside them. 'Hobbling along, trying to keep pace, he started to sing "Tipperary" in what, for his age, was a remarkably powerful voice. Encouraged by the troops, he continued with "Pack Up Your Troubles', both songs sung in word-perfect English that had obviously been painstakingly learned from our fathers.'

Holding was handed a large bottle of beer by a very small girl. Bill Brodie was the recipient of a bunch of rhubarb. So many flowers were tossed into John Matthew's car that he thought it was beginning to resemble a hearse. It was all so different from what Matthew had been led to expect. 'We were told that as soon as we crossed the Belgian frontier we should watch for saboteurs, and if we saw anyone lurking by the side of the road we were to shoot first and ask questions afterwards.'

By nightfall the BEF's leading motorized elements had reached the Dyle Line. Montgomery's 3rd Division arrived in the dark to find the position allotted to it already occupied by Belgian troops who, mistaking their new allies for German parachutists, opened fire and seriously wounded one soldier. The Belgians were understandably jittery, since the town of Louvain had been heavily bombed earlier.

All day the BEF's convoys had jammed the roads into Belgium. The Royal Horse Artillery officer, Anthony Rhodes, was in one which drew up at the frontier to await darkness before proceeding. 'We congregated in little clumps, smoking and chatting near the vehicles. . . . Some German bombers came over while we were waiting and our reaction seemed typical of the first day of the war. We did nothing; we just stood glaring up at them hoping someone would blow them to bits.'

Nobody seemed surprised that the Luftwaffe had made no attempt to hamper the BEF's advance. This was because it was an advance which suited the German strategy. When Hitler heard that the Allies had swept forward to the Dyle, in the fashion of a bull reacting to a matador's cloak, he exulted: 'I could have wept for joy, they had fallen into the trap.'

The Balloon Goes Up

The German Air Force, banned by the Treaty of Versailles and reborn in February 1935, had been rebuilt with the same rapidity as the Wehrmacht. Commanded by Hermann Göring, one of the Richthofen squadron in 1918, it soon achieved a strength close to 2000 aircraft and 20,000 personnel. By May 1940 it had comfortably doubled that number of planes and was operating from 400 airfields. The RAF had 89.

In the May Blitzkrieg the Luftwaffe's role was not that of a strategic weapon. Instead it was used mainly in support of the powerful German ground forces as they swept through Luxembourg and into Belgium and Holland. Airfields and communications centres were the main targets of the bombers, and by the end of the first day's fighting the Dutch Air Force had lost 62 of its 125 planes, mostly destroyed on the ground, and the equally small Belgian Air Force had suffered similarly. Allied airfields also came in for sustained attack, and road and rail junctions in the northern sector of the invasion were bombed, but the Luftwaffe kept the bulk of its fighter aircraft as an umbrella over the vulnerable columns of Panzers as they chugged into the Ardennes.

What the world was witnessing, on that first day of Blitzkrieg in the West, was unprecedented domination of the battle area by air power. As John Terraine has pointed out in his history of the air war, the results 'were not merely gratifying to the German leaders but also psychologically devastating to the opposition, seizing for Germany an initiative which she never lost throughout the campaign'.

It was an initiative grabbed swiftly in Holland and Belgium. Widespread use was made, for the first time on such a scale, of special airborne operations to drop parachutists and land glider-borne storm troops on airfields, bridges and fortified posts in order to clear a path for armour and motorized infantry.

Holland, with a larger population than Belgium's but an army of 250,000 which was only one third as strong, placed much defensive reliance on the flooding of large areas and the destruction of bridges over its many canals. Thorough and occasionally subversive action by the German troops often bypassed such planning by the Dutch, whose government reacted to the invasion by banning alcohol, the use of the telephone and listening to German radio as part of its package of emergency restrictions.

By the time the people of Brussels were scanning the headline in *La Nation Belge* ('The Germans Are Back') serious inroads had been made into Belgium's defences, again by a combination of daring and cunning. The day's most spectacular coup was the capture of Fort Eben

61

Emael, the linchpin of the Albert Canal defences where Gamelin confidently expected the German attack to be held. Completed only in 1935, it was the world's most modern fortification but, crucially, it possessed no defence against assault from the air. Fewer than a hundred crack German troops landed unopposed on the roof by glider, and at a cost of only six dead immobilized the fort and its 1200 defenders until German columns broke through the next day. So within thirty hours the Allied plans were already looking vulnerable.

Because of the difficult terrain things went less rapidly in the area of the Manstein Plan's knife thrust, the Ardennes. Germany, a nation which in 1933 had been forced to conduct Army exercises with cardboard models of tanks, was able on 10 May to put into the field ten Panzer divisions, a total of 2574 tanks, the biggest concentration ever. Seven of these divisions were aimed at the Ardennes, bearing out Guderian's dictum (*'Klotzen, nicht kleckern'*) that it was better to strike with fist than fingers. France actually possessed numerical superiority in tanks (Britain's contribution was so small as to be negligible), and its heavier models also had thicker armour and bigger guns. But the Germans were better in three vital areas – speed, radio communications and, above all, leadership. Highly mobile and completely self-contained, each Panzer division was an army in miniature, with its own rifle brigade, artillery, anti-aircraft battery, engineers, signals, supply organization and even reconnaissance aircraft.

The passage of the three Panzer divisions of Guderian's 19 Corps through Luxembourg was smoothed over the previous days by the filtering into that tiny country of German 'tourists' on bicycles and motorbikes. In a little over four hours Luxembourg was over-run, at a cost to its bewildered population of six policemen and one soldier wounded.

At the height of the advance on 10 May the armoured column, though closed up to a degree where it would have suffered enormously under air attack, still stretched more than a hundred miles from head to tail. The mountainous and wooded countryside, made more difficult by demolition work on the narrow roads, did far more to hold up the German assault than did the flimsy opposition. As Guderian noted, 'The resisting power of cavalry against Panzer divisions proved insufficient.'

Erwin Rommel, leading the 7th Panzers, had forecast in a letter to his wife on the eve of the invasion, 'Everything will go all right.' Two days later he wrote again in joyful confirmation, 'I've come up for breath for the first time today. . . . Everything wonderful so far. Am way ahead of my neighbours. I'm completely hoarse from orders and shouting. Had a bare three hours' sleep and an occasional meal. Otherwise I'm absolutely fine.'

Back in Berlin, William Shirer noted, the reaction to the great new assault was muted that weekend; 12 May was 'a typical Sunday with no evidence that the Berliners, at least, are greatly exercised at the battle for their thousand-year existence. Cafés have been ordered to close at 11 p.m. instead of 1 a.m. That will get the folk back home before the night air-raids start, though we've had none yet. Also, dancing has been *verboten* for the time being.'

In her Suffolk village, soon after hearing of the Lowlands invasion, Margery Allingham noticed 'the windows began to rattle faintly in their frames as they used to all the time when I was a child and there were big guns in Belgium before'. With air attacks expected any moment, she stored away what she called 'my only valuable', the manuscript of her latest novel, in a biscuit tin and took it to bed with her.

Though the papers for that weekend in Britain carried adverts from the resorts, such as 'Ramsgate: Your place in the sun for holidays as usual', the government was urging people to avoid all unnecessary travel over the Whitsun weekend and, where possible, to stay at work. In its issue of 11 May, the *Times* said, 'The workers of Britain will give their answer to the new Nazi aggressions by willingly foregoing a much-prized holiday. But for Hitler thousands of them would have gone off this weekend to the seaside and the country. Instead they will be on duty and, it is safe to assume, putting into their work everything they can.'

The main story in Britain's papers that day was the installation of the nation's new leader. Well aware, by the afternoon of 9 May, that he might become Prime Minister, Churchill maintained that the prospect 'neither excited nor alarmed me. . . . I was content to let events unfold.'

Since Churchill had been a champion of his brother, the Duke of Windsor, during the Abdication crisis, King George VI did not favour him, and suggested instead Lord Halifax. However, the departing Chamberlain informed the King that Halifax had already declined at a meeting held at Downing Street earlier that day between Chamberlain, Halifax and Churchill. 'Thus then, on the night of 10 May, at the outset of this mighty battle, I acquired the chief power in the State,' Churchill wrote later. 'As I went to bed about 3 a.m. I was conscious of a profound sense of relief. At last I had the authority to give directions over the whole scene. I felt as if I were walking with destiny, and that all my past life had been but a preparation for this hour and this trial.'

7

Nuns by Parachute

*The Teuton hog of Europe is breaking out of his sty . . . if we can
hog-tie the brute for six months, we've got him.*

Cassandra, *Daily Mirror*, 13 May

'Despair in Berlin' trumpeted the *Sunday Chronicle* on 12 May. The
following morning's *Daily Mirror* informed Britain: 'Allied Advance
Goes On'. To the extent that the BEF was still moving up into Belgium
this was true enough, though already they were beginning to run into
refugees heading for France. The *Mirror*'s man, Bernard Gray, encountered the better-heeled vanguard as he drove towards Brussels
on 11 May. 'One didn't notice [the refugees] much this first day. For
the people who were leaving were the people with money to run big
motor-cars. The rich, as usual, were getting out first.' In Brussels
itself, Gray noted, 'The streets were packed, tram cars crowded to
capacity. The sun shone. Women wore their smartest spring clothes.
It seemed a very happy world, with the Germans a long way off and
victory very near.'

In fact the Germans were drawing closer by the hour and defeat
loomed. Desperate attempts by the poorly equipped French Air Force
and French-based planes of the RAF to destroy bridges left unblown
by the Belgians, and over which the Wehrmacht was pouring, only
caused further heavy losses to squadrons which had already suffered
grievously. On the first morning of the Blitzkrieg 114 Squadron's
Blenheim bombers had been caught on the ground at their airfield
near Rheims. Inside ten minutes six were destroyed and the remaining ten shot up so badly that they were unserviceable. Later that day
32 Battle bombers attacked advancing German columns. Thirteen
were shot down by anti-aircraft fire and none of the others escaped
damage. Only one of eight Battles returned from another mission.
Forty-two RAF losses were recorded on 10 May, another 44 on the

11th, a further 48 on the 12th, and on the 13th 71 of the RAF's rapidly disappearing and heavily outnumbered air arm were shot out of the sky. So in four days just over half the RAF's 400 French-based planes had been lost, and Sir Cyril Newall, Chief of Air Staff, was stating the obvious when he told the commander in France, Air Marshal Sir Arthur Barrett, 'I must impress on you we cannot continue indefinitely at this rate of intensity.'

The ten squadrons of Hurricane fighters provided the only bright moments in the air. They claimed 42 'kills' in 208 sorties on 10 May, but after three days had lost almost half their 96 machines. Back in Britain the C-in-C of Fighter Command, Sir Hugh Dowding, refused to commit any of his 19 Spitfire squadrons to the air war, wisely hoarding his most precious commodity for the forthcoming Battle of Britain, while the War Cabinet endorsed Bomber Command's decision to bomb Germany by night rather than support the French.

By mid-May the men of the BEF were complaining that the initials RAF stood for Rare As Fairies, an understandable comment but dismissive of the bravery shown by aircrews as they set off on what amounted to suicide missions in outgunned and outmoded aircraft. None were braver than the five crews of No. 12 Battle Squadron who volunteered on 12 May to attempt the demolition of two bridges over the Albert Canal left unblown by the Belgians. Only one plane returned, but so determinedly did they press home the attack in the face of withering fire that the RAF's first two Victoria Crosses of the war were awarded posthumously to Flying Officer Donald Garland and his crew, Sergeant Thomas Gray, who damaged one of the bridges by crashing into it. A German officer who interrogated one of the captured survivors of the attack told him: 'You British are mad. We capture the bridge Friday morning, you give us two days to get our flak guns all around it and then you come along and try to blow the thing up.'

There were similar grievous losses among the French Air Force. It had only 700 war-ready aircraft on 10 May and its subsequent decimation fulfilled the predictions of its deeply pessimistic commander, General Vuillemin, described as 'a pilot of the last war who had gone to seed'.

The virtual destruction of such air cover as the Allies possessed had a crippling effect on the morale of the Belgian Army, buffeted on the ground and from above. Soon they were streaming back to the BEF's defence line, mingling with refugees and affording the British soldiers grim amusement. In Wavre, on the right flank of the BEF's twenty-two-mile frontage, Brigadier William Holden estimated that the

Belgian troops outnumbered refugees. 'Many were without boots and happy to get behind our lines.' Much of the Belgian artillery was pulled by horses or mules. Joe Hooker, a Royal Engineers sapper, thought one retreating column looked as if it had just marched out of the Crimean War, with its covered wagons and two-wheeled carts. 'They also had "tar-boilers" cooking soup as they went along, chimneys smoking.' When Les Boyce, an RASC driver, asked one Belgian gunner what the two crates – one filled with chickens, the other with puppies – aboard his wagon were for, he was told 'Food'. Many of the men and animals on these retreating columns were so exhausted that the medical orderly Derek Ramsdale saw soldiers asleep in the saddle and horses leaning against each other for support, a grim foretaste of what the BEF would soon suffer.

The combination of exhaustion and demoralization sometimes had tragic consequences. Alf Hewitt, whose company of the South Lancashires was guarding a canal bridge just behind the Dyle Line on the outskirts of Brussels, was sent on a night patrol:

We crawled around the fields from 7 p.m. until about midnight. When we got back to the canal there was about a quarter of an hour to go until we were due to come back through the lines. So the sergeant leading us said we could have a smoke. There was a small side road that led down to the canal, so we went down there towards a low wall at the edge of the water. One or two sat on the wall and we lit up.

Then we heard troops approaching. This corporal of ours strolled to the road, looked and told us they were Belgians. We had seen them over the past few days. They used to go up ready for war and come staggering back afterwards absolutely defeated after taking a terrific hammering from the Germans.

The Belgians went past the top of the road, about fifty yards away. It was bright moonlight. Suddenly they came to a ragged halt and before our eyes they threw themselves on the floor facing us and began firing at us, pouring fire into us. There was nothing we could do but retaliate. We weren't a rabble like they were, we were well-trained infantry. We had two Bren guns. The action went on for about a minute and then somebody among them blew a whistle and they stopped firing and we sorted ourselves out.

With their first volley we had two killed, one sitting on the wall, name of Martin, fell over backwards into the canal and we never recovered his body. Then there was a fellow named Bill Smith, who had joined up with me. I was lying in the gutter and he was on the pavement just above me. The machine gun they had firing ploughed straight into us. I heard a clunk as they hit his helmet. My own helmet was jerked round a bit but five bullets went straight through Smith's head.

When we had a count-up this Belgian officer was crying like a baby. Said his men had seen the moonlight shining on our helmets and took us for Germans, since they weren't Belgian helmets. We killed seventeen of them and wounded many more. It showed we were a bit more efficient than they were. It was regrettable but we were rather pleased. That was our first action at close quarters and we had come out of it well.

Other forms of communication proved a problem because of the British Army's reluctance to use two-way radios. The choice of BEF headquarters or command posts was therefore governed by the location of civilian phone lines or cables. Major Ralph Rayner of the Royal Signals, sent to Brussels from England on 10 May to organize a signals centre at the British Embassy, found that the Belgian telephone operators were still working peacetime hours. On Sunday, 12 May he was unable to raise anyone before 9 a.m. having been trying for the previous eight hours. When Rayner eventually contacted the engineer-in-chief of the public telephone system their meeting was a brief one. The official pleaded a headache, promised to return later but was never seen again, having joined the flood of refugees.

The signals lieutenant, Toby Taylor, was required to lay wires through the centre of Brussels.

It was all so daft. If we put them on the road the trams cut them in half. I remember trying to lay some cables through the grounds of the Royal Palace because that was a short cut to our positions. When I got the sentry on the gate to let me in there were some rather pretty girls playing tennis, of all things, who told me the King wouldn't like it if I started laying cables through his gardens. So the gates were slammed and I had to find somewhere else.

When Gort moved a slimmed-down headquarters into Belgium on 11 May his Director of Military Intelligence, Major General Frank Mason-Macfarlane, was forced to get his news from the British Embassy, who were getting it from the BBC, who in turn were being fed the wildly optimistic bulletins of the French High Command. Even the journalists on the spot were reduced to attempting to find out what was happening by listening to radio bulletins. The *Daily Mail*'s Paul Bewsher joked: 'The BBC may prevent us being captured by telling us where the Germans are.'

Montgomery overcame the communications problem by jamming messages on the end of his walking stick and thrusting it through the window of his staff car for his personal despatch rider to deliver, though even this was not a foolproof method because of congested roads and the increasing frequency of air attack. The swelling flood of refugees caused the worst obstructions and brought heart-rending sights which deeply moved the British troops. Brigadier George Sutton felt 'It would be a hard-hearted person who did not stop to pity these people and a chicken-hearted one who would not risk his life to defeat the scum who cause such misery.'

Major Peter Hill wrote to his wife in Banstead, Surrey,

The last few days have not been pleasant and, my dear, it is no use pretending otherwise. . . . I had to attend dying and injured refugees after they had been bombed. My first dead were a child of five and her grandfather. I don't want to try and be horrific, Betty, and soldiers expect terrible things in war, but when one sees the pitiful plight of innocent people we have only one idea – carry the same total warfare into Germany and smash them in pieces for ever.

After witnessing an air raid on Louvain, Tom Bristow watched refugees flooding out of the town.

As they filed past, their faces were a picture of hopeless misery. They appeared quite oblivious to us, just walking on with glazed eyes staring straight in front of them. I felt tears welling up in my eyes as I noticed a small boy – he could not have been more than six – with his head almost completely bandaged, clutching his mother's skirt for guidance with one hand whilst the mother was nearly exhausted from pulling a handcart, piled high with bedding and a few other treasures, up the slope. I told her to look after the boy and leave me to get her cart to the top of the hill and on to the Brussels highway. I could see no logic in undertaking a fifteen-mile trek just to get to another place that could prove to be no safer than the one this crowd were leaving.

The woman whose cart I had hauled was about the same age as I was. I wondered where her husband might be – perhaps he was already in uniform or perhaps he was in that desert of rubble that had yesterday been houses. Giving the woman what assistance I could helped me to shake off the feeling of guilt that we were at least partly responsible for the desolation being caused.

Major W C Giblett and his men handed out their chocolate and sweets to the children and cigarettes to the adults 'until we had no more to give', and Captain Alan Bell Macdonald provided beer in an abandoned bar being used as a headquarters: 'Oh God, it is dreadful – one lot sat while I served them beer and let them wash, then they went on, dejected and hopeless. It gets me down so much I could cry.'

Major John Matthew's troop-carrying unit had permission, when returning empty from the front in Belgium, to offer lifts at their discretion. 'But it was a difficult job. One dare not stop where they were very thick, as one got besieged, chiefly by the young and active. There were far too many young and able-bodied men among the refugees and quite a lot of Belgian Army officers and men too. None of them got lifts from us.'

Any form of transportation was pressed into service by those fleeing. Joe Hooker of the Royal Engineers spotted three dust carts ('nice and shrapnel-proof') full of people and wondered: 'Perhaps it was the mayor and corporation escaping.' Hooker also watched a man propelling his invalid chair, 'twiddling the handles hard'. André Maurois was struck by

the cyclists in their thousands, one troop for each village, the priest at its head, postmasters and railwaymen in their uniforms, young girls and children thoroughly enjoying the excursion. . . . Village firemen had brought their families away on the fire-engines. Some old men were huddled together in a hearse, the feeblest of them stretched out in the place where the coffin goes.

Captain Basil Bartlett spoke to a cyclist who had done the same journey on the same machine twenty-five years previously – 'But in half the time'.

For Anthony Rhodes there was a horrible fascination in seeing the refugees' sense of priority: 'Pots with withered plants in them, pictures in gilt frames, quilts and cloths . . . there were birds and beasts and fishes of all descriptions and on one pile I saw a monkey sound asleep. One man had a donkey to pull his cart and he sat on top of a gigantic pile of gimcrackery looking just like the muleteer in the drawing from *Don Quixote*.'

Gregory Blaxland watched the departure of the occupants of a farmhouse commandeered by his company:

Two carts were produced and piled high with possessions, and then a crippled old lady was hoisted up with the aid of us soldiers and placed in a chair facing backwards on the top of the load. She was in an uncontrollable fit of sobs. An infant was also shoved aboard. This left the householder, two sturdy women and a boy of about ten.

The householder, who had taken an understandably sullen view of our occupation, beckoned me into the kitchen, showed me sides of salted pork hanging against a wall and indicated they were ours. I made gestures of thanks and asked '*Où allez-vous?*' He shrugged his shoulders. He departed pushing one cart in league with the ten-year-old and his two women pushed the other. For the first time I felt sorry for the Belgians.

Joe Patterson noted 'a touch of the *Marie Celeste*' in the abandoned villa where he established his Regimental Aid Post: 'I found everything just as it was. On the table was the newspaper of 10 May, fateful day, there was milk in a saucepan and coffee in the pot. Upstairs the beds were just as the people had left them. There must have been three little children here. Their toys are all about and their clothes here and there.'

Heading towards the Dyle Line, the French transport officer Denis Barlone was incensed by the road jams. 'What are the army traffic control doing?' he wondered. 'Everywhere traffic-blocks! In 1917 the service worked perfectly. Have we unlearnt the lessons of the last war?' Many British soldiers commented on the number of young male refugees pushing bicycles with bright red blankets strapped to the pannier. Joe Hooker's feeling that the blankets were 'almost a badge of office' was not far wide of the mark: they were, in fact, Belgian Army deserters. Robert Holding of the Royal Sussex Regiment was convinced they were German SS men infiltrating the Allied lines. Rumours such as this about the presence of spies and Fifth Columnists (a phrase which originated in the Spanish Civil War when a general advancing on Madrid boasted he had four columns under his command and a fifth, composed of Franco supporters, inside the city) added further to the chaos and confusion.

Undoubtedly there were those in Allied territory sympathetic towards, or actively working for, the Nazis, but their influence did not begin to measure up to the strength attributed to them. The German ploy of dropping dummy parachutists ahead of their advance into Belgium and Holland became a horror story of nuns descending from the sky sporting hobnailed boots and seven o'clock shadows, and of priests toting sub-machine guns. Advertising hoardings for brands of salt and chicory were torn down because it was rumoured they were message and guidance boards for the invaders. Poisoned sweets were reputed to have been dropped at the Gare d'Austerlitz in Paris, killing a child who ate one. Fear spread like a plague and it would all have been grimly amusing if the consequences had not so frequently been fatal. The despatch rider Don Ellingworth witnessed the summary execution of a woman hanging out washing because it was thought she was communicating with a German plane circling overheard. Farmers cutting their fields or householders mowing their lawns risked death if the direction of the cut happened to point towards a gun position or troop concentration.

Lord Normanby, intelligence officer of the 5th Battalion Green Howards, had so many suspicious characters awaiting interrogation that he thought his office resembled a doctor's surgery. Lieutenant Colonel R L Clarke came across a dejected figure wearing civilian shoes and an ill-fitting battledress, sitting blindfolded in a chair and guarded by two military policemen. It transpired he was one of the

British Embassy staff in Brussels who thought he would have a better chance of getting to a Channel port dressed as a soldier.

As Major John Matthew approached his divisional headquarters late one evening he came across the following scene:

At the entrance and silhouetted against the sunset were a very tall, heavily built priest and a little elderly peasant, each of them with two soldiers with rifles cocked and fixed bayonets pointing straight at their chests. They were suspected spies awaiting interrogation. Later on, as I came out of the HQ buildings in bright moonlight, the smaller one was being questioned by a French liaison officer, with a revolver pressed into his tummy, and as I passed the little man just collapsed in a heap under the strain. Shortly afterwards they were marched off under escort, whether for further interrogation or for shooting I don't know. Probably the latter, as in a very short time the escort came back without them, one of them wearing the priest's hat.

S L Rhodda's convoy was passing a straggle of refugees

when I saw a pigeon fluttering away from a bloke. An oldish woman behind him bent down, whipped off one of her hefty clogs and hit him over the head with it. He disappeared under half a dozen struggling refugees, all yelling and cursing. A couple of Redcaps drove up and whisked him off. About five minutes later, as we moved off, we heard a small burst of rifle fire. An officer and the Redcaps then came along the column warning us to watch out for spies releasing pigeons carrying information to the Germans.

Ronnie Noble, the Universal News cameraman, said, 'People like me with war correspondent tags were under heavy suspicion. People would look at us twice.' He also witnessed an incident when two men in an open sports car were stopped at a French road block. They claimed to be golf professionals from a club near Brussels, but when they were unable to produce suitable identification they were marched behind a nearby house. 'A few minutes later I heard four shots,' wrote Noble. '"They should carry identification cards" muttered a French sergeant. "The —— Fifth Column is everywhere".' Noble confessed, when he saw some nuns, that even he checked to see if they were wearing boots.

When word reached England of parachutists disguised as nuns Margery Allingham's reaction was that 'since a nun is not a familiar figure in my village and the arrival of one by bus, much less by parachute, would have occasioned considerable interest, not to say suspicion, the information had a touch of pure fantasy about it very hard to stomach at first'. There was also a touch of fantasy about

Kenneth McDougall, a Dundee labourer, who was fined 10s 6d for telling a woman he was a German parachutist.

The 12th Royal Lancers, the armoured car regiment which had been the first BEF component into Belgium, pushed well to the east of the Dyle Line and had its first contact with German tanks on Whit Sunday, 12 May. The following night the Lancers made the first of what were to be many British withdrawals, and on 14 May the six road bridges over the British section of the Dyle were destroyed. The BEF stood ready to receive the enemy.

The Dyle, little more than a brook until widened by damming, was not at all the well-prepared defensive position the British commanders had been expecting. On the extreme right flank of the BEF sector, in the small town of Wavre and a few miles from the battlefield of Waterloo, the 1st Battalion The Royal Scots had to break into pill boxes near the river because whoever held the keys of these defensive positions could not be found.

On its left flank the BEF's defences ended at the university town of Louvain, painstakingly rebuilt with American aid after its destruction in 1914. Since the Dyle ran through Louvain's centre, the British position had to be based on a railway line along the eastern outskirts and linking, to the north of the town, with the Belgian Army. It was against Louvain that the main German thrust in this area came on the afternoon of 14 May, and it was here that Montgomery had already stamped his unique brand of leadership on the situation. His biographer, Lord Chalfont, recalled,

All day he was out with his units, solving problems, making decisions, giving orders on the spot. At teatime he would return to his headquarters, assemble his staff and give orders for the night and the next day. Immediately after dinner he retired to bed, with orders that he was not to be disturbed. On one occasion the Germans actually entered Louvain in a night attack and the duty officer, mistakenly believing this to be a crisis of which the divisional commander might care to be appraised, woke him with the news. 'Go away', said Montgomery crisply, 'and don't bother me. Tell the brigadier in Louvain to turn them out.'

Colonel Graham Brooks recalled awaiting the arrival of the Germans at the Dyle:

It is a curious feeling watching the country beyond the river, knowing that somewhere behind it are the Boches. How far away are they now? How long before you get a glimpse of them? The first hint was movement of animals. Away on high ground beyond the river, herds of cows began to move obliquely away from the road. Animal movement is most helpful to the artillery observer. Sure enough, motor cyclists soon came into view, then an armoured car or two. The next to appear were marching infantry. Over the crest they came, a glorious target. Dennis Clarke (in charge of the command post) waited until at least two hundred were in sight on the forward slope. . . .

In some ways the Hun infantryman has not changed. Though our shells were dropping among them, men were falling and others running for safety, more infantry kept appearing over the crest, just as they used to come doggedly on in the last war without using any intelligence. This continued for some time before they changed their plan. In the meantime we had done useful execution. Those were the first shells fired in anger on the Dyle.

Attacks against the British defences were pressed with little armour but great determination, and it was here that the first Army Victoria Cross of the war was awarded. When the enemy got across the Dyle near Wavre, Second Lieutenant Richard Annand of the Durham Light Infantry mounted a lone sortie hurling grenades, and was wounded. Annand led the repulse of a second attack and, on withdrawing once more, learned that his batman had been hit and left behind; he went back for the injured soldier and carted him to safety in a wheelbarrow before collapsing from his own wounds.

Although not being hammered from the air as severely as the Dutch in the north and the French on the River Meuse to the south, the British were already suffering the helplessness of being attacked and observed with virtual impunity by the Luftwaffe. The Rev. Ted Brabyn, a First World War veteran and Territorial Army chaplain, was conducting an open-air service in Belgium on Whit Sunday, 12 May, when the sirens sounded. 'At once all the troops put on their tin hats except me, who felt that, as the padre taking the service, I would have to remain bareheaded,' Brabyn remembered. 'Being almost bald, I felt great comfort when they sang

Cover my defenceless head
With the shadow of Thy wing.

A Green Howards officer found 'a sort of sinister fascination' in being bombed: 'We used to argue, when we had time for it, which were the greater menace, the bombs or the guns. I belonged to the school that favoured the bombs. I preferred to see what was coming my way to a shell that landed alongside unannounced.' S L Rhodda found no fascination at all in his experiences when he was bombed just outside Louvain: 'The radio operators and myself dived into a trench-like brick-lined pit, which had obviously been used for storing pigswill, and we found the CO had beaten us to it. True to their nature, the Jerries came over regularly every hour afterwards. The CO warned us by checking on his watch and we would all shelter in the pit as the odd bomb fell nearby.'

The *Daily Mail*'s Paul Bewsher reached one town minutes after it had been bombed and found

a scene of horror and desolation . . . In the main street three buildings were in flames from top to bottom. Men called me to help and I dashed into a large department store. In the floor there was a huge hole filled with flaming debris. From this smoke and flame came the faint, wailing voice of a child crying *'Au secours, au secours.'* While people frantically threw buckets of water on the fire and tried to smash open the floor beside the hole, a Belgian *gendarme*, a British officer and a middle-aged civilian went down to the cellar from a small door above the pavement . . . they then carried out a little boy of six, with bloodstained face and hands, who nodded his head and said *'merci'* politely as he was laid on the table.

After such horrors it was little wonder that a terrible fate awaited many German airmen who were shot down. When British troops arrived at one crash scene they found all the occupants of the bomber dead and an elderly woman kicking and spitting on one of the corpses. The sapper, Joe Hooker, watched a German fighter crash-land: 'The pilot was badly wounded and came out calling "Doctor, doctor", but as he held on to his revolver they gave it to him.' Major Ralph Rayner of the Royal Signals was in Brussels on the evening of 14 May when three parachutists landed in the square of Porte de Namur 'and were literally torn to pieces by the crowd'.

Though the British held firm against bombs, shells and ground assault their position on the Dyle was imperilled by collapses on either side. At 11 a.m. on 15 May Holland surrendered, shattered by the previous day's atrocity bombing of Rotterdam which laid waste to a square mile of the city centre, destroyed 20,000 buildings and killed 980 civilians. Under the heading 'Dutch Govt. Flees', the *Daily Mirror* reported that Queen Wilhelmina had arrived in London 'with a gas mask slung over her back and wearing a plain black coat and skirt'.

In the following day's edition, carrying a report from the French High Command that the situation was 'serious but not critical', the *Mirror* commented that the French, rather like football managers in later years, were 'cool, determined and quietly confident'. In reality the situation was cataclysmic. The great River Meuse, behind which the French had taken confident shelter, was already breached by the night of 12 May by contingents of German infantry. Twenty-four hours later General Alphonse Georges, in charge of the North-East theatre of war, rang Gamelin to tell his C-in-C there had been *'un pépin assez serieux'* (a rather serious hitch) in the Meuse defences. That 'hitch' had become a gaping hole by midnight on the 14th, with German tanks on the river's west bank and the ill-trained and low-quality French troops demoralized by concentrated artillery and the Junkers JU87 'Stuka' dive bomber which had so recently devastated the armies of Poland.

Defenders of what were considered impregnable positions were broken and driven in headlong retreat – though at great cost to the Germans, too. However on 14 May the Battle of France was in effect lost. The 9th and 2nd Armies of Corap and Huntziger were in chaotic flight as the Panzers gathered themselves for that historic armoured breakthrough across northern France.

At 7.30 a.m. on 15 May, before he had had the opportunity to read the comment in that morning's *Times* that 'the German have not yet made contact with the bulk of the British and French forces', Churchill took a bedside telephone call from his opposite number, Reynaud: 'He spoke in English and evidently under stress. "We have been defeated." As I did not immediately respond he said again "We are beaten. We have lost the battle." I said "Surely it can't have happened so soon?" But he replied "The front is broken near Sedan. They are pouring through in great numbers with tanks and armoured cars."'

8

'Run, Run Like Hell!'

It was an ideal war for the intellectual. The ordinary ranker didn't know what was happening.

Harry Dennis, East Surrey Regiment

Communications may have been difficult and information sparse, but with the campaign a week old it was clear the BEF had its head in a noose. Steps had to be taken quickly to extricate the army.

The order to withdraw from the Dyle Line was transmitted in several ways to soften the blow. Harold Foster of the Grenadier Guards was told the plan was to entice the Germans forward, attack them from the flanks and cut them off – exactly, in fact, what the Germans were in the process of doing to the British. Bill Brodie recalled 'our spirits were lightened' when his signals section was told the withdrawal was intentional in order to lengthen the enemy's lines of communication. Being a colonel, Graham Brooks was slightly better informed – but no less puzzled: 'To leave this magnificent position on the Dyle, when the BEF had its tail right up – it couldn't be true. . . . Everyone on the Dyle had the impression that the BEF was top dog over the Hun. Still, we thought, we'll be back here again very soon.'

Arnold Johnson's troop-carrying company had just eaten supper when orders were received to pack up and get out, with no explanation offered. 'I was getting a bit fed up,' said Johnson. 'Keeping the ordinary soldier in ignorance was a great mistake. Esprit de corps was founded on pride in what one was doing and a sense of belonging to a family of comrades in arms. Without this we felt lost and isolated.'

Lieutenant Colonel Brian Horrocks, who on 10 May had hurried from his job as chief instructor at the Camberley Staff College to take command of the 2nd Battalion Middlesex Regiment at Louvain, and had begged a lift in a dental truck to help him get there, was one officer who made a practice of explaining to his troops what was happening around them – because, he considered 'the modern soldier. . . . will give of his best only if he understands the reason for what he is doing'. Horrocks also attempted to explain to the silent crowds of Belgians watching the pull-out, telling them, 'Don't worry. We will come back.'

Of that scene in Belgium Anthony Rhodes wrote,

There were no cheering people this time, they all realized well enough that they were being left to the Germans once again. But they did not jeer or catcall. They just stood quietly and gloomily at street corners watching the great sea of British vehicles flooding the streets, all struggling to get into their city and out of it, like rats escaping through a hole.

The civilians sometimes found it difficult to accept that they were being deserted. One man spat at the staff car carrying Brigadier Merton Beckwith-Smith of the 1st Guards Brigade. The despatch rider Don Ellingworth, who witnessed this incident, said, 'The Brigadier did his nut, in fact he was going to pull his revolver.'

The dislike, even before the Belgian surrender, was often mutual. When Gregory Blaxland's company left the flax farm where they had been staying near Courtrai their departure was enlivened by the frantic gesticulations of the farmer demanding a colossal sum for the use they had made of his flax as bedding. 'No one felt sorry for the farmer,' Blaxland wrote. 'The Belgians had that effect.' Even a Church of England chaplain, the Rev. Gough Quinn, found the people of Brussels hard to take: 'They didn't seem to mind what happened in the war, provided the town was not damaged. I must have been asked a dozen times if we were going to defend Brussels. I got pretty sick of their poor spirit and finally took a malicious pleasure in telling them that we certainly should fight, even if every building had been destroyed.'

Toby Taylor, who had been upbraided for attempting to lay cables through the Royal Palace grounds on the BEF's arrival in Brussels, faced more complaints as he prepared to blow bridges on the withdrawal through what King Leopold had pleaded should be declared an open city: 'It was rather like blowing Westminster Bridge in London. One chap came up to me and told me he had to get over to the other side, where he lived. I told him that was his bad luck. They just weren't interested, they had their job to do and whether it was us or the Germans it didn't make any odds.'

There was passing popularity for a company of the 3rd Battalion Grenadier Guards who, on rounding a street corner, ran into an enthusiastic welcome from a cheering crowd. On checking his map, the company commander found they had taken a wrong turn and were heading back towards the German Army. He ordered an about turn in stony silence.

So rapidly was the Allied front disintegrating around them that, whichever way they faced, the BEF risked running into trouble. A letter from an unnamed officer in those same 3rd Grenadier Guards paid full tribute to the enemy:

There is no doubt that the German firepower is something wonderful. The co-ordination between their dive bombers, artillery, mortars and machine guns is astounding. Lastly the efficiency of their tanks and the speed with which mechanized units follow up a breakthrough; coupled with all this the Fifth Column and the parachutists gives one an awful feeling of insecurity behind one's lines.

The letter might also have mentioned the imaginative and daring leadership of the Panzer general, Guderian, and his colleague, Rommel, who was comparatively inexperienced but learning very fast the art of armoured warfare, having been given command of the 7th Panzer Division only in February 1940. Guderian, known as Hurrying Heinz to his adoring tankmen, insisted on carrying out his theory that 'only leaders who drive in front of the troops will influence the outcome of the battle'. That was an outlook shared by Rommel, and it came close to costing both men their lives during the heady and hectic days of the breakthrough.

The only leaders capable of wrecking the German success were not British or French, but Hitler and the more cautious of his generals. Guderian, who almost single-handedly had been responsible for the creation of the Panzers in the face of doubters, was outspoken and often short on tact as a result of the struggles he had undergone to transform the dream of armoured power into reality. As an officer cadet he had been dropped from a choir because, being tone deaf, he sang different notes from the others. Now, in May 1940, he was fifty-two and things had not changed. On 15 May his immediate superior, General Ewald von Kleist, ordered Guderian to halt his three Panzer divisions, which formed part of the armoured group named after Kleist – an officer of the old school who held the job which Guderian felt, with good reason, should have been his. Clearly, no love was lost between the two. Told to hold his tanks in the bridge-head over the Meuse until further orders, Guderian complained, 'I would not and could not put up with this order since it entailed the abandoning of surprise and all our initial success.' So he phoned Kleist, pleading for the cancellation of the halt order. 'The exchange of opinions was very lively and was repeated several times,' he noted.

Kleist agreed to a further twenty-four hour advance to consolidate the Meuse bridgehead for infantry to follow up, which Guderian took as carte blanche to order his tanks to advance 'to the last drop of petrol'. They covered forty miles, leaving supply columns and support troops far behind. The same day Rommel did even better with a fifty-mile advance. It was all too much for Hitler. The gambler who had backed the Panzer plan suddenly lost his nerve, worried that the racing columns of armour would be encircled by counter-attack and destroyed. On the evening of 17 May General Franz Halder, Chief of Staff of the German High Command, commented in his diary, 'A most unfortunate day. The Führer is terribly nervous. He is frightened by his own success, is unwilling to take any risks and is trying to hold us back.' The same morning Kleist had flown to see Guderian and, without even wishing him good morning, began to berate him for disobeying orders. He reimposed the halt order which had been insisted on by his own superior, von Rundstedt, who in turn had been affected by Hitler's nervousness. Guderian, shocked that Kleist 'did not see fit to waste a word of praise on the performance of the troops', waited until his visitor paused to draw breath, 'then asked that I might be relieved of my command'. Though taken aback, Kleist nodded.

Guderian's resignation was rapidly overturned on von Rundstedt's orders, and an accommodation worked out whereby the Panzer general would be permitted to carry out 'a reconnaissance in force' while leaving his headquarters where it was. Off went the tanks and their weary but jubilant crews – exhaustion made acceptable by the enemy's obvious disintegration – while back at his operational headquarters Hitler was still full of trepidation on 18 May. 'He rages and shouts that we are going about it the right way to ruin the entire operation and are running the risk of defeat,' Halder wrote.

Certainly, had Guderian suffered any severe rebuff in his westward thrust he would have faced execution by Hitler for persistent disobedience. As it was, the 'hideous, fatal scythes' (as Churchill called them) of Operation Sickle Cut encountered little resistance. Had the efforts of the French armour been co-ordinated, Hitler's worst fears might have been realized, but four armoured divisions (of 150 tanks each) were committed piecemeal against seven German ones averaging 260 tanks apiece. On 14 May the 1st French Armoured Division was ordered into action near Dinant but, able to average only four miles an hour along roads clogged by refugees and fleeing troops, ran out of fuel halfway towards its destination. Rommel's tanks swept past while it was at a standstill, and later the French tanks were over-run and cut to pieces. The 2nd and 3rd Divisions, severely disrupted by air attacks and road congestion, were never available in sufficient force to make any significant contribution. The 4th Division was under the command of Charles De Gaulle, a forty-nine-year-old, 6ft 5in. colonel nicknamed 'La Grande Asperge' (the Big Asparagus). De Gaulle had assumed command of the division, so new that it did not yet possess a divisional staff, only on 11 May. Officers met their crews for the first time on the way to the battlefield as De Gaulle threw a scratch force of three battalions into action at the town of Montcornet, north-east of Laon, on 17 May, the day the Panzers were halted. Initial success against infantry caused confusion on this vulnerable German flank, but lack of support of any kind forced De Gaulle to break off what never amounted to anything more than a raid, and withdraw.

So the Panzers swept ever deeper into France, filling up at public petrol stations when they outstripped supply facilities. On 18 May Guderian's 'reconnaissance' crossed the River Somme and took Péronne, where several French staff officers, intent on finding the position of their own troops, were made prisoners. The tanks rumbled past huge posters, inspired by Reynaud and intended to maintain morale, showing a map of the world with the British and French empires splashed in red and carrying the slogan '*Nous vaincrons parce que nous sommes les plus forts*' (We'll win because we're stronger).

Masses of French troops were persuaded to lay down their arms by nothing more than shouted orders from the turrets of passing tanks. Once, when fifteen undamaged French tanks fell into his hands, Rommel incorporated them into his own column, still with their French drivers. Captured officers, he noted, were mainly concerned about permission to keep their batmen. In his diary he wrote: 'Civilians and French troops, their faces distorted with terror, lay huddled in the ditches, alongside hedges and in every hollow beside the road . . . nowhere was any resistance attempted.' One irate French officer, plucked from a traffic jam and ordered to accompany Rommel, was shot when he refused. '*Vous êtes Anglais?*' one woman asked Rommel as he stood in a village street. When he said no, German, she cried, '*Oh, les barbares*' and hurried indoors, head buried in her apron.

On an airfield outside Amiens a unit of RAF Hurricanes took off hurriedly as Panzers appeared on the perimeter. At Albert a battery of Royal Artillery, possessing only training ammunition in any case, was captured neatly drawn up on the town square. And Lieutenant

Charles Lamb of the East Surreys, who had been accidentally shot in the face by an Allied sentry during a visit to the Maginot Line, was popped into the Panzers' 'bag' in the act of leaving hospital in Abbeville to rejoin his battalion.

Responding to Reynaud's dramatic telephone call of the previous day, Churchill flew to Paris on 16 May to find the situation 'incomparably worse than we had imagined'. At a meeting at the Quai d'Orsay with Reynaud, Gamelin and others, Churchill asked the whereabouts of the French strategic reserve to plug the Panzer breaches – and was told: 'We have none.' Stunned, the British Prime Minister moved to the window to consider the implications of that comment, where he was greeted by the equally depressing sight of French Foreign Office staff preparing for the evacuation of Paris by trundling wheelbarrows of documents on to bonfires. (They could have spared themselves the trouble; a complete set of duplicates fell into German hands.) Churchill attempted to cheer up the French leaders by agreeing to their request for more RAF fighters, but told them firmly, 'It is the business of the artillery to stop tanks.'

Needing to stem the rot from within as well as the tanks from the east, Reynaud had decided, hours before meeting Churchill, to get rid of Gamelin. The man he wanted as replacement was Maxime Weygand. Inevitably, since Reynaud was a notoriously poor judge of people, the choice was disastrous. A seventy-three-year-old cavalry-man who had never commanded troops in action, Weygand had retired as French C-in-C in 1935 only to be recalled in 1939 to take charge of French troops in the eastern Mediterranean. He was a small, dapper man whose high cheekbones and sparse moustache gave him an Oriental look, though his liking for riding breeches, enormous boots and brass spurs brought comparison with an aged jockey or, in the opinion of General Spears, 'Puss in Boots'.

Weygand received the secret summons to return home in Beirut on 17 May and arrived two days later, having to be helped from his aircraft when the undercarriage collapsed on landing – not the happiest of starts. Weygand was lively enough physically, sprinting across a hundred yards of grass at his first meeting with his General Staff officers and then taking the stairs four at a time *en route* to the conference room. At least that was a contrast to Gamelin and his sidekicks, paralysed by indecision since the German invasion began. One of the most severe problems of French command was that, with General Alphonse Georges in charge of the North-Eastern theatre of operations (the only area where hostilities were taking place), there were, in effect, two French C-in-Cs who, furthermore, detested each other.

Georges had suffered severe head injuries in the bomb attack of 1934 which killed King Alexander of Yugoslavia, and many thought he had never fully recovered. Certainly his ability to comprehend the enormity of what was happening around him was flawed. He burst into tears after the French front was broken on the Meuse, and when General Huntziger of the 2nd Army asked Georges on 14 May which way he should retreat he had to wait several hours for the reply: 'Do for the best.' Although the Duke of Gloucester thought Georges 'a smart-looking old boy with about twenty-eight medals' and he was the proud owner of an enormous Cadillac, he was debilitated and stupefied by the German breakthrough. Yet Gamelin was content to leave conduct of the battle to Georges and had to be prodded by his Prime Minister into issuing an Order of the Day on 17 May urging his troops to die rather than concede any more French soil. On 20 May, the day the first Panzers reached the Atlantic coast, at the seaward end of the Somme near Abbeville, Gamelin handed over command. 'He appeared relieved that so heavy a weight had been lifted from his shoulders,' wrote his replacement, Weygand. 'We parted without the least sign of rancour on his side.'

Having installed a seventy-three-year-old as his top soldier, Reynaud next turned to an eighty-four-year-old, Marshal Philippe Pétain, the First World War hero, to join the fray as his Deputy Prime Minister. 'Poor old boy,' mused Alexander Werth in Paris. 'Fancy being dragged into all this at his age.'

By Friday, 17 May, the end of the first week's fighting, Gort knew that he faced being cut off by the Panzer thrusts. In the confusion of retreat, snarled up on the roads by hapless refugees, under mounting air attack and in peril from marauding German columns, many British units became lost or marooned. Les Shorrock's memories of those days were of 'constant harassment, noise and confusion, and never seeming to remain in one place for more than a few hours'.

Late on the night of 18 May Bill Brodie was called over by General Brooke and ordered to identify some troops withdrawing past 2 Corps headquarters. Brodie told the corps commander they were the Coldstream Guards, at which Brooke said to his staff officers, 'When Corps HQ is in front of the Brigade of Guards it is time for Corps HQ to move.'

Harold Foster, the Grenadier Guards warrant officer, remembered,

It was a time of confusion for us all. At one point my platoon were in position on a canal by a bridge which had been laid with explosives ready for demolition. It was my job to set off the charge when given the order. For the following twenty-four hours I seemed to be inundated with messages . . . 'Blow the bridge at 1000 hours' . . . 'On no account will the bridge be blown', and so on, until I was fed up with the damned bridge.

Foster also received a written message ordering him to destroy all the ammunition which could not be carried by his platoon when they pulled back. 'I queried this order with Company HQ and was told it was correct. So we took the ammunition from our truck, breaking open the watertight seals on the boxes before dumping it into the water. This soul-destroying task had hardly been completed when I got a further message from Company HQ: "On no account destroy the ammunition".'

At one stage the 1st Guards Brigade headquarters only discovered at dawn that it was retreating the wrong way, back east towards the enemy. 'We pulled into a field to check maps and location,' said the despatch rider Don Ellingworth. 'One man was taken short and went into a copse but he was back in seconds, pulling up his trousers and telling us that the field on the other side of the copse was full of Germans. That's where we lost all our equipment, because we pulled out in a hurry and the lorry wouldn't start.'

Lacking anti-tank weapons, the British often resorted to desperate measures. S L Rhodda watched soldiers constructing a barricade of 'old carts, wardrobes and other bits of furniture which wouldn't have stopped a determined rent collector mounted on a strong pushbike'. One British unit puzzled, and briefly halted, some German tanks by laying dinner plates upside down in the road to resemble mines.

Driving a lorryload of exhausted troops, Tom Bristow got out during a traffic delay to stretch his legs and ruminate on the lunacy of what was happening:

I looked at the dim forms reclining full-length in the back. How I'd like to change places with one of them, but not one of them could drive. I wondered what they would do if I should get wounded or killed; push the bleeding thing, I suppose. In all that time we had spent saluting, digging and constructing barrack squares, we could have taught every man to drive. It was in keeping with the trench war mentality of those who had no time for new-fangled things like tanks and planes. The bayonet was the thing.

Soon Bristow's lorry came across a group of Belgian soldiers, all with bicycles and heading back towards the front. Balanced on the

Pillar of Fire

handlebars were gallon jars of rum and other items of British rations. They pointed the way to a nearby field where a mass of rations had been dumped.

The sight was simply unbelievable – smashed boxes and ripped-open cartons strewed large areas with their litter. Seated amongst all this mess were quite a number of Belgian soldiers drinking from the gallon jars, all of them in varying degrees of drunkenness, who invited us to have a drink with them, holding up the jars and waving them. There were at least four of them who were out cold, sprawled among the litter as though part of it. All the attractive items had been claimed long before. There was no tinned milk, no bully beef, no tinned stew, no tinned beans. In fact the only tins there were some small round ones containing Marmite. No one apparently wanted the stuff but I loaded three boxes of them onto the truck. There were plenty of cartons of tea packets and spilled bags of sugar, from which I salvaged some. A jar of rum joined the Marmite.

Fatigue was taking a severe toll by the end of the first week's fighting. As he watched the vehicles of the 4th Division pulling back into his regiment's reserve area behind the Dyle, Gregory Blaxland said, 'I was shocked to find them laden with corpses, but after staring at them hard and seeing some movement I realized that the bodies they carried were not dead but fast asleep. . . . How soon would we be in a similar state?'

As S L Rhodda pulled back with a group of Hussars they passed three infantrymen on a small ridge near the road.

One of the officers shouted that we were the last British troops and that the enemy was just behind. One of them was fast asleep; one was trying to dig a slit trench, at the same time attending to a little wood fire with a mess tin of water on it; and the third was lying down behind a Bren gun with a good supply of magazines beside it. I couldn't see the face of the bloke asleep but the other two were really clapped out. They never moved, spoke or blinked when the officer spoke to them. The poor sods hadn't the faintest hope against what was on our tail.

Exhaustion affected even the highest ranks. Major General H C 'Budget' Loyd, in command of the 2nd Division, began to show signs of severe strain at a corps conference on 16 May. 'He was desperately tired and sleepy,' reported Brigadier William Holden of 1 Corps. 'He quietly protested against every proposal put forward and the situation was becoming very acute. All he would say was "It cannot be done" or "It is not an operation of war". He then collapsed and a doctor was sent for.'

Joe Patterson, medical officer of the 2nd Manchesters, noted in his

84

diary for 18 May: 'I took some bromide last night. I was in a state of jitters. I was jumping at every squeal of tyres and roar of engines.' Although he found the men of his battalion 'in grand form and very cheerful', Patterson developed a strong dislike for the regimental padre: 'This ruddy parson gets me down. He is a wet and sits there reading his Bible, the silly bun-faced wet that he is. If he mucked in now and then and filled a few sandbags he would be better occupied.'

'All the beasts are very worried with the din,' he wrote to his wife next day. 'Only the little birds keep on singing and don't seem to mind.' Sapper Joe Hooker, filling sandbags under a heavy barrage on 17 May, recalled: 'Over all were the nightingales down in the misty valley, singing, singing all night above the gunfire.' At the BEF command post at Premesques, a house with large grounds and a lake, Lieutenant James Hill recalled, 'I achieved one of my ambitions by seeing a golden oriole.'

Despite their own plight, the British soldiers were deeply concerned about the piteous condition of abandoned livestock and pets. Les Cannon recalled an overnight stop at a farm being rendered sleepless 'by the hideous lowing of neglected cattle'. Lieutenant Colonel Graham Brooks remembered how

Civilians, in their panic, had left their animals behind: cows, pigs, dogs, cats, even birds in cages. Some of these animals were left shut up, others were roaming about. . . .

First trouble came with the cows. The poor brutes needed milking; as their udders became distended and sore, they raced about the place bellowing pitifully. Our chaps did their best to milk them but we were all busy digging and fighting and the cows were legion, so it was an impossible task. . . . I therefore decided to shut up the few we could manage to milk and shoot the rest. . . .

Next came the dogs. It was pathetic, searching deserted houses, to find dogs chained up, locked up, going mad for want of food and water, terrified by bombing and the noise of our guns. Finally we deputed Sergeant Watts, himself a dog lover, to go round and put them out of their misery. You would see him, pipe in mouth and rifle in hand, stroll into a house. Then you would hear a crack. Out would come Watts, pipe still in mouth, jerk his thumb towards the house and say to a gunner, 'Bury that poor dog, son.'

The chickens we ate, the goats we milked. The pigs were the least trouble. They wandered about as they pleased. . . . Eventually when orders came to retreat we shot the pigs as well and soaked the carcasses of all dead animals with petrol, for nothing must be left of use to the Boches.

The plight of the refugees reminded General Brooke of the abandoned cattle. He described them in his diary as 'agonising humanity drifting aimlessly' and noted with dismay how they were cluttering the lines of communication 'on which all hopes of security rest'. However, by no means all the civil population took to the roads. Colonel Palmer Cook was struck by the way some farm workers carried on with their jobs while the fighting erupted around them. Once, during a bombing raid, he and his troops 'rather shamefacedly observed from our hiding places in ditches and under farm wagons and our own lorries a young French girl unhurriedly bringing in the cows at milking time'.

Lieutenant Colonel James Birch and his 2nd Battalion Bedfordshire and Hertfordshire Regiment were dug in along the Tourcoing–Courtrai road, overlooked by a huge block of flats where 'the people were sitting at their windows watching the fun'. Birch noticed that some women who were hanging out washing were staring hard at something. 'Looking carefully with my glasses I saw the bottoms of a few Boches who were crawling up a ditch near the gardens. The presence of civilians on the battlefield I found to make an atmosphere of unreality throughout the operations.'

Ronnie Noble, the Universal News cameraman, was filming at an anti-tank gun emplacement near Louvain 'with artillery shells flying in both directions, a dog fight up above and an occasional burst of machine-gun fire up the road' when someone was spotted advancing along the road. 'Gradually this figure got bigger. It was an old woman carrying a bucket of tea and three loaves. Without a word, she put them down beside the gun, smiled, turned round and went back. So brave.'

Noble's initiation into action came when his car, a Humber with a driver provided by the Army, was blocked by the flood of refugees. He climbed on to an *estaminet* roof to get some shots of the crowds.

Through the view-finder I saw an incredible scene. As one man, all the refugees in the road dived for the ditches – in a split second or so the road was clear. I heard the roar of aircraft, big black shadows flew over me and the machine-gun bullets hit the road and the ditches alongside. . . .

Then all was quiet until I heard the moaning from the people who were either hit or so afraid they could no longer control themselves. A young woman jumped and ran towards the building I was standing on. She stopped right under the camera and stood beating her head and hands against the wall, and then gradually she slid to the ground in a faint. . . .

Then I saw a child of about five appear from the ditch and stand in the centre of the road. He looked around and I could see the panic in his eyes from where I was. Fear held him tight where he stood. I heard a roar of aircraft above; then through my view-finder I saw an old lady clamber into the road. I pressed the trigger and panned the camera from left to right as she ran along the road. She grabbed the child in her arms and flung herself into the ditch. As she hit the ground the shadows swooped along the road pumping their noisy death into the ditches.

Noble recalled in later years, 'It sounds terrible to say this, but some of the best shots were when you'd see people dive or jump into the ditches, leaving prams at the side of the road.'

Having managed to remove the accumulated grime of several days with an al fresco bath in a rusty cistern, Bill Brodie found a hairdresser's shop in Wambrechies still in business. 'At a critical point the air-raid siren wailed and the barber, his assistant and the bevy of customers made a bolt for the door, leaving me in the chair complete with a large towel – and half a haircut! I carried this incomplete coiffure until I reached a barber in England.'

The Stuka dive bombers, with wailing sirens fitted to their wings, were the most unnerving of the German aircraft. 'Every one that came down gave the impression of diving directly at you,' recalled Alfred Baldwin. Sapper Jack Toomey devised an anti-Stuka plan: 'Never look a dive-bomber in the face. Pray hard and run, run like hell for the nearest ditch and dive in. I got quite used to diving in the end, could make a flat dive from the middle of the road or a power dive from a lorry in one motion.'

Tom Bristow provided a graphic description of what it felt like to be under attack by Stukas:

High up in the sky about thirty planes were flying in a circle as if playing 'follow my leader'. Three had peeled off from the circus and were diving for the very spot where we were sitting. They looked like filthy vultures, their undercarriage not being retractable so that their landing gear reminded one of the cruel talons in which they held their victims. What was held between the wheels, however, was not a victim but a big fat bomb. My eyes became riveted on that bomb . . . it held a strange fascination for me, it was my executioner. And I could do nothing about it. I had no fear of dying, just a wonder of what it would be like . . . the bomb was now so low that I imagined I could reach up and catch it and at that moment my muscles began to react; I turned swiftly on to my stomach, clasped my hands together behind my neck so that my arms would protect my ears, then buried my face in Mother-Earth and waited for the inevitable.

I was getting annoyed with that bomb; why was it taking so long? An eternity seemed to be passing, why didn't the bloody thing get it over with? I heard a terrific crump and the ground shook. My head went up, turning towards the sound, and I saw a few trees and a lot of soil defying gravity forty yards away. Some of the stuff that had gone up started to rain down as I shouted in my relief at the second plane coming down, 'He's missed me.'

The spell was broken. I sat up and watched what really was a spectacular display, regarding it as a show put on by the Luftwaffe for our special benefit. They'd never again be able to scare me stiff with their banshee screamers but at the same time I'd never welcome their attentions.

Despatch riders found themselves favourite targets of strafing planes. Don Ellingworth was near Ninove, heading back towards his brigade headquarters, when he was jumped. 'This plane with black crosses came after me. How he didn't get me I don't know. The bullets passed either side of me along the road. I managed to escape by driving into an orchard and hiding under a tree.' Tom Willy rode into Courtrai just as the last bombs of a raid were falling. 'One of the Stukas had levelled out and I could have shaken hands with the gunner. As he saw me he turned and fired but I got up against a wall and the burst went over the top of it.'

With little opposition and a wealth of targets to aim at, the Luftwaffe could afford to be selective. Lieutenant Gregory Blaxland was relieved, during his retreat, that

such aircraft as could be heard appeared to have no interest in us – until I found myself staring at the demon face of an air gunner. His plane, which I think must have been an Me110, came from behind us at such speed and at such low altitude that its swish became audible at the exact moment that I was presented with a close-up view of this awful, grinning face. It leered from a turret facing rearwards and there was a gun attached to it, spouting forth golden orbs. Luckily, ditches were available on either side of the road and I was at the bottom of the one on my side long before the thought of returning fire entered my head.

The Military Police corporal Reg Phillips had two even narrower escapes from death by shells and bombs. The first came when he was sheltering in a corrugated iron shed near Petit Vimy:

There were three boys from the Royal Scots Fusiliers with me. You could poke your fingers through the corrugated iron, it was so rotten, so I thought that wasn't the place for me because the shelling was very bad. I made instead for a haystack, turned round, there was an explosion and the shed I had just left was a hole in the ground. I ran from the haystack into a cottage and got under the fireplace because it was the most solid place there. All of a sudden there was this terrible thump on the top of my tin hat and I thought 'This is it' but it was just a brass clock falling off the mantelpiece.

Phillips's second escape came when Dornier bombers caught up with him in a wood. Having walked a long way and suffered painful feet, he had his boots tied round his neck.

I was with Sergeant Pete Holden, my pal, and a Grenadier sergeant, Bob Emmington. I was lying against Bob's feet and my boots were each side of my ears. My face was in my spats and I thought I would move up alongside Bob because I didn't like where I was for some reason. I hadn't been in my new position ten seconds when we were straddled by three bombs. Pete had moved into my place and his brains were coming out through a hole in his tin hat and over my boots. We buried him there when it was quiet.

On Sunday, 19 May the retreating British suffered their worst single blow from the air. German planes bombed and set ablaze the historic fortress town of Tournai, which lay astride the escape route, before turning their attention to the civilian and military traffic choking the roads. The 2nd Battalion Gloucestershire Regiment and the 4th Battalion Oxfordshire and Buckinghamshire Light Infantry, both part of the 48th Division, lost 194 and 48 men respectively when they were caught in the open. A travelling circus, trapped in the chaos, was also badly hit and the sight of wounded and crazed elephants plunging through the carnage added to a nightmare scene containing another unexpected element.

Two asylums near Tournai had released from custody all but the most helpless and dangerous cases, and to Brigadier George Sutton of 125 Brigade fell the task of resolving what to do with them:

The decision to release came from the Belgian government and while it may be protested that lunatics, of all people, might well have been left to Nazi care, it must be remembered they were in what was fast becoming a battleground and could not be left vulnerable. The lesser cases thus became free to wander the countryside and naturally their behaviour was unusual and they became suspect. There were a number of helpless ones and the decision what to do with them was left to me. I could not arrange their removal and so was given the authority to have them painlessly destroyed, but even the most hard-bitten medico quailed before the task. We were saved in the end because some of the priests who ran the asylum volunteered to stay with their charges, and putting both priests and patients in the inferno appealed to me more than the other solution.

The signals sergeant Bill Brodie knew that matters were now serious because messages began to bear higher and higher priority endorsements. Yet dozens of these messages could not be delivered because nobody had any idea of the location of the units concerned. The reluctance, or inability, to tell the Allied troops what was happening deepened the confusion.

The French transport officer Denis Barlone noted in his diary for 16 May. 'The men want to know where I am leading them but I conceal the fact that we are returning to France.' The 1st Battalion The Loyal Regiment, retreating from the Dyle Line, marched a total of fifty-four miles in three days, during which they prepared for battle four times only to be moved on again before finally reaching the BEF's new defensive line on the River Escaut (or Scheldt as it was known in Belgium). Little wonder they were sceptical about digging in yet again. Tom Willy's unit was preparing defensive positions near a crossroads 'when the old lady came out and played hell with us for digging up her garden. To crown it all, when we had dug the trenches we moved on again and never even used them. All we ever did was move back. We never made contact, always moving back.'

The 2nd Battalion Sherwood Foresters had one bizarre experience as they fell back towards the new regrouping line. Marching into a small town, they were astonished to be met by the burgomeister in full regalia. He offered them the town's surrender, only to realize to his horror that they were not Germans.

In the midst of confusion some things still functioned. Lord Sysonby, second in command of the 1/5th Battalion Queen's Royal Regiment, was handed by a despatch rider an envelope marked 'MOST SECRET AND URGENT'. Its contents notified him that a planned meeting of his division's Old Etonian Society would not now be taking place. Reg Phillips, a former policeman, was handed two letters from a mailbag rescued from an abandoned lorry: 'One was from the Income Tax and the other was from the police back home asking if I would make a regular donation out of my pay to their Widows and Orphans Fund.'

By 19 May the Allies had completed their withdrawal behind the line of the River Escaut, described by Captain Basil Bartlett as 'a curiously inadequate ditch behind which to fight a decisive battle'. Brigadier George Sutton did not think much of it either: 'Either through treachery or stupidity the French or Belgians responsible had let too much water out of it and in parts the muddy bottom was showing.' Ditch or not, the British troops, sandwiched between the tottering Belgian Army to the north and the French 1st Army to the south, were in sore need of a rest. Lieutenant Miles Fitzalan-Howard, with Montgomery's 3rd Division, had managed eight hours' sleep in five days. John Matthew, the RASC major and a Cambridge man, recalled he had 'the greatest difficulty in remembering the simplest things, let alone complicated orders. On one occasion I fell asleep as I was being given orders.'

Toby Taylor of the East Surreys had no doubt that many of his men slept as they marched: 'By linking arms two outside men could march a man between them as he slept, and later change over. On one or two occasions sleeping men walked straight off the road into a ditch. I remember walking half asleep straight into the backside and bristling tail of a very large French Army horse.' After falling off his motorbike several times because of exhaustion Don Ellingworth ran the machine into the side of the road, pumped six bullets into it, slashed the tyres, climbed into the camouflage netting on top of a wireless van and finally got the sleep he craved.

There was no rest for driver Tom Bristow, whose transport officer ordered a rifle parade in a wood beside the Escaut in steady rain with an air raid going on:

We were getting nervous and wet but the TO carried on moving from man to man, squinting down the barrels of the rifles, lost in a dream world of his own. At last he had finished, but we had not escaped yet. He started talking, telling us that many years ago he went to see a Charlie Chaplin film. He had never laughed before so much in his life until this parade. I wondered just what the TO thought of his performance. Was it an example of calmness under fire in his eyes? Whatever it was, it had frightened us more than the Germans could. The fool could have got every driver killed and then he would have been in a mess.

There was precious little rest, either, for Lord Gort, who felt by the night of 19 May that 'the picture was now no longer that of a line bent or temporarily broken but of a besieged fortress'. With his lengthy supply lines from ports in Normandy and Brittany now cut by the Panzer thrust to the coast, Gort's mind turned more and more to falling back towards the nearer Channel ports in readiness for an evacuation, and he warned the War Office in London of the need for such thinking 'as a last alternative'. The message had already penetrated. The same day, 19 May, that Gort sent his message, the War Office had opened joint discussions with the Admiralty about the 'possible but unlikely evacuation of a very large force in hazardous circumstances'. The code name allotted to the talks was Operation Dynamo.

9

Battle at Arras

We were all impressed by how efficient the Germans were, the way they went through Poland. But no way did we believe they could do that to us.

Alfred Baldwin, 65th Field Regiment, Royal Artillery

The campaign was only eleven days old when, on 20 May, the first Panzers came in sight of the Channel. In that time Guderian and his strike force had done what the German Army failed to accomplish in four years from 1914 to 1918. The dust-covered and weary architect of success arrived to take in the view himself and called it simply 'This remarkable day'. Alfred Jodl, chief of Hitler's operations staff, said the Führer was 'beside himself with joy and he already foresaw victory and peace'. Hitler's nervousness in reining back the tanks was commented on by an officer in the 1st Panzer Division on reaching the coast: 'We had the feeling such as a fine racehorse may have, of having been held back by its rider, coldly and deliberately, then getting its head free to reach out into a swinging gallop and speed to the winning post.'

Guderian's sickle cut virtually decided the battle of northern France. The military historian Captain Basil Liddell Hart considered that the way Guderian and his tankmen pulled the German Army along after them 'produced the most sweeping victory in modern history'. That the Allies were unable to comprehend the speed of collapse is perhaps best illustrated by the fate of General Henri Giraud, who had replaced Corap as commander of the shattered 9th Army of the Meuse on 16 May. Three days later he was captured – by tanks, according to Giraud himself, by men of a field kitchen unit according to the War Diary of the 6th Panzer Division. Ewald von Kleist, in charge of the armoured group which breached the Meuse, was reading a report of Giraud's appointment monitored from French radio 'when the door opened and a handsome French general was ushered in'. He introduced himself as Giraud, saying he had set out in an armoured car to look for his army and instead found himself in the middle of German forces far ahead of where he expected them to be.

Units of three under-trained and wretchedly equipped divisions of the BEF only recently landed in France – the 12th, 23rd and 46th – were rushed forward to bar the path of the Panzers and to prevent consolidation of the gap punched in the Allied defences. The town of Arras, where the BEF's general headquarters had been located since its arrival in France and which bore sentimental memories of British success in the First World War, was the key pivot. Its loss would enable the Germans further to broaden the hole in Gort's southern flank. The commander of the 12th Division, Major General Richard Petre, was hurriedly taken from his division and placed in charge of what was called, in the popular military jargon of that time, Petreforce. It consisted of the 23rd Division, 36th Infantry Brigade and the Arras garrison, whose main component was the crack 1st Battalion Welsh Guards, virtually the only experienced soldiers in the force. The 23rd Division, like the 12th and 46th, possessed neither signals nor artillery, only one Bren gun per platoon, one anti-tank rifle to each company and no anti-tank guns. Fewer than half the men had ever fired a Bren gun and a quarter of them had not even completed basic rifle training.

The poor training and, especially, lack of equipment caused the virtual annihilation of the 7th Battalion Royal Sussex Regiment, part of the 36th Brigade, when it found itself in the path of Rommel's 7th Panzers on 20 May. The battalion carried only thirty-two rounds for its anti-tank rifles. When they were expended the Royal Sussex tackled the tanks with Bren guns and rifles, and at their surrender after a day-long battle there remained only seventy of the battalion's original strength of 701 to be taken into captivity. An official history of the BEF condemns as 'both tragic and wasteful' the commital of these and other soldiers of little training at such hopeless disadvantage.

As success piled on devastating success the German propaganda machine invited Berlin-based foreign correspondents to the front. William Shirer of CBS was among those to be impressed:

One of the sights that overwhelms you is the vast scale on which the Germans bring up men, guns and supplies unhindered. . . . And what a magnificent machine keeps them running so smoothly. In fact that is the chief impression you get from watching the German Army at work. It is a gigantic, impersonal war machine, run as coolly and efficiently, say, as our automobile industry in Detroit. Directly behind the front, with the guns pounding daylight out of your ears and the airplanes roaring overhead, and thousands of vehicles thundering by on the dusty roads, officers and men alike remain cool and business-like. Absolutely no excitement, no tension. An officer directing artillery fire stops for half an hour to explain to you what he is up to. General von Reichenau, directing a huge army in a crucial battle, halts for an hour to explain to amateurs his particular job.

Morale of the German troops is fantastically good. I remember a company of engineers which was about to go down to the Scheldt River to lay a pontoon bridge under enemy fire. The men were reclining on the edge of the wood reading the day's edition of the army daily paper, *Western Front*. I've never seen men going into a battle from which some were sure never to come out alive so – well, so nonchalant.

On 20 May, returning to Germany, Shirer's group of correspondents came across a batch of British prisoners near Maastricht:

They were a sad sight. Prisoners always are, especially right after a battle. Some obviously shell-shocked, some wounded, all dead tired. But what impressed me most about them was their poor physique. . . . The English youngsters, I knew, had fought as bravely as men can. But bravery is not all; it is not enough in this machine-age war. . . .

I asked the English about that. There were six of them, standing apart – all that were left, they told me, from a company that had gone into battle near Louvain.

'We didn't have a chance', one of them said. 'We were simply overwhelmed. Especially by those dive-bombers and tanks.'

'What about your own bombers and tanks?' I asked.

'Didn't see any.' The answer was chorused.

Three of the men had dirty, bloody bandages over one eye. One of the three looked particularly depressed and stood there gritting his teeth in pain. 'A shame', his comrade whispered to me. 'He's lost the eye. Feels pretty rotten about it'. . . .

On the whole, though, despite the shell-shock, despite the black future as prisoners, they were a cheery lot. One little fellow from Liverpool grinned through his thick glasses. 'You know, you're the first American I've ever seen in the flesh. Funny place to meet one for the first time, ain't it?' This started the others to make the same observation, and we had a good laugh. But inside I was feeling not so good.

The news that Gort was even considering falling back to the coast caused consternation in London. The Chief of the Imperial General Staff, General Sir Edmund Ironside, was appalled. He felt the BEF should fight its way south through the Panzer thrust and rejoin the French on the River Somme, and this opinion received Churchill's whole-hearted support at an emergency meeting of the War Cabinet held late on the afternoon of Sunday 19 May. It was decided that Ironside should travel immediately to present the War Cabinet's views to Gort. Early the next morning the CIGS was putting his case that 'the right and indeed the only possible course for the BEF is at once to march in the direction of Amiens fighting all enemies met on the way'.

According to Ironside, 'After some thought, Lord Gort did not agree.' The surprise was that the embattled Commander-in-Chief needed to devote any thought at all to such a fatuous instruction. Quietly, he pointed out to Ironside (who has been described as 'an excellent man for African adventure . . . but with an apparent self-confidence as CIGS which turned out to be unjustified') that by disengaging the seven divisions facing the enemy on the Escaut he would precipitate the collapse of the tottering Belgians on the BEF's left flank and thus guarantee disaster.

Gort attempted to soothe Ironside by telling him he already had plans in hand to launch a limited attack southwards from Arras the next day, 21 May, with the only two divisions he still held in reserve, but that the effort would have to be approved by, and co-ordinated with, his immediate superior as head of the Allies' Army Group One, General Gaston Billotte. Gort considered Billotte, who had given the BEF no orders for eight days, was 'just jelly – he has nothing and does nothing'.

Pausing only to collect Gort's Chief of Staff, Lieutenant General Henry Pownall, Ironside set off angrily for Billotte's headquarters under the Vimy Ridge near Lens where, after a tiresome journey on roads blocked by refugees, he found Billotte with General Georges Blanchard, commander of the French 1st Army. Pownall thought the two French generals were 'in a proper dither' and Ironside considered them 'in a state of complete depression'. When the trembling Billotte voiced his despair about halting the Panzers, Ironside, whose 6ft 4in. stature earned him the inevitable nickname Tiny and whose indiscretions matched that stature, seized the Frenchman by his tunic buttons and administered a vigorous shaking. The startled Billotte accepted the British proposal to attack the next day and promised French support. When Ironside conveyed the good news to Gort, the C-in-C insisted that the French would never attack. The CIGS shared Gort's despondency after his visit: 'God help the BEF. Brought to this state by French incompetence.'

While Ironside was berating Billotte, Gort was briefing the man he had chosen to lead the improvised force, Major General Harold

Franklyn. Dubbed Frankforce, it nominally consisted of two infantry divisions, the 50th and Franklyn's own 5th; Petreforce troops already installed around Arras; and the 1st Army Tank Brigade. The orders were to block the roads south of Arras, cutting off the thrusting Panzers from supplies and communication.

What Franklyn was able to muster at the start line near the historic First World War location, Vimy, on 21 May for the first phase of the attack in no way resembled the strike force envisaged by such as Churchill and Ironside. The nearest the BEF could offer to an armoured force, the 1st Tank Brigade, which had trundled off into Belgium from its headquarters in Arras after the outbreak of hostilities, had covered 120 miles in five days with little time for maintenance before finishing back where it started. As a result, of the hundred tanks Franklyn anticipated only seventy-four were serviceable. Of these fifty-eight were Mark Is, armed only with a medium machine gun. The other sixteen were Mark IIs, later christened Matildas, carring a 2-pounder gun and the thickest armour of any tank operating at that time. Infantry support consisted of two footsore battalions of the Durham Light Infantry, who had suffered during the withdrawal to the Escaut Line because of lack of transport. Between tanks and infantry – and supporting artillery and motorcycle platoons – there was no means of communication except by word of mouth or hand-delivered message. There was no air cover. Nor, as expected, was there any French support for the push south. Their troops would not be ready, Gort was informed late on the night of 20 May, until the 22nd at the earliest.

So at 11 a.m. on 21 May the force moved in two columns across the great sweep of country stretching away from Vimy Ridge and towards the land to the west of Arras. With no opposition encountered in the first three miles the tanks forged ahead, leaving the infantrymen toiling – and frequently limping because of blisters collected over the previous days – far in the rear. After a brisk exchange of fire with tanks which turned out to be French near the village of Duisans, the British columns turned to the south of Arras and had a stroke of luck. The armoured spearhead of the 7th Panzer Division had just passed through, heading west, and one of the columns came across a procession of lorry-borne infantry. The startled Germans, young and battle-inexperienced Nazis of the SS Totenkopf (Death's Head) Division, were startled when their anti-tank shells bounced off the Matildas' armour. It was reported afterwards that one tank had suffered fourteen direct hits from 37mm shells 'and the only indication the crew had of being hit was a red glow for a few seconds on the inside of the armour plate'. The SS broke and ran, and when the Durham Light Infantry finally got to the scene they rounded up some four hundred dazed prisoners.

That was the high point of British success. Rommel, back chasing up a lagging rifle regiment instead of leading the tank spearhead, came across the chaos as he moved forward once more and criticized the demoralized German troops for 'jamming up the roads with their vehicles instead of going into action with every available weapon'. It was, he admitted, 'an extremely tight spot', and before Rommel got out of it he lost his ADC, Lieutenant Most, killed at his side.

Soon, however, Rommel was able to halt the British by the introduction of devastating firepower in the shape of 88mm guns normally used for anti-aircraft purposes. Firing over open sights, these weapons proved too much even for the armour of the Matildas. The commanders of the two British tank battalions were killed, one when he left his vehicle to make hand signals to his men after wireless failure. The first British tank attack of the war penetrated ten miles, and forty-six tanks (62 per cent of the total) were lost in the nine-hour battle.

By 6 p.m. the Stukas were in action against the infantry caught in the open. Unopposed by Allied planes, they carried out their work at leisure. After one forty-minute attack, a subaltern of the 8th Battalion Durham Light Infantry said, 'The chaps were absolutely shattered.' Though few were hit, many had to be kicked to their feet in order to pull back to their assembly area of that morning near Vimy Ridge, under a pounding from tanks and artillery as well as the Luftwaffe.

The attack, a forlorn venture from the start, could only be termed a crippling defeat since it virtually eliminated the BEF's armour in that area. Yet it achieved an impact far out of proportion to its merit. The 7th Panzers' War Diary recorded 'a very heavy battle against hundreds of enemy tanks and following infantry'. Rommel, whose division suffered 378 casualties that day, the heaviest by far of the campaign in France up to this moment, was convinced he was under attack by vastly superior forces. Even less did he realize that what he was facing was every British tank fit to do battle.

What was presented to the world as 'the Arras counter-attack' had two far-reaching consequences. First, apprehension about the damage and panic inflicted that day was in the forefront of the thinking of Hitler and his High Command when the famous 'Halt Order' was issued to the Panzers on the outskirts of Dunkirk three days later. And second, anger and resentment among the SS at reported atrocities against those of their comrades taken prisoner was one of the main causes of two massacres of British captives at the end of the same week.

An official history of the BEF has termed the Arras battle 'a haphazard affair, more a swipe in the dark than a deliberate attack. Yet it came at a time when a swipe offered the only alternative to an ignominious retreat, and certainly the troops made it a glorious swipe.'

As the clash at Arras began to take shape Weygand, too, embarked on an eventful day. Undeterred by the dramatic fashion of his arrival by air from the Middle East, the new French C-in-C decided to fly north (a clear land route being unavailable because of Guderian) to consult personally with his field commanders and other Allied leaders.

Arriving at Le Bourget on the northern outskirts of Paris just before dawn, he was dismayed to learn that nobody appeared to know anything about the trip. Eventually, riding in a light bomber with a fighter escort, Weygand got away. The formation came under antiaircraft fire before landing at the Allied airfield at Norrent-Fontes near Béthune, where he received another shock. The sole occupant, a French private, told his chief officer, 'They've all pissed off', and then asked what he should do about all the aviation fuel left behind.

Eventually Weygand and his ADC found an ancient truck and set off in search of a telephone. 'The difficulties we had already met with on our journey gave me some idea of the disorganization I might expect to find reigning when I reached HQ,' he wrote later. Since the transport sent to collect him had suffered a brush with the German Army, Weygand made his own way to the appointed meeting place, the mayor's office in Ypres town hall. It was three in the afternoon before he got there, Weygand having witnessed at first hand the clogging effect on the roads of a civilian population on the run. Even so, none of the other key figures – King Leopold, Gort and Billotte – had yet arrived. Gort was not even aware that this crucial conference was taking place, for the signal about it had failed to reach him.

When Leopold and Billotte turned up, Weygand insisted that the best chance of Allied recovery lay in an immediate push to the south by the forty-five cut-off divisions in a bid to rejoin France's main body of troops. Billotte was probably still in a state of some agitation, having just received from Churchill a scathing comment on his own statement that the French preoccupation was with stopping holes. On the contrary, Churchill informed Billotte through British aides at the general's headquarters, 'We had to punch holes, not stop them. . . . It was ridiculous to run away from places because a few enemy appeared. If enemy tanks got through, one should let them through and then shoot them up.' Weygand's wild optimism could only have served to agitate Billotte still further.

The Ypres meeting was a waste of everybody's time, apart from emphasizing that a parting of the ways was imminent. Weygand noted signs of 'profound discouragement' in Leopold as he proposed a further withdrawal by the King's forces (to cover the projected southward thrust by the BEF) which would have left the Belgians retaining only a small fraction of their own country. Gort, now alerted, hurried towards Ypres but Weygand could not wait to meet him as he was due in Paris next morning to report his plans to the Allied leaders, Reynaud and Churchill. Weygand made the return journey in similarly hairy fashion, by motor torpedo boat from Dunkirk – where he embarked during an air raid – to Cherbourg via Dover. Through the exhausting journey Weygand nursed and developed a bitter belief that Gort had deliberately snubbed him, a belief which exacerbated the differences already appearing between French and British. In his memoirs Weygand maintained that he did not learn until after the war that Gort's absence was unwitting.

Gort arrived in Ypres that night to learn second-hand from Billotte of Weygand's dismaying intentions regarding the BEF. The only important consequence of his belated arrival was that Billotte, having waited with increasing impatience for Gort, set off in the dark for his headquarters. Frustrated by the slow progress his driver was making on the crowded, blacked-out roads, Billotte took the wheel himself, collided with a truck and died after lying in a coma for two days. With his death disappeared the only Allied commander with first-hand knowledge of what became known as the Weygand Plan.

While Billotte was fighting for his life no decision was taken about a successor. So three days elapsed before a decidedly shaken Blanchard, commander of the French 1st Army, was promoted to take charge of the beleaguered northern forces. The French transport officer Denis Barlone was unimpressed with Blanchard because of his 'marked taste for photographers, for whom he frequently poses'. That disposition to show off had evaporated when Brooke saw him on 24 May, the day of his assumption of command:

He was standing studying maps . . . and I gathered the impression that he might as well have been staring at a blank wall. . . . He gave me the impression of a man whose brain had ceased to function. The blows that had fallen on us in quick succession had left him 'punch drunk' and unable to register events. I was badly shaken and felt that, if he were to take over the tiller in the present storm, it would not be long before we were on the rocks.

Despite the rigours of his twenty-eight-hour journey Weygand breezed back to his Vincennes HQ for the 22 May summit meeting, impressing Churchill and Reynaud by the 'brisk, buoyant and incisive' exposition of his plan which would sweep aside the enemy and restore the Allies' fortunes. The three leaders parted in optimistic mood, having shuffled and committed forces which simply did not exist or were, at best, incapable of carrying out the expectations imposed willy-nilly upon them. Churchill, a determined seeker of silver linings in the darkest clouds, repeated his instructions to the BEF for an attack southwards the next day, 23 May, prompting the bitter comment from Gort's Chief of Staff, Pownall, 'The man's mad.'

Churchill was not the only one suffering from hallucinations. Weygand issued a stirring Operation Order No. 1 whose main call, for the northern Allied armies to stop the Germans from reaching the Channel coast, ignored the fact that they were already there.

Those responsible for providing information for media dissemination were also guilty of delusion. On 21 May the *Daily Mirror* announced: 'French Drive Nazis Back' and the following day: 'Bombs Rain on German Troops'. In Arras General Petre and his garrision were irritated by a BBC bulletin on 20 May announcing that the town they were about to defend was already in German hands. 'The next effort of the BBC was to say that Arras was recaptured by French troops,' Petre noted in his official report of the Arras siege. 'This turned irritation into annoyance as only two or three liaison officers and eleven Zouaves could be induced to help in any way in the defence.'

The rest of the French troops in Arras, described as 'for the most part elderly depot personnel . . . not prepared to help in the defence of the town', moved out before the German assault, as did BEF headquarters personnel and others not regarded as vital for the purpose of fighting. 'Useless mouths', as they became known, were as well out of the way, especially in view of the shortage of provisions.

For his defence of Arras, Petre was able to muster the 1st Battalion Welsh Guards, 5th Battalion Green Howards, 8th Battalion Royal Northumberland Fusiliers, a company of chemical warfare engineers, detachments of the Pioneer Corps and military police, a few light tanks, a company of 25mm guns and a battery of 25-pounders. This shortage of artillery proved an embarrassment when, on 20 May, about thirty German tanks moved into position south-west of Arras and began to refuel in full view of the defenders.

The barricades inherited by the Green Howards when they got to Arras tended towards the primitive. The road block taken over by A

Company was nothing more than a set of level crossing gates, and B Company's (previously guarded by a sergeant of the military police and a group of GHQ clerks) was so fragile that while a Green Howards officer was making an inspection a French country bus rounded the corner and crashed clean through it. In contrast, D Company's consisted of three steam engines wedged into the narrow road and proved so effective that a damaged British tank retreating into the town was forced to blow itself up outside this massive obstacle.

It was only with reluctance that the British made use of houses as firepoints. This reluctance sprang partly from the ban imposed during training the previous winter on damaging private property, and partly from a natural respect for the unfortunate householders. When Sergeant George Griffin of the Welsh Guards was ordered to defend a crossroads he moved his anti-tank rifle into a house and knocked a hole in the wall of what had been a child's bedroom. Before positioning the gun he wrote a note on a calendar apologizing for the mess he had made.

Heavy air raids on the town started on 19 May, and during the destruction of the railway station two trains loading civilians preparing to flee the coming battle were struck, with heavy loss of life. As German infantry began to infiltrate, various ruses were employed to fool the defenders. Petre noted, 'It was usually the approach of some individual in a car disguised as a French officer or with the car disguised as a refugee car.' Cattle were stampeded over any area the attackers suspected of being mined, and the success rate at installing snipers within the town caused such casualties and consequent jitters that orders were issued to shoot all stray dogs following a scare that they were being used by the Germans to convey messages. Major Will Lacy of the Green Howards had great difficulty preserving from would-be executioners an Alsatian he had adopted.

The usual rumours abounded about Fifth Columnists, and at the height of the battle George Griffin arrested a man he thought looked a typical spy: 'He couldn't have done it any better if he had tried. He had thick glasses, a camera and a black Homburg hat.' Griffin woke up his superior, Lieutenant the Hon. Christopher Furness, to ask what should be done with the man. 'Take him out and shoot him,' ordered the irritated Furness. Griffin recalled, 'I took the bloke outside and told him to clear off. I couldn't have shot him, any more than I could have carried out the order to shoot all dogs.'

The Welsh Guards rapidly became skilled at rooting out infiltrators. On one search Sergeant D H Griffiths was told of a group of Germans in a garden. Despite the fact that he had an arm in plaster because of a football injury Griffiths had himself hoisted to the top of a high wall, spotted the Germans hiding on the other side and killed two by dropping grenades on them, an act which won him the Military Medal.

As food ran short the Welsh Guards' padre, the Rev. C H D Cullingford (described in one regimental diary as 'a born thief'), led plundering raids on abandoned shops in the town. An officer of the Green Howards came across Cullingford loading supplies on to a lorry through the shattered window of a large provisions store. 'He was embarrassed at us finding him engaged in such an unclerical occupation as daylight shopbreaking and was at pains to explain that if there must be looting it was better it should be done in an organized manner by an officer and best of all by a padre.'

An ornamental lake in the gardens of the Palais St Vaast in the centre of Arras was used for drinking and washing until a bomb emptied it, after which water tended to be in shorter supply than wine. The Green Howards' medical officer, Dr Frank Allen, cleaned up after treating the wounded in the palace cellars by washing his hands in a barrel of beer, and Lieutenant Frank Pearce of the same Yorkshire regiment took to shaving in champagne.

The Frankforce attack on 21 May resulted only in Arras coming under even heavier shelling, and the defenders were no better off as a result of a French assault launched towards Cambrai the next day by an infantry regiment supported by two armoured reconnaissance groups. This venture, originally part of the Frankforce scheme but postponed for twenty-four hours because the French had problems of assembly and organization, scored heartening early successes and penetrated as far as the outskirts of Cambrai. Then, just like the British effort, it petered out against strong artillery resistance and bombing; after twelve hours the French were back behind their start line.

It was on this day, 22 May, that Petre noted, 'By now much of Arras was burning, which made its occupation far from attractive. On the other hand it stood as a strong hinge for the forces on either flank. For some reason the enemy seemed not prepared to tackle it seriously and consequently its value was undoubted.' Life became less attractive for the defenders next day under an even heavier air raid. The War Diary of the Welsh Guards reported 'the bombers coming over in relays and going through a solemn performance of circling and diving as if it was an exhibition turn'.

Four hours after Petre had been ordered to hold Arras to the last round and the last man, Gort changed his mind and decided to extricate the garrison before it became encircled. The message to evacuate was sent at 0130 on 24 May, Empire Day, and was passed on inside Arras with appropriate urgency: 'Wake up, get up, pack up.'

An evacuation convoy under the protection of the Bren gun-carrier platoon of the Welsh Guards ran into trouble at dawn, finding their escape route blocked by a German detachment on high ground overlooking the road. Forty soft-top lorries crammed with troops had nothing to conceal them except a shroud of mist rapidly thinning as the sun rose. The stage was set for gallantry and it was unhesitatingly occupied by Lieutenant the Hon. Christopher Furness, in charge of the Bren gun-carriers. As the lorries attempted to turn in the cramped road to seek another escape route, Furness led his carriers forward, telling an astonished transport corporal, 'I'm riding into battle this time. I'm going to have a go at them.'

Furness, known as 'Dickie', was the son of the shipping magnate Viscount Furness (Family motto: I'll Defend). A rider to hounds, driver of fast cars and all-round sportsman, he was a popular officer with his men. Guardsman Tom Griffiths recalled how, in the bitter winter of 1940, Furness organized a competition in his platoon to see who could build the best snowman. 'He was a good officer, one of the boys,' said Griffiths. 'Being in the Guards you didn't get many like that.'

The *Daily Mirror* war correspondent, Bernard Gray, remembered the 'permanently mischievous look in his eye' and the fact that Furness never worried about clashing with authority. In January 1940, returning from leave with two whippets he planned to use for coursing in France, he had managed to ship them across the Channel by the simple expedient of tying a label to each dog reading: 'For Lord Gort'.

Furness had suffered a slight shell splinter wound the previous evening when his patrolling carrier was fired on by a British gun, but it would have required something much more serious to prevent him tilting at the enemy. By this time only five of the platoon's ten carriers were serviceable for action and as they moved through the mist towards the sound of firing two more had to pull out, one with a broken fuel valve and the other with a jammed gun. The remaining three vehicles, whose three-man crews were commanded by Furness himself, Sergeant George Griffin and Sergeant Ted Hall, advanced through a company of Northumberland Fusiliers pinned down by the fire from the German post, situated in front of a couple of haystacks. Griffin's carrier took into action an extra passenger, a youngster called Williams who, because the name was so common in the Welsh Guards, was identified by the last two digits of his service number, 17. Because the carrier already contained its full complement of three, '17'

Williams had to ride on the outside. As they came under fire he was urged by Griffin to get off but, lying on a ledge nursing a Bren gun, he said, 'No fucking fear, I'm browned off with this. I'm going to have a bundle with you blokes.'

Furness led the three carriers in a Red Indian-type attack, circling the haystacks, hurling grenades and scattering enemy troops. Tom Griffiths, gunner in Hall's vehicle, remembered, 'Furness was standing up in his carrier waving his revolver. Asking for trouble, wasn't he?' Furness leaned over the side to grapple with a German, shooting him with the revolver. 'Fire was very hot indeed by this time, pinging on the plates,' said George Griffin. 'It was suicide to stand up.' All three occupants of the Furness carrier were killed and when Griffin's vehicle, its driver also hit, crashed into the back of it and stalled, things also looked grim for them. 'Two Germans came out from the post and started walking towards us,' said Griffin. 'Perhaps they thought we were finished too. Anyway, I had a lovely clear shot and wiped them out with a full magazine.' Then Griffin's wounded driver ('I've never seen a wound like it', Griffin recalled. 'You could see the white bone all the way down his arm.') managed to restart the carrier and they withdrew. 'I was going to raise myself and give the two-finger sign, I was so frustrated,' said Griffin. 'But then a burst of machine-gun fire on the plates made me change my mind.'

Griffin was the only guardsman of the ten who went into action in the three carriers to escape unwounded. His extra passenger, '17' Williams, was killed by an anti-tank bullet through the chest. All three carriers were knocked out or damaged and eventually abandoned.

Furness's act saved the transport of the 1st Battalion Welsh Guards from destruction and earned him a posthumous VC. Five months later his father, Viscount Furness, also died and the family fortune was due to pass to the divorced Lieutenant Furness's small son. Tom Griffiths, evacuated from Dunkirk on a hospital ship, was contacted by the Furness family because the officer had left no will and a witness to his death was needed. 'So they sent me a two shilling postal order with a letter asking me to go to the Commissioner of Oaths in London to swear him dead, which I did.'

On and near the Vimy Ridge to the north of Arras the British suffered severely from air attack on their exposed positions. The diary notes of Lance Bombardier Eric Manley of the 92nd Field Regiment, Royal Artillery voiced the outrage felt by many at the one-sidedness of the air war:

20 May: Where is the RAF? We are obviously at the Germans' mercy. No wonder they conquer countries overnight. Where are our planes? Where is the Ack-Ack? We feel this is futile and most of us are cursing England for such a humiliating situation. . . . 1820 hours. 28 heavy enemy planes pass over in formation. Don't really know what they are but we lie in the grass at the roadside and feel absolutely abandoned. Surely this can't be what was expected of us? Twenty more following them. Fifteen more. Still no British to be seen. Bombs fall on the road about 300 yards away. As I write, 18 more, followed by a formation of 12. . . . We move off under brutal attack from the air.

22 May: Enemy planes are so thick and unmolested that we have a very hot time. Most of the lads are pretty demoralized and disgusted. Still no sign of the RAF coming to relieve us but we are told they are doing good work somewhere else. It is hard to believe . . . and little consolation.

23 May: Up to the end of the Ridge. An air attack prevents us moving . . . enemy tanks said to have broken through and coming straight for us. We change our position, with much anxiety. No sooner do we get into position than there is a terrific air attack. Jerry evidently intends to have us. Bombs fall all around and shake the house that serves as a Command Post. One blast threw me down the stairs.

With what has been described as 'multiple and far spread groups of grimly trudging British soldiers' pulling back through the bleak mining country north of Arras, Lord Gort's despatches noted: 'Thus concluded the defence of Arras, which had been carried out by a small garrison, hastily assembled, but well commanded, and determined to fight. It had imposed a valuable delay on a greatly superior enemy force against which it had blocked a vital road centre.'

The Arras withdrawal might have marked the conclusion of that particular battle, but it signalled the onset of bitter recriminations between British and French. Gort had undoubtedly done the sensible thing by pulling out his soldiers before they were encircled at Arras, but this act effectively scuppered the Weygand Plan for an attack to the south. It thus offered the French command the opportunity to shift the blame for catastrophe away from their own doorstep. The first Churchill knew of the Arras retreat was from Reynaud at midday on 24 May, and he replied at once that such a withdrawal 'would be absolutely contrary to our wishes'.

Late that night another reproachful telegram from the French Premier told Churchill that 'contrary to formal orders confirmed this morning by General Weygand the British Army has decided and carried out a withdrawal of 40 kilometres in the direction of the ports'. In fact, because of the pressure and presence of German armour south and south-west of them, the British retreat was away from the ports and towards the rest of the BEF behind the line of the River Escaut.

Whatever the direction, the situation was bleak. General Brooke's diary for 23 May summed it up: 'Nothing but a miracle can save the BEF now, and the end cannot be far off.' Brooke concluded his night's writing with a tribute to the opposition which the German propagandists would have found priceless if they had succeeded in getting their hands on the diary: 'It is a fortnight since the German advance started and the success they have achieved is nothing short of phenomenal. There is no doubt that they are most wonderful soldiers.'

10

Cointreau and Cigars

You can't fight against armour when all you have is a rifle.

John Farrer, Bedfordshire and Hertfordshire Regiment

In order adequately to man his new thirty-two-mile front on the Escaut, Gort had to commit all seven divisions available to him in that area. With nothing in reserve it was a situation of much risk, and the C-in-C attempted to bolster the morale of his soldiers by circulating a message as the British tanks attacked near Arras: 'News from the south reassuring. We stand and fight. Tell your men.'

The opportunity to stand and fight would not long be denied, but frequently the soldiers had to abide by the frustrating order not to fire at low-flying aircraft for fear of drawing even heavier attention. Bill Brodie, the signals sergeant, recalled sitting in a foxhole with an anti-tank rifle and Lewis guns awaiting the reported arrival of Panzers. 'Suddenly two huge German planes flew across my sights at 1000 yards. I could see clearly the swastika on their tails and I debated whether I would get a Military Medal or a court martial if I pulled the trigger. I decided that I would more likely share a string of retaliatory bombs with the rest of the Section, so I lost my chance.'

Major Julian Wright, second in command of the 2nd Battalion Sherwood Foresters, was annoyed when, having dispersed his troops in a wood opposite the village of Ligny, a British armoured car regiment settled in the village.

They walked all over the place in the open, started chasing hens and shooting at cattle and put out several light automatics. I was thankful I had cornered the liquor. Worse followed, for a Boche plane came over well out of range and every gun opened up. . . . I went at once to their CO and asked him to stop such nonsense. He said he would do so but there was not much improvement.

Next day, after the armoured cars had left, the Sherwood Foresters were attacked from the air.

It was on the Escaut that Alf Hewitt of the 1st Battalion South Lancashires, who had joined the Army vowing to kill Germans and had succeeded so far only in shooting Belgians, saw his first enemy:

We dug in behind a man-made ridge of soil and sand from river straightening and dredging and were told this was where we were going to make a stand. Right opposite us, about 600 yards away, was a natural ridge and the Germans were behind that. We hadn't seen any, but they were there. We had the whole brigade there, Black Watch on our left, Royal Fusiliers on our right. Further north, the Guards. We were quite strong behind there, at least we thought we were.

On the second morning I was with Tim McCormick, a mate of mine, on the forward slope of the ridge. The rest were dug in behind the crest, sleeping. Tim and I were smoking and chatting and all of a sudden, right in front of our eyes on the far bank of the river, was a German soldier, walking along with hands in pockets, unarmed, just strolling along. Every army unit has got its idiot and the German Army is no exception. They had their Wallys the same as we had and this was definitely a Teutonic Wally. He was about 40 yards away and he was the first German I had seen. I watched through binoculars as Tim lined him up. It was like shooting a rat in a barrel.

On 21 May two more Victoria Crosses were won in repelling heavy assaults on the Escaut. When the Germans gained a foothold across the river south of Tournai, Company Sergeant Major George Gristock of the Royal Norfolks went forward to deal with a machine gun post. He was immediately wounded in both legs by fire from the opposite bank, his right knee smashed, but he still managed to drag himself forward and wipe out the machine gun crew of four with his rifle. Gristock died of his wounds before he knew he had been awarded the VC.

Under cover of early morning mist the Germans also got across the Escaut between the 3rd Grenadier Guards and the 2nd Coldstreams. Two counter-attacks failed to dislodge them, and when a hitherto uncommitted company of the Grenadiers launched a third attack it promptly lost three officers, including Lieutenant the Duke of Northumberland. As the leaderless guardsmen went to ground Lance Corporal Harry Nicholls rushed forward, firing his Bren gun from the hip. Already struck in the arm, Nicholls was knocked down by a head wound but crawled up to a ridge overlooking the river and opened fire on Germans massing there before collapsing under two more hits. Only one officer and four men were left of Nicholls's company, but his bravery forced the attackers to abandon their lodgement and Nicholls was awarded what was thought at the time to be a posthumous VC. Four months later came news that he was recuperating from his multiple wounds in a prisoner-of-war hospital.

The BEF's casualties mounted as they came under sustained attack that day. Guardsman James Stevenson of the 3rd Grenadiers remembered:

They were mortaring us. My mate got a little blue hole in his throat and the back of his head blown off. I had seven shrapnel wounds in my left leg. When I got to the building being used as a field dressing station they brought in a chappie who had just had the bridge of his nose blown off. That had shut his eyes, so after we had been attended to he more or less carried me and I showed him the way until we got transport to Dunkirk.

At last finding use for what he called 'medical comforts' for the wounded – 'one bottle whisky, one of brandy' – in his kit, Dr Joe Patterson discovered they had been consumed by his stretcherbearers, members of the regimental band in peacetime, and replaced with light- and dark-coloured tea.

Dr Ian Samuel, unit surgeon of the 6th Field Ambulance Unit found himself working under increasingly difficult conditions. In the retreat from Brussels his company came across a hotel which appeared suitable for commandeering as an emergency hospital:

I entered the hotel and to my amazement found night life in full swing. What shocked us most of all was some Belgian officers, immaculately garbed in well-creased and valeted tunics, entertaining their womenfolk. However, the proprietor spoke fluent English and after he had fully convinced himself of the urgency of the situation – a great shock as he imagined the scene of the fighting to be very remote – he let us bring our casualties into the ballroom . . . he also produced lashings of hot tea and hot water for dressings and bottles. His restaurant was taken over for our operating theatre and it was admirable in every way, his freshly laundered table napkins making grand operating towels.

Knight's next stop, a hamlet called Doulieu, was much less salubrious. He and his colleagues were inundated with so many casualties, civilian as well as military, that when all the barns and stables were filled the stretchers had to be laid in the fields. During twenty-four hours at Doulieu they received more than six hundred injured and wounded and under atrocious conditions operated continuously, including eleven amputations, some with a carpenter's hacksaw. 'And a very excellent instrument it was,' Knight remembered.

Although the task of the German 6th Army attacking the Escaut was ostensibly that of a foil, to divert the Allies from impeding the progress of von Rundstedt's armour sweeping round behind them, many units pressed home the assault bravely and suffered heavy casualties. The War Diary of the German XI Corps described the fighting of 21 May: 'The British have established themselves in a most masterly fashion. They fire from every hedge. Each house is a fortress. They defend themselves tenaciously until a shot fired at close range or a bayonet thrust kills them. But the men from Lower Saxony are even more tenacious in the assault and are not afraid of fighting man to man.'

The following day saw the Germans attempting to cut their losses by tactics of infiltration rather than direct assault. The sign of an impending attack was the firing of white Very signal lights to let their own gunners and aircraft know where they were. Lieutenant Peter Hadley found a menacing quality in them:

These Very lights went up at regular intervals, always in our direction and each time appearing a little closer than before. Of the enemy himself there was never a trace. To troops who had as yet had no experience of actual fighting this silent and relentless advance seemed uncanny and rather frightening. If only we could have caught one fleeting glimpse of the human beings who were firing those Very lights we should have felt that we were at grips with something tangible; but as it was one gained only the impression of a mysterious force approaching closer and closer.

Nerves were also strained by the constant presence of Henschel spotter planes, hovering unimpeded just out of range of BEF bullets.

Though Tom Bristow could see no reason why the Germans had need of a Fifth Column 'when their observation planes were flying about unmolested all day', the most alarming rumours about spies and traitors continued to cause chaos. Willy Lescène, a French liaison officer attached to the Manchester Regiment, suffered a particularly trying time. Because his kit had been blown up he was forced to dress in a strange assortment of khaki breeches, blue stockings, blue tunic and British tin hat. 'He got arrested on average three times a day as a suspected spy', reported the RAMC captain, Joe Patterson. 'Once he stole a bike and rode away with the Germans shooting at him, and then had to run the gauntlet of our own chaps shooting at him as well.'

The Rev. Gough Quinn's padre's uniform also got him into trouble with some suspicious French troops, whose officer arrested him. Quinn, who was to become the first Church of England chaplain in this war to win the Military Cross – for bravery in the retreat to Dunkirk – was kept under guard overnight and next morning loaded on to a lorry to be taken to the French brigade HQ along with two other suspects:

One was a Jew who had fled from Germany and the other appeared to be a mental defective. Both had been constantly under arrest during the past week. I wonder what happened to them afterwards. Presently I was told to put on a handkerchief to blindfold myself and we came to Brigade HQ. We were taken out of the lorry, still blindfolded, and made to stand a long time while enquiries were made about us. Then we were put into a lorry and taken to Divisional HQ. Here again we spent an eternity waiting about. We were left with an escort while the officer went off to report, and we certainly needed an escort, not to stop us from escaping but to protect us from the gallant *Belges*, whose courage rose to the occasion. We had to be moved to save us from a mobbing. One of my fellow prisoners got a rather nasty knock on the shoulder with a stick. I managed to see a good deal under my handkerchief.

Eventually the padre's blindfold was removed, to his delight, by a friend from his regiment and he was released. But, he wrote, 'I felt pretty annoyed about it.' Quinn, who was killed in 1943 at Salerno, was fortunate on that occasion to escape with his life. The French transport officer Denis Barlone noted in his diary on 22 May: 'Our orders are to shoot all spies and strangers who are unable to justify their presence in the zone . . . No fuss or bother, merely keep an account of the total number dealt with.' Even the Grenadier Guards, who had suffered much sniping, executed 17 men in civilian clothes suspected of being German Army infiltrators.

German Jews who had fled persecution in their homeland were particularly vulnerable. Those in Belgium on 10 May were rounded up and had their identification documents confiscated, only to be released without their papers as the Allies retreated. 'So now we have on the road a flood of Germans, without papers, speaking no language but German,' reported Captain Basil Bartlett of the Field Security Police. 'It's my job to sift the genuine ones from the frauds. It's an impossibility, of course.' By 21 May Bartlett was complaining, 'I have nowhere to detain suspects. It looks as though I may have to have them either shot or released.'

The exasperated Bartlett was eventually reduced to anti-Semitism:

I hesitate to say that Hitler knew what he was about when he persecuted them. But he had provocation. They're not at all the sort of Jews we know in England, nor indeed the fine cultivated Jews of Vienna. They're the riffraff of the East. They are quite unscrupulous. They'd steal the hat off your head and as good as tell you so. If you show the slightest sympathy with their sufferings – which have been appalling – they at once start asking you to do impossible things for them, and abuse you if you don't. They all seem to have money. They arrive on foot in an exhausted condition and beg for food. And yet, when you come to search them, they usually have thousands of francs in cash and credit notes on half the capitals of Europe.

However, Bartlett showed compassion, too, in his thankless task: 'A farmer and his family were brought in under escort. They have faulty wiring in their farm and, in consequence, were suspected by the troops billeted on them of signalling to the enemy. I think they were innocent. The family was badly scared. I sent it back home in a car.'

War correspondents were also at risk. Percy Philip of the *New York Times*, fair-haired and blue-eyed, was dragged out of a train by French troops, accused of being a parachutist and narrowly escaped being shot out of hand. Maurice Nöel of *Le Figaro* was dragged from his bicycle, told by an Arab soldier 'I can tell by your accent that you are not a Frenchman' and beaten up when a search revealed a box of indigestion powder which was assumed to be explosives.

With supply lines severed Gort told Anthony Eden, the Secretary of State for War, on 23 May that there were less than three days' supplies left for his army, and very little ammunition. His telegram added, 'Belgian Army also in very bad state for supplies and asks us to supply 400,000 rations daily which I am unable to do.'

One commodity not in short supply, because of local stockpiling, was petrol, and drivers showed extreme bravery in transporting fuel and what ammunition could be found to where it was most needed, often under shelling or attack from the air. Stan Smith, a driver with the 13th Line of Communication, said, 'I was mainly ferrying petrol in jerry cans but I was young and didn't worry that much. We came under fire and got strafed a lot. Some got hit and blew up. You had to take your chances.' Bill Edwards, whose father had been a driver in the First World War, took parental advice and carried half a bottle of rum hidden in the cab of his lorry. He had need of the drink when driving the leading petrol-carrying vehicle in a convoy of twelve which strayed into no man's land: 'I have never gone through anywhere so deserted. It was eerie. Suddenly a GHQ car came tearing up, said we were in danger and told us we had been under shellfire for three miles. As we were turning round a house near me flew apart.' Which was when Driver Edwards reached for his rum.

John Carpenter, an eighteen-year-old Royal Artillery subaltern and, in his own description, 'very much an innocent abroad', considered lorries loaded with ammunition 'fairly safe unless you got a direct hit',

Above: The BEF's new weapon was the Bren Gun, ineffective against the new German weapon, the Panzers. (*Imperial War Museum*)

Below: Belgian citizens turned out in jubilant force to welcome the British Army into their country. (*Imperial War Museum*)

Left: Lord Gort, Commander-in-Chief of the BEF, with the Supreme Allied Commander General Gamelin. (*Imperial War Museum*). *Top right:* General Gerd Von Rundstedt, Commander of the German Army Group A, which included most of the Panzers. (*Imperial War Museum*). *Centre right:* Heinz Guderian, the Panzer general adored by his soldiers. (*Imperial War Museum*). *Below:* General Brooke (centre), Commander of the BEF 2 Corps, flanked by his divisional commanders Montgomery (left) and Johnson. (*Imperial War Museum*)

JU87 Stuka dive bomber (*above*) which caused such terror to civilians and troops alike (*below*). (*Imperial War Museum*)

Above: British troops make their way through the Dunkirk streets towards the beaches. (*Times Newspapers Ltd*). *Below:* Little was left standing in Dunkirk by the time the Germans moved in. (*Studio Boursin, Dunkirk*). *Opposite:* Comparatively peaceful moment in the embarkation from Dunkirk's East Mole. (*Times Newspapers Ltd*).

Rifles against bombs – the BEF defend themselves with the only weapons they possess. (*Hulton-Deutsch Collection*)

The orderly queues on Dunkirk beach as Allied troops await evacuation. (*Hulton-Deutsch Collection*)

The ones who did not get away – the debris and the dead left behind. (*Imperial War Museum*)

Left: Blazing oil tanks cast a pall over Dunkirk and its beaches. (*Camera Press*). *Right:* The long thin line as troops wade out to rescue ships. (*Imperial War Museum*)

The rescued tr[oops] came home in e[very] type of craft. (T[imes] *Newspapers Ltd*)

Royal Navy destroyers packed hundreds of men onto and below their decks. (*Times Newspapers Ltd*)

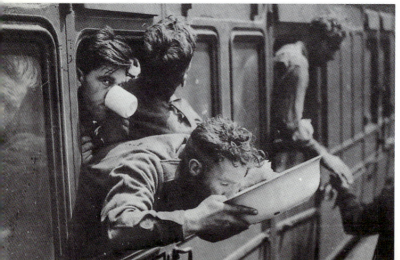

Home at last. [The] survivors of Dun[kirk] take a drink of [any]thing to hand. (T[imes] *Newspapers Ltd*)

so he slept on top of ammunition boxes in the back of one truck 'for want of a better place'. Carpenter, who had undergone his baptism of fire by helping to unload explosives from a blazing train, was deputed to scour the countryside for ammunition. 'We used to find quite a lot, actually,' he recalled.

It became increasingly necessary to forage for food as supplies ceased to flow. On 21 May Captain Alan Bell Macdonald noted: 'Our method of living is literally on the country, a sort of licensed pillage – the villages being deserted. We all just help ourselves as we feel inclined. Last night dinner was delicious. It all seems rather dreadful, but then *c'est la guerre* as they say.'

Joe Hooker of the Royal Engineers reported 'living like kings' in the deserted village of Rumes after sending out foraging parties ('a polite name', as he said, for looting when led by an NCO). He called his time in Rumes 'two gorgeous days, with more than we could take on board, and the best wines, including champagne'. They even broke open a petty cash box but were disappointed to find only a few coins. Clothing was also a let-down: 'It was all women's and children's, so there was not much we could refit with.'

Tom Bristow, who confessed that, as company mechanic, he was 'more or less a freelance and was often able to mix business with other exploits', came across a brasserie in one village which had so far escaped looting. 'We found it was still well stocked with groceries and liquor so we declared an armistice and, seated cross-legged on the floor with a crate of champagne between us and a lump of cheese, we had a private wine and cheese party until we'd had enough of swilling the gassy stuff. We were still sober enough to collect a goodly supply of groceries and stagger out to our trucks with them.'

Having been invited by the owner to clear out his cigar factory rather than leave the stock for the invaders, the troops and officers under Lieutenant Colonel Graham Brooks were allocated two hundred each. 'In our command post dugout the pungent aroma of cigars almost drowned the smell of earth, unwashed bodies and musty battledress,' said Brooks.

When news reached him of a NAAFI depot being abandoned Brooks sent three lorries to plunder whatever they could.

They returned with a haul of a quarter of a million cigarettes, tins of cocoa, apricots and pears, slabs of chocolate, soap and all kinds of toilet requisites. The drink was the disappointment. There was no beer, no whisky. The only alcohol left was Cointreau – three cases of it, which we decided to keep under strict control. Every man was issued with several hundred cigarettes. Once they had got a 'fag' again they had no use for the cigars – they started throwing away whole boxes which the officers salvaged and smoked.

Having been on duty all night I emerged from the command post at dawn to see a batman sitting on a box in the courtyard cleaning his officer's boots. There was an enormous cigar in his mouth. He took a glance at a Boche plane overhead, paused in his work, stooped to pick up a bottle and raised it to his mouth. To my horror, I saw it was a bottle of Cointreau. At four o'clock in the morning.

There were no such constraints on the liquid refreshment available when Bill Brodie's signals office was established in a wine and spirit warehouse at Armentières – merely a shortage of food:

We were surrounded by thousands of bottles of wines and spirits of every description but not a thing to eat. . . . The arrival of some tepid corned beef stew did not help much. We had neither mess-tins nor knives and forks. Eventually, like a crowd of cannibals, we squatted round the dixie and with improvised ladles we helped ourselves in rotation. Somebody found a case of tomato juice and we finished with a bottle each.

Others fared even worse. John Farrer of the 2nd Battalion Bedfordshire and Hertfordshire Regiment found only a stone jar of pickles when he went foraging, and noted glumly: 'You can't eat *them* without something.' Harry Dennis of the East Surreys recalled the joy with which he and his mates welcomed the arrival of a supply lorry after they had gone hungry for a couple of days. 'They had all this tinned stuff in the back and threw it out, yelling, "Two men per tin." We opened it up and it was bleedin' beetroot.'

But even beetroot might have been welcomed by Sam Wright of the 6th Green Howards:

From leaving Rumacourt on Sunday morning [19 May] sleep and food have been at a minimum. From 3 a.m. Sunday to 3 a.m. Monday I had a bare two hours' sleep in a garden and during this period two meals consisting of two slices of bread and a slice of meat roll. The other meal was two slices of bread and cheese with the addition of some chocolate and jam. I slept from 3 a.m. to 4 a.m. and then had a meal of scrounged and looted food – jam, bread, cakes and biscuits – not at all adequate. On Monday we rested until 1.30 p.m. and had bully beef and a slice of bread at 6 p.m. and a mouthful of tea at 11 p.m. Again no sleep until 5 a.m. having some bacon, beans and tea before sleep. . . . There was a shortage of liquids – no water, half a pint of tea and a mouthful of wine in thirty-six hours.

With enemy armour by now posing a threat to the Channel ports at his back, and the area to the south of his main line of defence held by scratch formations – Polforce, Usherforce, Woodforce – cobbled together with soldiers not normally expected to go anywhere near the scene of action, there was no option for Gort but to fall back again. It was only twenty-four hours since the C-in-C had issued the heartening instruction, 'We stand and fight.' Now, in accordance with agreement reached at the Ypres meeting on 21 May, Gort ordered a withdrawal to the line on the Franco–Belgian frontier named after him and which the BEF had spent most of the previous winter constructing. He issued the instruction with bitterness in his heart, complaining to his corps commanders of the 'complete lack of effort' of his French superiors and calling the commitment of his reserves to the Battle of Arras 'a desperate remedy in an attempt to put heart into the French'.

Captain Basil Bartlett spoke for most of the BEF when he said, 'I was stupefied to find that we're again moving.' He considered the BEF by no means a beaten army. 'But it's a bewildered army. Since its first trek into Belgium it's done nothing but retire, take up a position, fight and then retire again. It's had no rest at all.' Alfred Baldwin's artillery unit first heard of the latest withdrawal when they were suddenly ordered to fire off all their ammunition. 'When we limbered up the guns and pulled out, our battery major stood at the gate and shouted at the drivers, "Don't panic." I don't recall any panic – all I was aware of was a great haste.'

Elsewhere there were clear indications of panic. In Wortegem Lieutenant Peter Hadley was confronted with a disorderly mob of British troops, 'grimy, bloodstained and obviously badly scared', who told him the Germans were just behind them. 'And they hurried on', said Hadley, 'looking (if truth be told) very much like the popular British conception of the Italian Army.'

As Lieutenant Gregory Blaxland and the eight-man remains of his East Kents platoon pulled back from the Escaut fighting they were overtaken by a large body of troops. 'They were not exactly in a state of panic but were clearly in no mood to halt, and when the last of them had passed we all felt the dire drawing power of their suction.' At a road junction Blaxland came across an officer attempting to staunch the rate of flow. 'He was an elderly brigadier and was imploring the men to end their retreat in a manner from which it could be deduced they were not under his command. He had recourse to oratory: "We can't let this beastly fellow Hitler win the war. We've got to stop him somewhere. Why not here?" The retreat continued.'

There was panic, too, as observed by the signaller, S L Rhodda, when a despatch rider came racing along the road wearing a gas mask.

The gas alarm was sounded, everyone donned their masks and the motorcyclist was halted and asked where the gas attack was taking place. 'He said he was wearing the mask because someone had stolen his goggles. The officer blessed him with some non-religious language and sent him on his way.'

Even the officers tended not to be kept informed of the reasons for withdrawal. Captain Alan Bell Macdonald of the 32nd Field Regiment RA noted, 'Here we go again – at midday came the order to up sticks and off we set. No reason given. . . . I am frankly puzzled by our retreat and definitely scared.' George Sutton, in command of 125 Brigade, also felt unease. 'I couldn't help comparing this "coming out of the line" with the same process in the last war. In those days the feeling was one of safety and of freedom from enemy interference but here we felt unsafe and were constantly interfered with by enemy action.'

So, after a nightmare two weeks, the BEF – exhausted, mauled, disillusioned – pulled back behind the Gort Line, from which they had moved forward so exuberantly on 10 May. The grim trend was even getting through to the newspapers back home. The *Daily Mirror* of 23 May could find no more heartening propaganda news than 'Nazis Lose Their Cattle', a story recording an outbreak of foot and mouth disease in Germany.

After reaching the coast on 20 May the Panzers paused, partly because of the need to rest, refit and regroup but also because the German High Command was not sure what to do with them next. Should they be directed south against the Somme and Paris, or north towards the Channel ports and the isolated Allied armies?

On 22 May the order came: head north. Some of the armoured units were by now down to half strength because of losses and breakdowns, but even if all five divisions had been reduced to 50 per cent effectiveness von Kleist's strike force could still have mustered more than six hundred tanks with plenty of infantry support. Had von Kleist, or his superior von Rundstedt, possessed the vision and daring of Guderian the war could have been won on that day. But Hitler and his top generals, alarmed by the British counter-attack at Arras the previous day, still held the reins tight. Kleist removed one of Guderian's three divisions, the 10th, into reserve and did not permit the others to roll northwards until 1300 hours on the 22nd. Guderian ordered his 2nd Division to capture Boulogne and the 1st to attack Calais. The 10th, of which he was suddenly deprived, was to have taken Dunkirk at the same time.

Such was the lack of co-ordination in the Kleist Group that General Georg Hans Reinhardt set off with the 6th and 8th Panzers towards the same two ports. By nightfall on the 22nd Guderian's 2nd Division, after another staggering advance of more than forty miles, was on the outskirts of Boulogne; but the 1st Division suffered opposition from French troops and – a rare event – assault by British planes, causing Guderian to complain, 'The enemy air force was very active, bombing and machine-gunning, whilst we saw very little of our own Luftwaffe.' Although he had made much better progress towards Calais Reinhardt was ordered to leave the port to Guderian, and he protested to von Kleist about the bitter disappointment of his troops at having to 'give this victory to the neighbour who is still a long way back'.

In Boulogne itself the evacuation to Britain of 'useless mouths' – largely GHQ personnel evacuated from Arras, plus assorted anxious refugees – had been under way since 19 May. Several war correspondents were stranded in Boulogne, and since they neither knew what was happening nor were able to file stories the *Daily Mirror*'s Bernard Gray suggested to Evelyn Montague of the *Manchester Guardian* and Kim Philby of the *Times* that they scrounge a car and go over to Le Touquet for a game of golf. 'We went along to the Public Relations Office to get permission,' wrote Gray. '"Le Touquet?" said the officer then in charge. "Of course, old boy. Delighted for you to go normally. But it's a bit difficult at the moment you know. The Germans are there." We gave up the idea of playing golf.'

Hasty arrangements were made to bolster the Boulogne garrison by despatching two battalions of Guards, the 2nd Welsh and the 2nd Irish, plus anti-tank personnel. On 21 May the guardsmen were on manoeuvres in Surrey; thirty-six hours later they were fighting a real enemy in France, and thirty-six hours after landing at Boulogne those who had managed to get away were back in England.

Their commander, Brigadier William Fox-Pitt, under orders to defend Boulogne 'to the last man and the last round', organized a hurried defence in the hills which surround the port, incorporating some of the 'useless mouths' into his force but failing to co-ordinate resistance plans with French troops on the spot. Driven back into the port area, the British were ordered to evacuate on the afternoon of 23 May, and by 2100 those who had not been cut off got away on destroyers which plucked them dramatically to safety after exchanging fire with German tanks and batteries on the way into and out of harbour. Some six hundred of the seven hundred Irish Guards were rescued, but the Welsh left one company stranded outside Boulogne and two others in the sprawling dock area. So intense was the fire laid down on the British warships that the commanders of *Vimy* and *Keith* were both killed. In a miniature version of what was soon to follow further up the coast at Dunkirk the Navy lifted off most of those able to get away, though the worst of the wounded had to be left behind because of a shortage of stretchers and a mob of panic-stricken British and Allied military non-combatants had to be driven back at bayonet point by Marines when they attempted to rush *Whitshed* as she berthed. It was reported, 'Many of them were drunk . . . at least three officers (one British) were quite incapable of carrying out their duties.'

French resistance in the heights of the old town was crushed next morning, medieval fashion, with a scaling ladder after an 88mm gun had been brought up to breach the ancient walls of Boulogne. The British in the port area fought on until soon after noon when, because of the danger to refugees and wounded, the cause was given up as hopeless.

Understandably, there was French bitterness at British failure to inform their Allies in Boulogne of the intention to retreat, and embarrassment in London over what had happened was to prove costly in the battle for Calais which followed. The 30th Infantry Brigade under Brigadier Claude Nicholson had been hurried to Calais, together with the 3rd Royal Tank Regiment, and ordered to operate offensively towards Boulogne. By the time Nicholson arrived in the early afternoon of 23 May Calais had been bypassed and surrounded, and soon after midnight, with the last of the British pulling out of Boulogne, Nicholson, too, was ordered to prepare for evacuation.

Stung by Reynaud's vigorous complaints at the British pull-outs from Arras and Boulogne, Churchill countermanded the Calais evacuation instruction 'for the sake of Allied solidarity' and sent a testy message to Anthony Eden: 'Are you sure there is no streak of defeatist opinion in the General Staff?'

The embattled Nicholson was assured from London on 25 May that 'the eyes of the Empire are upon the defence of Calais and His Majesty's Government are confident that you and your gallant regiment will perform an exploit worthy of the British name'. Having taken the decision to sacrifice the garrison of Calais to buy time for the BEF (a decision which he admitted made him feel 'physically sick'), Churchill laid on the rhetoric in encouraging Nicholson: 'Every hour you continue to exist is of the greatest help to the BEF. Gort has therefore decided you must continue to fight. Have greatest possible admiration for your splendid stand.'

Nicholson rejected two German offers of an honourable surrender to avoid unnecessary waste of life before the battered town and its defenders finally gave up on Sunday, 26 May. Nicholson, deeply depressed by the belief that he had failed his country, died a prisoner of war, while Churchill maintained long afterwards in his memoirs that the defence of Calais saved the rest of the British forces in France from encirclement. It was not an opinion shared by Guderian: 'The defence of Calais had no effect on the operations against Dunkirk. No delay in the advance arose from the defence of that fortress.' In other words, the bravery of the 30th Brigade had been a useless sacrifice.

The day after Calais fell it was still much on Churchill's mind. He sent a message to Gort that the port might be recaptured by a bold counter-attack 'since very likely the enemy tanks are tired. . . . Perhaps they will be less formidable when attacked themselves', a comment which showed that Churchill and Hitler at least had one thing in common – an inability, at that stage of the war, fully to appreciate the merit of the Panzers.

It was Hitler who greatly aided the escape of the BEF with one of the most controversial instructions of the war, the Halt Order which pulled up the Panzers a mere ten miles from Dunkirk. The order was put into effect on 24 May, as the last British were departing from Arras, and it required the German armoured columns to stop at the line of the Aa and other canals stretching inland from Gravelines, just to the west of Dunkirk, down to St Omer. When the first Panzers got to the canal line the twenty-mile stretch was covered by only one British battalion and many bridges were still unblown. Bridgeheads across the water were rapidly established on 23 May and, once the Germans were across, there was nothing to stop them severing the BEF's line of retreat to the one port still open to them.

That chance of finishing off the British and French troops was thrown away as the Panzers were instructed to pull back across the Aa. Although the order came from Hitler and was passed on by von Rundstedt, it was maintained by the Führer's Chief of Staff, Keitel, that he was 'unjustly credited with the responsibility for making the wrong decision'. Keitel was at the meeting when the High Command sought Hitler's approval for a halt and claimed that the generals 'did not have the guts to accept responsibility for it themselves'. After the war captured commanders like von Rundstedt and Guderian found it expedient to shift the blame on to their late leader. Von Rundstedt told his captors that he 'raised an immediate protest' while Guderian (more understandably) professed to have been 'absolutely speechless', but at the time von Rundstedt, as commander of Army Group A which included the bulk of the Panzers, appeared to share Hitler's anxieties about the rapidity of the advance, as he had already demonstrated on the halt of 16 May. The anxieties were based on a reluctance to commit the armour into what Hitler remembered from his own experiences of the First World War as the marshy plains of Flanders. There was a further reason for husbanding the precious armoured columns. They would be needed soon for Plan Red, the drive to the south and Paris. Then, too, the British tank attack of 21 May at Arras had alarmed the German High Command out of all proportion to its achievement. They were still nervous about suffering the consequences of over-confidence, despite the clear indications of a smashing victory which persuaded Rommel to write to his wife on the day of the Halt Order, 'By my estimate the war will be won in a fortnight.'

Von Rundstedt voiced suspicions after the war that Hitler's decision had been taken in order 'to help the British', basing this opinion on remarks alleged to have been made by the Führer on a visit to his HQ in which he praised Britain as a world power and intimated a willingness to strike an alliance. But there exists no evidence to support the theory that Hitler secretly hoped the British would get away.

Finally, there was the intervention of the vainglorious Hermann Göring, the Luftwaffe C-in-C, who pleaded for his airmen to be given a chance to finish off the trapped Allies. Since the Luftwaffe had much closer ties to the Nazi Party than did the Army, Hitler could well have taken this into account in acceding to Göring's request. Now the responsibility for eliminating the enemy would be left to the dismayed commanders of an air arm whose pilots were in urgent need of rest after a fortnight of non-stop operations.

On 25 May the CBS Berlin correspondent, William Shirer, noted: 'German military circles here tonight put it flatly. They said the fate of the great Allied army bottled up in Flanders is sealed.' Lord Gort was of much the same mind. After cabling Eden, 'I must not conceal from you that a great part of the BEF and its equipment will inevitably be lost in the best of circumstances', he confided to his aide, Captain the Earl of Munster, 'You know, the day I joined up I never thought I would lead the British Army to its biggest defeat.'

That defeat was very much in the mind of the King in his Empire Day broadcast on 24 May, when he told the nation, 'The decisive struggle is now upon us . . . let no one be mistaken, it is no mere territorial conquest that our enemies are seeking. It is the overthrow, complete and final, of this Empire and of everything for which it stands, and after that the conquest of the world.'

The King then called for a day of national prayer on Sunday, 26 May. He attended a packed service at Westminster Abbey while outside a crowd of two thousand, unable to gain admittance, held their own open-air prayers. Inside the Abbey, Churchill recalled, 'I could feel the pent-up, passionate emotion, and also the fear of the congregation, not of death or wounds or material loss, but of defeat and the final ruin of Britain.' In France the medical orderly Derek Ramsdale, no better informed than most of the BEF, noted, 'It was not until we heard that we were being prayed for that we realized how bad things must be.'

11

The Useless Mouths

When Frenchmen and Englishmen are in trouble together and arguments break out, the Frenchman is often voluble and vehement, and the Englishman unresponsive or even rude.

Winston Churchill

Sunday, 26 May, the National Day of Prayer, was a grim one for British leaders on both sides of the Channel. Even the weather was grey, an overcast morning in France giving way to a steady downpour. Apart from the rain, all that fell on the BEF from the sky this day were thousands of leaflets telling them they were encircled. Major Alan Johnson of the Royal Engineers recalled, 'The leaflets were in bad English saying we should lay down our arms and surrender as they, the Germans, knew how to treat a gallant enemy. We laughed at this and made a bonfire in the farmyard of much of this paper.'

Gort, exasperated at the inability of the War Cabinet to grasp the desperate plight of his army, had pleaded that General Sir John Dill, the Vice Chief of the Imperial General Staff, be allowed to come and see for himself. The request was a shrewd one. Dill had commanded the BEF's 1 Corps until his recall to become Ironside's deputy less than three weeks before the German invasion started. As soon as Gort demonstrated that he was fighting the Germans on an eighty-seven-mile front with seven divisions, Dill cabled Churchill on 25 May: 'There is NO blinking the seriousness of the situation.'

Things moved rapidly next day as the truth finally sank in. Dill returned home to find himself promoted to CIGS in place of Ironside, who was made C-in-C Home Forces and charged with implementing plans for the defence of Britain against possible invasion. Following an early morning War Cabinet meeting Gort was told that, since neither the BEF nor the French appeared to possess the strength to fight their way through to the south in accordance with the Weygand Plan, there was 'no course open to you but to fall back upon the coast . . . you are now authorized to operate towards the coast forthwith'. Thus Reynaud's gloomy comment to Sir Ronald Campbell, the British Ambassador in Paris, that British generals always made for harbours in an emergency was being borne out.

Gort was told that Reynaud, who was in London for talks with Churchill that day, would inform Weygand of the British decision to head for the sea. Relieved finally to be offered official approval for what he had known for a week was inevitable, Gort informed his Corps commanders of the evacuation decision. Brooke's opinion was that 'It is going to be a very hazardous enterprise and we shall be lucky if we save 25 per cent of the BEF.'

At their lunch meeting following the Westminster Abbey service, Churchill and Reynaud discussed at length the French request for more RAF fighters. The subject of embarkation was not raised by the British Prime Minister. As far as the French were concerned, the bridgehead around Dunkirk was to be held with no thought of further retreat. When they eventually found out what was going on, the French – with some reason – considered Britain guilty of deception. Weygand complained that Churchill had been playing a double game since 16 May and insisted that his now-abandoned plan to attack south would still have worked 'if the British had not continually looked back towards the sea'. He echoed his Prime Minister with the opinion 'They do not know how to resist the call of the harbours.'

Having said farewell to Reynaud on this busy 26 May, Churchill gave the green light for Operation Dynamo, the plan to save the BEF by sea which, with admirable foresight and without French knowledge, the British had been urgently preparing with a skeleton staff at Dover in case of catastrophe. The Admiralty order to implement Dynamo went out a few minutes before seven that evening, but in fact by the time the formal opening of the evacuation was decreed almost 28,000 troops had already been safely shipped back from Dunkirk, France's third largest port.

Since they had no choice in the matter, the BEF were fortunate that it was Dunkirk towards which they were retreating. It boasted formidable old fortifications, was surrounded by marshes which could be flooded, and the beaches stretching away to the east of the town formed the largest continuous expanse of sand in Europe. The beach and sand dunes were in places up to a mile wide, providing excellent assembly areas for large groups. It was among those dunes in the seventh century that St Eloi built the dune church from which Dunkirk took its name. The chapel became a shrine, a fishing village grew up around it and in 960 the village became a port when Baldwin, Earl of Flanders, surrounded it with a wall. Stormed by the French, Spanish and British over the centuries, it was destroyed time and again. Now the town of St Eloi's dune church was to suffer once more.

Colonel Gerald Whitfeld, the BEF's Assistant Adjutant General, was sent to Dunkirk on 20 May with orders to evacuate at his discretion as many superfluous personnel as he considered necessary. Whitfeld's report provides a graphic account of the drama and difficulties in Dunkirk, even before the implementation of Operation Dynamo.

Provided only with a staff captain, a clerk and two sections of military police, Whitfeld was overwhelmed by the enormity of his task from the day he arrived as masses of what he called 'unwanted mouths' swarmed into the port. Whitfeld noted 'a somewhat alarming movement towards Dunkirk by both officers and men', adding, 'They hurried into the report centre at a speed which made one suppose that the enemy were at least only a few yards behind them. It was clearly impossible for me to check up on the credentials of so many arrivals . . . as the food and water shortage was acute, I had no option but to send them on to the United Kingdom.'

Whitfeld was bitterly critical of the discipline and morale of many among these early departures, even those supposed to be in command. 'In many cases the officers departed for the boats, leaving their men behind to be rescued later by members of my staff. Officers whom I detailed for jobs which might delay their departure for a day or so disappeared and, I have no doubt, embarked for England without permission.'

Whitfeld also complained about the 'unsatisfactory conduct' of military police, apart from the two sections under his immediate charge.

These men awaited the arrival of darkness, left their positions and embarked without obtaining permission. The conduct of the RASC Ambulance calls for even greater condemnation. On more than one occasion these men drove their ambulances down to the docks and slipped away in the dark on to the boats, leaving the wounded or empty ambulances on the quay. It is due to this disgraceful conduct on the part of certain RASC drivers that the evacuation of wounded at one time almost failed to function.

Eddie Barry, a former Co-op van boy from Swansea, was an ambulance driver operating between the makeshift hospital, a château on Dunkirk's outskirts known as the Chapeau Rouge because of its red dome, and the docks. Even before Göring received permission to unleash the Luftwaffe, Dunkirk was suffering daily bombing and convoys of ambulances had to make their way to the waterside via the back roads because rubble blocked the main streets. 'Often we would load the ambulances and then be told to wait because the hospital ships had to move out due to air raids,' Barry remembered. 'Sometimes I had chaps in my ambulance over a day waiting to get away. When some of the drivers abandoned their ambulances and went on board the rescue ships we had to go down to the docks and pick up the empty vehicles.'

At first Dunkirk was used as a supply port, but bombing soon rendered unloading a difficult, dangerous and eventually impossible task. 'It was more than the ships' companies could stand and the working parties finally broke under the strain and scattered,' Whitfeld reported. On 23 May an Admiralty party arrived with enough explosives to blow up the main docks if it should prove necessary. 'As, however, the enemy were now carrying out that demolition for us,' said Whitfeld, 'it appeared to me full use might be made of these explosives to prepare at least some of the bridges in Dunkirk for demolition.' When he put this idea to the French he was told by one senior naval officer, 'So you wish to blow up the town, do you?'

Relations between the Allies in Dunkirk were particularly difficult. The British were concerned only with evacuation, but the French regarded the port as a fortress, a base from which to launch the counter-attack which would undermine the German advance on Paris. There was, too, a sentimental attachment to Dunkirk as its most northerly city – 'a sort of French Merseyside', as a BBC TV documentary later termed it. Because it was a naval base, Dunkirk was commanded by an admiral, Jean-Marie Abrial, with headquarters situated in a bomb-proof dockside bunker known as Bastion 32.

The French naval staff were nettled at the numbers of British officers and men milling around, and attempting to enter, Bastion 32 since it was already overcrowded, so Whitfeld set up an office in the town until it was destroyed by bombing on 27 May. He did not find the breakdown of morale under bombing surprising. 'I am doubtful if even the best-disciplined troops could have stood such attacks for long, so I am not surprised that small bands of men, utterly helpless and lost, were reported to me as wandering about Dunkirk trying to find shelter from the next raid.'

As if he did not have enough worries, Whitfeld was involved in constant argument with his Allies.

The French were ever ready to bring to my notice cases of alleged misbehaviour by British soldiers. These complaints were made with some venom. The majority were made against men who were wandering about trying to find their way to the docks and often in the last stages of exhaustion. . . . I was finally obliged to point out with some asperity that the French soldiers were looting British lorries, stealing without question any car or motor bike they happened to see and in fact taking away from the dumps intended for the British troops all food supplies.

Such was the grim situation when the order to implement Dynamo was issued.

The sailor charged with that implementation was Admiral Sir Bertram Ramsay, the Flag Officer Commanding Dover. Ramsay's headquarters were located in the maze of tunnels dug into the chalk cliffs overlooking Dover and the Channel during the scares of the Napoleonic Wars. His operations room, which had once housed a dynamo to provide power for the complex and was known as the Dynamo Room, now lent its name to the plan to lift the BEF from the other side of the water.

Ramsay, according to his biographer 'a very dapper, brisk little man', was the son of a Hussars colonel but a naval man all his life. He was, until Dynamo, officially a failure, having been retired in 1938 at the early age of fifty-five with the rank of rear-admiral. The retirement came about because, appointed Chief of Staff to the C-in-C Home Fleet, Admiral Sir Roger Backhouse, he had an early clash of principles and personality with his chief and was relieved of the job at his own request. The retirement lasted a matter of months. With the Munich crisis of 1938 Ramsay was recalled to duty – by Backhouse, incidentally – and ordered to put Dover in working order as a naval base in case of war.

A first-class organizer and methodical planner, Ramsay was appalled by what he inherited, describing the conditions as 'quite hopeless'. The harbour needed dredging and the only signal station in the port had been converted into a public lavatory. His office had no telephone, typewriter or books and his staff had to take calls in the hotel where they lodged. With the outbreak of war the eighty-vessel force planned for the Dover Station consisted of only seven destroyers and twelve minesweepers. Things had not improved greatly by May

1940. On the day of Dynamo's implementation the only inshore craft available to Ramsay for lifting off troops were four Belgian passenger launches and the small boats of the Dover Command such as drifters and contraband-control motor vessels. It was greatly to his credit, and an achievement which made him a key figure in the Dunkirk evacuation, that Ramsay, the careful planner, pulled off his finest success in an operation entirely extemporized.

In ordering Ramsay to implement Dynamo 'with the greatest vigour' the Admiralty estimated that some forty-five thousand troops might be saved, 'after which it is probable that evacuation will be terminated by enemy action'. But the evacuation went on for nine historic days, calling for the sort of sustained effort never foreseen. As one of Ramsay's staff said, 'It was like being told to run a hundred yards at top speed and then when you'd done that find you'd got to carry on and do a mile at the same pace.'

As early as 13 May the Admiralty had requested details of all privately owned motor pleasure boats between 30ft and 100ft long which had not already been offered to the war effort or requisitioned. Although this was, in fact, a routine measure rather than an indication of apprehension about the ability of the BEF to halt the German advance, a week later Churchill himself was suggesting at a War Cabinet meeting the assembling of 'a large number of small vessels in readiness to proceed to ports and inlets on the French coast'. Later that same day, 20 May, Ramsay chaired a meeting in his Dover headquarters to consider 'the emergency evacuation across the Channel of very large forces'.

Just how rapidly that emergency was approaching was apparent from the windows of Ramsay's office on Thursday, 23 May. The explosions from the attack of the 2nd Panzer Division on Boulogne could be clearly seen. Three days later, with naval personnel hastily summoned from evening church services on the National Day of Prayer, Dynamo was officially launched.

Because the shoals off the French and Belgian coast, not to mention the presence of enemy aircraft, torpedo boats and submarines, precluded the involvement of heavy warships, destroyers played a vital part in the evacuation. At the outbreak of war the Royal Navy possessed 202 destroyers. However, because of the demands of other theatres of war such as Norway, convoy duty and the unexpected losses suffered in the evacuation of Boulogne (only one of the eight destroyers committed there escaped undamaged), the Admiralty was able to supply no more than forty of these ships for Dunkirk. Their duties did not, at first, include the transportation of troops. That was supposed to be left to passenger ferries whose crews were experienced in Channel crossings, plus assorted drifters and coasters.

An indication of what awaited the rescue ships was the experience of the *Mona's Queen*, an Isle of Man packet steamer which headed for Dunkirk late that Sunday evening. The vessel was riddled with shrapnel from shore batteries and attacked by dive bombers. Her captain, Mr R. Duggan, reported, 'I could see that the nerves of some of my men were badly shaken. I did not feel too well myself . . . but on being asked if they would volunteer to go in they did so to a man and I am glad to say we took off as many as *Mona's Queen* could carry.'

By now the BEF, Belgians and French had been compressed into a bag-shaped area, its nose south of Lille and the mouth opening on to the Channel from Gravelines in the west to Nieuport in the east. The bag was rapidly shrinking into a corridor, with British troops fighting on both sides of it to preserve an escape route to the sea, a large body of French facing encirclement at Lille and the Belgians in increasing disarray in the north-eastern segment of Allied territory.

At this moment, 27 May, Churchill attempted to bolster Gort's morale with the message: 'Presume troops know they are cutting their way home to Blighty. Never was there such a spur for fighting. We shall give you all the Navy and Air Force can do. . . . No one can tell how it will go but anything is better than being cooped up and starved out.' Churchill could not resist ending with the mild reproof that 'cannon ought to kill tanks and they may as well be lost doing that as any other way'.

Some of the BEF's cannon had been accomplishing just that as the Germans closed in on them. When Lieutenant Eric Loveluck's artillery section became detached from the rest of the 115th (Leicester) Army Field Regiment, he was asked by the colonel of a pioneer battalion of the King's Own Royals to help him hold off some light tanks which had inflicted heavy losses on his command defending the La Bassée Canal at Merville near Lille. The German armour had just broken off its attack and was drawn up in the square of a nearby village, Le Saar, not suspecting that Loveluck was training his two 1915 vintage 18-pounder guns in their direction from a farm on the edge of Merville. Equipped only with a map which he estimated was '250 or more miles to the square inch', Loveluck and his number two, Lieutenant John Caven, guessed the range of some three kilometres so exactly that their first air-burst shrapnel shell exploded over the heads of the dismounted crews, to be followed by enough shells to inflict severe damage.

The Useless Mouths

Next morning, expecting some reaction to his success, Loveluck climbed the tower of the village church to scan the surrounding country for any enemy activity. 'Suddenly the air around me was alive with German fighters and light bombers,' he recalled. 'I fired my revolver at the planes in fury, they were so close. I must have been seen by a pilot whom I had missed only by inches for he turned and climbed before diving at me with guns blazing. Clearly discretion was the better part of valour and I leapt inside one of the bigger bells, only to be nearly deafened by the noise of the hail of bullets striking it.'

On the following day an attack was launched, this time by medium tanks, and Loveluck's guns smashed another five of these before, running short of shells, they were themselves put out of action with the loss of one dead and four wounded among the gun crews. Loveluck, who won the Military Cross for his leadership and bravery, next teamed up with the crew of a 25-pounder which they towed away from the risk of capture under cover of darkness. Loveluck was thankful he had read German at Cambridge when they ran into enemy troops who pointed an anti-tank gun at them.

I flung open the roof hatch, yelled some choice abuse at the unsuspecting *Feldwebel* and he leapt to attention and saluted as we swept through. It just shows what discipline can do! At the time I was wearing the service dress of a captain in the Royal Northumberland Fusiliers, yet he swallowed it hook, line and sinker. Incidentally I was so attired because on a recce by motorcycle on 27 May I had crossed a bridge in the dusk and, alas, the bridge was not there, so I was duly muddied and, frankly, stank. My troops scrounged for me and I had to masquerade either as a wing commander RAF or a Royal Northumberlands officer, an easy decision for me to make with the RAF unjustly blamed by the ignorant for lack of air cover.

There was bravery on all sectors of the British front as the Germans pressed home their bid to finish off the BEF. When the area around Ypres came under heavy assault the 3rd Grenadier Guards was one of the battalions ordered into a counter-attack, and Captain Roderic Brinckman's account of his involvement in that foray is typical.

Brinckman, who estimated that in the seventeen days since the original German onslaught he had not managed more than thirty hours' sleep, had originally expected the battalion to be withdrawn to Dunkirk for embarkation, and told his company sergeant major that he was looking forward to being home in time for Ascot. After downing a whisky and soda which his batman had conjured from somewhere (and which he was to need in view of what was to happen

129

to him that night) Brinckman moved forward for a late evening counter-attack against a German penetration.

'We moved off about 8.30 p.m., I having previously stuffed my haversack with primed hand grenades', said Brinckman. 'Suddenly we came across about twenty men coming towards us. They were of the Black Watch and going, as I pointed out to them, the wrong way.' They told Brinckman the situation in front was hopeless but he incorporated them into his advancing company anyway.

'Mortar shells began to fall,' Brinckman wrote in a letter to his mother.

It was now too dark to see all the company, and so I could not tell what casualties were occurring; we were in enfilade fire from machine guns from our left. A mortar bomb burst nearby and a bit went into my right thigh. I said to myself, 'This is the real thing.' Well, we went up the slope and I thought we must surely be near the objective. We got to the crest and had not gone far when a perfectly withering fire greeted us from our front at a range of about 150 yards. I don't know how many were hit and how many just dropped down for cover, but I received a bullet through the right shoulder and another through the left arm.

Despite suffering yet another wound, this time in the left thigh, Brinckman then led a bayonet charge.

We got amongst the Germans who immediately threw up their arms. One surrendered to me and then shot my runner in the back, so I killed him with my revolver and then bayonetted two more Germans. Their fire seemed to slacken and suddenly ceased. We were on the canal by a little house which seemed to have more Germans in it so we got down behind a hedge and suddenly I realized that I had only one sergeant and two guardsmen with me, and of these only one man was unwounded. I sent him back along the railway line with the message that we were on the position but would need more men to hold it.

The cottage seemed full of Germans. I threw a grenade through the window which quietened them. Another German fired point blank at us from the other side of the hedge. Sergeant Ryder got him. Some more Germans came across the bridge and I threw another grenade at them. I had a third grenade in my hand and with great difficulty managed to get the pin out, and then realized that I was getting weak and my right arm seemed paralysed. Ryder was wounded in the thigh and could not help me. With great difficulty I managed to transfer the grenade to my left hand. Then there seemed to be a silence round us. The other guardsman was dead. I said to Ryder, 'It's no use staying here till daylight, we will crawl back and try and find some more men.' We began – there was some sort of a moon – and we'd gone about fifty yards when I got another bullet from the cottage area which hit my right leg. Ryder was hit again too. I threw the last grenade, under-hand with my left arm, in the direction of the flash.

I now felt bad – I continued to try and drag myself toward where I thought we must have some men left but my arms were hurting too much. I seemed to be bleeding everywhere. . . . With great difficulty I managed to get a box of morphia pellets from my trouser pocket – I could not open it. Again with great difficulty I managed to get my key chain out of my pocket and opened the little gold knife and pried open the tin box. I took the lot. Soon I felt better, everything seemed quiet round me except for groaning men. I sat up and found I was bleeding hard from the right thigh – with difficulty I got out my field dressing and decided to put it over my wound and then make a tourniquet. I think I succeeded. When I woke up I was on a bed in the cottage. There was a dead German lying on the floor beside me. It was daylight and a very live German was standing at the foot of the bed!

Presently I was put in a motor car with a badly wounded German soldier and we were driven to the advanced dressing station. I felt very ill and was sick on the way. We arrived at a school house about 10 a.m. and I was laid on a stretcher amongst a lot of German wounded. A medical orderly who had been to London came and spoke to me in English. He was friendly and said that my wounds would be attended to as soon as possible but that naturally the Germans had to be done first. At 7 p.m. I was carried into another room and my friendly orderly said, 'We see that you are Aryan – if you had been a Jew you would have had to wait.' The German doctor was most efficient. My beautiful Hawes & Curtis silken underwear and shirt were just cut off with shears. They were, of course, a solid cake of blood. The only thing which was fit to keep was my battle jacket and that was in a pretty good mess.

When Bill Brodie's signals section pulled out of their Armentières wine warehouse they withdrew to another office established in Lomme, arriving in the early hours of 26 May.

Tired, unwashed and unshaved we were told that enemy tanks had broken through – and we were to stop them. Wearily I took twenty men along the road and we manned a cemetery wall. In front of us in the pale moonlight we could see the dusty road and behind the grey faces of the tombstones leered in the half-light. Then in the distance I heard a dull rumble. I counted my firepower and found I had one revolver and twenty rifles, as effective as peashooters against Panzerwagons. 'Load,' I ordered and twenty rifle bolts clicked. The rumble became a rattle and the ground began to shake as the first of the monsters came in view. It was fully sixty tons and carried a huge gun that traversed from left to right as it lumbered along.

'For —— sake, don't fire,' came a hoarse whisper and twenty-one heads ducked behind the cemetery wall. In the swirling dust we counted five cruiser tanks and let them pass. They bore no identification marks and they may well have been French. We never found out, but later a lorry load of German prisoners passed so the road was still in Allied hands.

Les Boyce was another who had a close shave with tanks. He and a friend, Frank Morris, were enjoying a Sunday morning cup of coffee on 26 May in a village café.

Suddenly the small daughter of the establishment came running in, crying *'Allemands, Allemands.'* We looked out the back of the house and there were the tanks, coming up the road. We rushed out and into Frank's lorry. All the others had gone. Nobody had bothered to come looking for us. I never saw our officers again. They just left us, that was it. We felt totally betrayed.

The Coldstream Guards lieutenant, James Langley, received a sharp reminder that the Germans were never far behind when he discovered he had left his walking stick behind at a previous rest halt. 'A despatch rider who volunteered to retrieve it returned with a bullet through the petrol tank of his motorcycle.'

It was to be another week or so before the Germans would catch up with Langley but many British – wounded, surrounded or simply lost – were falling into captivity. Norman Dixon, a Royal Engineers clerk, was hit in the stomach by shrapnel when his company was pressed into a rearguard action. 'I was the only one in our group to be wounded, so they picked me up and carried me for a while,' Dixon recalled. Then, when they were sheltering in a ditch, his commanding officer passed him a note, which he carries in his wallet to this day. It read as follows:

To: Spr Dixon
From: Major W F Anderson
I am very sorry but I do not see how we can possibly get you away with us as there are German infantry within 150 yards and our only chance, and that not a very good one, is to crawl. If we get away safe we will tell a nearby farm to look after you. If no one comes by 1800 hrs leave your rifle and walk in and give yourself up to either civil or military and you will be quite well looked after, I think.
Goodbye and good luck.

'Then these characters started crawling over me as I lay slumped in the ditch, saying cheerio,' Dixon said.

When they'd all gone I began to feel a little bit sorry for myself, but the strange thing was that none of my section made it back to England.
Eventually I began to think of self-preservation so I crawled along this

ditch, over a field and sat on the edge of a road. The first person to come along was a woman refugee with lots of bags. She sat down and gave me a drink and then walked off. Next was an open farm cart with some children on it and a priest. He stopped the car, dressed my wound and gave me a drink. I asked if I could go on the cart but he said no because it would then become a military target.

So I staggered along the road and knocked on the door of a cottage. The people opened the door and when they saw me slammed it in my face, which did very little for my low opinion of the French at that stage. I knocked on the next door and asked where the British were. They pointed down the road and closed the door, so I went a bit further down the road, saw some German vehicles and dived into a ditch. I got out again, set off once more and immediately ran straight into a whole lot of Germans. I hadn't got a rifle or anything, so they sat me down by the roadside and a captain who could speak English gave me a drink and told me they were going to be in London within a couple of weeks.

There were signs of massacres to come in the treatment of some British prisoners. Cyril King of the Royal Artillery's 92nd Field Regiment fell asleep in an abandoned house and was left behind in the retreat from Vimy. Teaming up with other strays he attempted to make his way across country towards Lille, but the group was surrounded and forced to surrender.

We were divided up and I was pushed along with a sergeant and one other man into a field occupied by many French troops, both colonial and white. Around this field slit trenches had been dug and lined with straw, presumably by the French as defensive positions but never used. Approximately twenty of us were lined up in front of these trenches and about twenty paces away a machine gun, handled by two Germans, faced us. At the sight of this some of the French colonial men begged for mercy, but I told myself that if I could not do anything else I would not show fear and waited for the firing to begin. But it never came, and after the German officer in charge had shouted some few words at us we were marched towards the road. Here we were greeted by shouts and jeers from the enemy – 'For you the war is over' and 'Where is the umbrella of Chamberlain?'

Every now and then we came across a position which had been set up to stop the advance, but of course it had been hopeless to stop such a steamroller. The tarmac was covered with shattered guns, pools of blood and mutilated bodies. I just could not bear to look.

Having taken on the 6th Panzer Division, despite being 'disgracefully under-equipped', Lieutenant H C F Harwood and a group of the 5th East Kents attempted to evade the German advance and get back to the Allied lines. But they were spotted crossing the

St Pol–Arras road and cornered in a wood. Though they resisted for a while, Harwood recognized the situation was hopeless.

A voice shouted from outside the wood 'Surrender or we will all of you shoot.' Beckoning to the remainder of the men scattered around me, we chucked away our rifles and advanced towards an opening in the trees. Personally, I was quite convinced we would be shot as we emerged one by one from the wood, but anything seemed better than remaining where we were – just waiting for the end to come.

I was the first to emerge, merely because I happened to be at the head of a rather jittery line of men. As I came out from the cover of the undergrowth into the open I saw a German officer or NCO (I couldn't tell the difference) approaching me and brandishing a revolver in lamentably reckless fashion. He was young and powerfully built with a fair moustache and very light blue eyes.

When the last man emerged from the wood we were lined up and thoroughly searched. The German wanted to know why my revolver holster was empty. For some unknown reason I felt quite ashamed to admit that I had never been issued with one. To have admitted this would only have added to the contempt which the Germans already had for British efficiency, and I was damned if I was going to play up to that pink-faced, blue-eyed creature. 'I chucked it away in the wood,' I said sulkily, going through the motion of throwing something away with my hands.

Having satisfied themselves that we had no arms or ammunition concealed on us, we were marched off, still in single file with our hands above our heads. The young German officer could speak a word or two of English and kept saying, 'You are lucky, my lads, the war for you is over.' He carried on in this vein for a time and then said something to his men, pointing at us with his revolver. 'Chamberlain ha! ha! Churchill ha! ha!' This joke was apparently too much even for German discipline. They roared with laughter and stared at us with unconcealed loathing. I stumbled along with my hands above my head, feeling too numbed to mind what anyone said. All I knew was that I was now a prisoner in German hands, and God only knew what was going to happen to me and the other poor wretches with me.

They were taken to a château which Harwood thought was a German divisional headquarters and sat about on the grass. Eventually Harwood was ordered into a Mercedes alongside the driver, 'a little rat of a man who kept up a torrent of abuse in German in which Churchill and, apparently, myself seemed to be on the friendliest terms. I felt duly honoured. Presently the car slowed down and I noticed we were approaching a disused chalk quarry. The little swine of a driver started to pay his holster. Was this the end of the journey, I wondered?'

The German officer in the car and the driver looked at Harwood and a fellow officer. 'Our faces appeared to crown their little act with success because the car began to gather speed again amid the almost hysterical laughter of our captors. I found out later that to instil fear of being shot was quite an irresistible stand-by joke for the Germans.'

Such were the numbers of prisoners and so great the booty being accumulated by the Germans that the opportunity frequently presented itself for captured BEF men to escape. Jack Toomey of the 42nd Division's postal unit was in a retreating convoy which came under attack:

Everyone went into a ditch except another bloke and myself who were jammed in the back of the lorry. We could hear machine gun fire and thought it was a quiet shoot-up by Jerry planes, but when tracer shells started coming through the roof of our lorry I knew I was wrong. Two shells took a knapsack from the box next to my head and threw it out of the back looking like cotton waste. Another went past my ear so close I felt the wind of it. I just sat and gave up all hope of coming out of that lorry alive.

However, I heard the noise of a tank chugging past the lorry and the shooting stopped. The bloke driving the tank saw us in the lorry and calmly tossed a hand grenade under the tailboard. After it had gone off and we found we were still alive we came out of that lorry with our hands in the clouds. There are pleasanter ways of committing suicide than fighting five tanks, an armoured wireless car and a plane with a rifle.

Well, they took us prisoners and while we were looking after the wounded the French opened fire and we were between the two, so back into the ditch we went. The main body of prisoners were run off to a nearby village. We lay in the ditch in a thunderstorm for two hours and then went back to our lines. So much for my 'escape' – more a case of getting left behind.

The escape contrived by J O Jones and his mates (unit unspecified) was a great deal more dramatic. His recollection, with original syntax and spelling preserved and entitled 'My Adventures at Dunkirk Has Far as I Can Remember', told how

The order came for a quick move. There was ten of us in this one lorry, the last one in the convoy. Night came, pitch black, but lots of noise and flashes. Something went wrong with the engine of our lorry and by the time we got it fixed up we found ourselves stranded, which way our chaps had gone we did not know, but we kept on the straight road until we came to some cross-roads and turned right, and oh! boy slap bang into a party of Jerries, about fifty strong, we were taken in no time, they made us drive to a big house. After taking our ammunition and rifles from us, they locked us up in a big celler. We spent the rest of the night in there, a bit downhearted, but ready for anythink, while there was life there was hope. We did a bit of spying, and found out that their was only four Jerries guarding us, God knows where the rest where, but it was in our favour, and our lorry was still outside. We enticed one of them in, and once the door was opened we made a rush for the others, poor old Bert it was his last rush, they got him between the eyes, that left nine of us, we soon made short work of the guard, Bert was avenged. Did we hop it in that lorry, our stuff was still aboard, rifles etc. Luck was with us, we took the right road, and came upon our boys about five hours later.

Tom Dabner, a driver with the 11th Durham Light Infantry, was ambushed with his vehicle, then ordered to help load it with wounded and follow a tank returning to its refuelling point that night. At a road junction Dabner turned left when the tank turned right, sped off and brought the British wounded back to safety.

The Royal Engineers major, Edmund Booth, was captured near Boulogne (while unarmed and on a bicycle) but escaped, only to be taken prisoner again as he and some twenty men of his Artisan Works company attempted to slip across country towards Calais. This time he was too tired to think of getting away again.

We were given food, bread and tinned meat, but otherwise the German soldiers did not pay much attention to us. Later we were marched up the road and joined another gang of prisoners, mostly Belgian and French. We walked for what seemed an incredibly long way in an entirely disorganized rabble. . . . It would have been perfectly easy to have slipped out of the line of march and to have lain hidden in a ditch or a copse but the weariness, fatigue and hunger of the past two days produced (in me, at any rate) a state of mind wherein it was impossible to think of anything but food and rest. When one reaches an advanced stage of exhaustion, planned thinking becomes almost impossible and all one wants is to stick with one's friends and to go on doing what everyone else is doing almost automatically.

At last, when I was feeling very nearly at the end of my tether, a lorry came along packed with officer prisoners. It was already full to overflowing but a kindly German soldier picked me up and lifted me on to the front mudguard. I really believe I was physically quite incapable of climbing up by myself. It was a perilous position but I was thankful for the rest.

The sheer misery of a predicament exacerbated by a thoughtless superior was graphically noted by the gunner, Alfred Baldwin.

On the night of the 27th it had poured with rain. We had lost our truck, struck by a shell, and all our gear with it. During the night we slept round the gun and all we had against the rain was a groundsheet over the gun and four of us were sleeping under that. At dawn our second-in-charge of

The Useless Mouths

the battery, Major Shrimpton, came round. He was shouting his head off about everybody being asleep and gave instructions to the gun sergeant to give us some PT to wake us up. We were so tired that was the worst thing he could have done.

It was often difficult to get troops on the march again after they had fallen out for a rest. Robert Holding of the Royal Sussex Regiment wrote of his own retreat:

At each halt no one bothered to fall out but simply collapsed wherever they halted and were immediately asleep, only to be awakened after a short eight minutes to drag themselves to their feet and stagger off once more. In one large village I awoke after one of these halts to find myself lying in the gutter which was running with what I hope was nothing more than dirty water, though at the time I neither knew nor cared.

Alf Hewitt of the South Lancashires recalled falling asleep at a night halt in a village street.

I had a vision that I was in a hospital ward with nurses all round me, dressed in white, the sides of the ward were white and there was a soft light over me. A sister bent over me and told me it was time to get up. I woke up and she turned into this sergeant who was booting me and everybody else. The soft light was moonlight on my face and the whitewashed walls of the cottages in the street were the white walls of the ward.

Hewitt, who had pulled out of the Escaut line without orders when his platoon commander told the men, 'Come on, let's get out of here', got lost in strange circumstances during the retreat.

We came under shellfire along a road and dashed into a big allotment just outside a village. As we lay there under this accurate fire we had had no food and most of us had run out of water. Growing all round us were lush beds of rhubarb. Naturally we were reaching out, snapping off sticks and eating them. Imagine the result, all that rhubarb going into empty stomachs. I must have eaten more than the rest of them. About two hours later the effects of the rhubarb got to me. I had to fall out, into a ditch, and the reaction was so violent that they went on and left me. I had such cramps I couldn't put my trousers on, so I walked alone across country with my trousers round my neck. I daren't put them back on again and I spent a couple of days all on my own.

On that fateful 27 May Rommel found time to write to his wife Lu: 'We're busy encircling the British and French in Lille at the moment. . . . I'm all right for washing. Guenther [his batman] takes good care of that . . .'. At the heart of this encirclement threat was Montgomery's 3rd Division, perilously exposed near Roubaix. The urgent

137

need to extricate this division coincided with an opportunity to shift it some fifty miles to where a gap had opened up between the northernmost BEF positions and the tottering Belgian Army. Even the confident Monty considered this 'the most difficult operation we had to do' in the whole campaign.

It involved a night withdrawal from contact with the enemy and a move without lights along country roads within a couple of thousand yards of the front, where a fierce battle had been raging all day. Lieutenant Colonel Brian Horrocks, commanding a battalion of the Middlesex Regiment, said of that night, 'I never felt more naked in my life', as the division edged through unknown country. Montgomery's biographer called it 'a little masterpiece in the art of war – an operation which, for sheer nerve and skill, deserves to stand alongside any of his celebrated later achievements'.

The move went without a hitch and the division was in its new position by dawn on 28 May. 'Imagine my astonishment', wrote Montgomery of that day, 'to learn that the King of the Belgians had surrendered the Belgian Army to the Germans at midnight while I was moving my division into the gap. Here was a pretty pickle! Instead of having a Belgian Army on my left I now had nothing and had to do some rapid thinking.'

12

'A Regal Judas'

The whole of Belgium seemed to have blossomed white. Everywhere there were white flags, linen of every description, flapping from lamp posts, windows and flagpoles.

Frank Farley, Middlesex Regiment

Bombarded mercilessly from the air and under fierce ground assault from an enemy who sensed collapse was at hand, the Belgian Army had battled as best it could to shore up the eastern flank of the shrinking perimeter around Dunkirk. With its own air force destroyed within forty-eight hours of the German invasion, Belgium appealed repeatedly for RAF help in driving away the Luftwaffe, but deteriorating communications and a reluctance on Britain's part to commit more of its precious fighter planes meant that most of the appeals went unanswered. During the fighting on the River Lys on 26 and 27 May the British Mission to the Belgian Army was bluntly informed that the demoralized troops would not hold 'unless they saw aircraft with English markings in the sky'.

On 25 May a deputation of Belgian politicians had begged Leopold to flee the country with them and establish a government in exile. The King refused, saying his place was with his people. It was a decision which, though subsequently heavily criticized, did much to help save the BEF, preserving for a further forty-eight hours defences which would certainly have given way if the Belgian Army had lost its commander-in-chief at that moment.

Britain's special envoy to King Leopold, Admiral Sir Roger Keyes, warned Churchill of the imminent disaster, as did the French liaison officer, General Champon, in a message to Weygand. 'The limits of resistance have very nearly been reached,' said Champon. 'Our front is giving way like a worn-out old rope.'

139

On 27 May Churchill wired Keyes,

Impart following to your friend [King Leopold]. Presume he knows that British and French are fighting their way to coast and that we propose to give fullest support from navy and air force during hazardous embarkation. What can we do for him? Certainly we cannot serve Belgium's cause by being hemmed in and starved out. Only hope is victory and England will never quit the war whatever happens till Hitler is beat or we cease to be a State. Trust you will make sure he leaves with you by aeroplane before too late. . . . Vitally important Belgium should continue in war and safety King's person essential.

Keyes did not receive the message until his arrival in England next day, 28 May, without Leopold. Churchill's assumption that Leopold was aware of the British embarkation plans blithely ignored the fact that neither the French nor the Belgians had been officially informed at that stage.

On the morning of 27 May Lieutenant Colonel George Davy, in charge of the British Liaison Mission to the Belgian Army headquarters, arrived at BEF Command HQ with the gloomy opinion that the Belgians 'would have packed up within twenty-four hours'. In fact Davy considerably over-estimated Belgian capacity for further resistance. By 2.30 that afternoon an official communiqué from Belgian High Command warned that its units were 'incapable of renewing the struggle tomorrow' and its Chief of Staff, General Michiels, admitted, 'I believe the Army is finished.'

By 5 p.m. an envoy in a white-pennanted car was on his way to seek terms for a cessation of hostilities. The German attitude was uncompromising: the vehicle was shot up as it passed through the lines and the demand was for unconditional surrender, with no alternative. The Belgians conceded, but managed to set the ceasefire for four o'clock next morning to give their Allies time to react to the news.

The reaction was virulent. Although they had been offered ample evidence and received adequate warning of the pending collapse, the French in particular were vehement in their denunciations. Weygand claimed 'the news fell on us like a thunderbolt', while his Prime Minister, Reynaud, raged that 'there has never been such a betrayal in history . . . it is monstrous, absolutely monstrous'. Leopold's picture was removed from the window of Cartier, the jeweller, in the Rue de la Paix and replaced with one of Queen Mary. Angry French people ejected from their houses bewildered Belgian refugees, who were jostled and jeered in public places. A sad, quiet demonstration by a group of Belgian exiles took place in front of the statue of Leopold's father, King Albert, in Paris. The Belgian national anthem was sung, wreaths were laid and to the statue itself were affixed black crêpe and the poignant message: 'Venerated King who made our country great, give us strength to wash away the shame with which your unworthy successor has covered our unhappy Belgium. We swear to avenge this treason.'

Alexander Werth, the *Manchester Guardian* man in Paris, raged, 'God, I always thought Leopold a bad egg', and ruminated on stories that the Belgian monarch had a German mistress supplied by the Gestapo. The general reaction in France, however, was more of bewilderment than anger. One Maginot Line gunner recalled his reaction on hearing the news: 'To us the British were a strange and unknown race but we felt the Belgians were part of ourselves . . . it was as if our best friend had let us down.'

Churchill, fully apprised of the dilemma of the Eton-educated Leopold, offered a far more restrained reaction, telling the Commons he had no intention of passing judgement on the King but warning the House that it must prepare itself for 'hard and heavy tidings'. Later, under French pressure to fall into line, Churchill would change tack and condemn Leopold in much the same terms as Reynaud had.

The British press vilified him as 'Traitor King' and 'King Rat'. In a stinging column headlined 'I Shall Betray', the *Daily Mirror* columnist Cassandra accused him of being 'a regal Judas', while the *Mirror'*s women's page carried a picture of Leopold alongside the heading 'The Face That Every Woman Now Despises' over an article which asserted: 'Women know that a handsome face often hides the heart of a devil.'

The reaction of the British troops, whose contact with the Belgian Army had largely been confined to witnessing their carousing, was similarly bleak. Captain Basil Bartlett felt, 'It's a relief they've packed up. At least we shan't be expecting them to hold positions which they never meant to hold.' Bartlett did concede that 'with their horse-drawn, 1914 artillery and totally inadequate air force they didn't stand a chance and they must have taken a hammering during the first few days of the campaign. But they ought to have done better.'

The signaller, Lawrence Vollans, felt sympathy for the Belgians as he withdrew through one small town.

From the upper windows of almost every house were hanging impro-vised white flags made of everything and anything, from sheets to handkerchiefs, so long as they were white. And on either side of the street filed long lines of Belgian soldiers, silent and dejected, no longer an army – their arms thrown away. Some of our lads booed them and I was sorry about that.

There was even admiration from Lieutenant Colonel Brian Horrocks, who was with a party of sappers preparing a bridge for demolition when news came of the surrender. The group contained a lone Belgian soldier. 'He might have been pole-axed,' wrote Horrocks. 'With a stricken look on his face he put on his equipment, saluted, and walked away towards the German front . . . It was a dramatic little scene which has remained in my memory ever since. The solitary figure of the Belgian soldier disappearing towards the enemy seemed to accentuate the shame of his country in defeat.'

The German reaction was, understandably, ecstatic. Wilhelm Prüller, with the 9th Panzer Division, noted in his diary: 'My eyes are wet for joy and pride in the Wehrmacht's accomplishments. Now comes the turn of those who are most to blame . . . We'll get you.' Despite the jubilation, German propaganda took care to congratulate Leopold for acting 'like a soldier and a human being' in sparing his country further suffering, and praised the King's 'brave soldiers'. But when General von Bechtolsheim, Operations Chief of the German 6th Army, drove through the Belgian defences to negotiate the surrender he said of the Belgian soldiers, 'Most of them seemed to be very relieved that the struggle had ended.' Summing up the campaign on that front he was equally scathing, claiming: 'The only real difficulty we had was the crossing of rivers and canals, not from the opposition.'

With the British need to consolidate a perimeter around Dunkirk now even more urgent, the decision was taken that men to defend it must be rescued at the cost of equipment if necessary. Guns were to be disabled, transport immobilized. Only what could be carried through or was urgently needed would be permitted inside the defences being assembled on the canal lines.

Basil Bartlett confessed he was 'stupefied' at the order to destroy everything. His Field Security squad smashed and fired shots into their cipher truck and burned all records. All around them a similar orgy of destruction was in progress. 'Under a clear blue sky, on a quiet country road, it was perhaps the most astonishing sight of all this queer war.' To Brian Horrocks it was 'a horrible sight – thousands of abandoned carriers, guns and pieces of military equipment of all sorts. It was a graveyard of gear.' When the 8th King's Own Royal Regiment was ordered to destroy all the battalion transport except his own staff car and one truck, Colonel Lionel Westropp considered: 'It was now clear to everyone that perhaps the greatest military disaster in history was about to take place.'

The gunnery colonel, Graham Brooks, considered it

a bitter moment for us all. To a gunner, the idea of destroying his guns is sacrilege. We were not disheartened, or even alarmed, at the plight of the army – we were embittered, enraged and ashamed.

I had never seen men so furious, never seen so much venom or determination put into obedience of orders. . . . If things *had* to be destroyed then, by God, they should be destroyed wholeheartedly! We burnt all documents and maps, except the maps required to get us to the coast. All kit, blankets and spare clothing were slashed, ripped to pieces with knives, torn to shreds and buried in the mud. We smashed all our artillery instruments except those small enough to be carried, and buried them. Tractors, carts and vehicles not required for the journey were smashed by shooting bullets through petrol tanks, removing car-burettors, taking off all fittings, breaking windscreens, slashing tyres to shreds, bashing radiators with pickaxes and then pushing the wreck into the water. Tears were in the drivers' eyes as they pushed a battered 'Alice' or 'Rosie' into the river . . . in the cottage where our headquarters were we smashed everything and gutted the place. Every cup, chair, table, window, we broke to pieces.

As the Royal Artillery's 2nd Medium Regiment began to destroy its weapons, Sergeant Jimmy Walsham witnessed a poignant scene: 'A limber gunner who in peacetime was responsible for cleaning his gun and keeping the steelwork burnished bright, collapsed to the ground and lay prostrate, crying his eyes out and making incoherent noises. His pride and joy for some five years was now scrap. He had to be carried and lifted on to a lorry.'

As he set off to walk to Dunkirk the Royal Artillery subaltern, John Carpenter, was under instructions to destroy all automatic weapons. These included some Bren guns which had been delivered in the middle of the battle and were still in their protective grease, and a Lewis machine gun of First World War vintage.

This was a curious weapon and had, I think, eighty-four working parts. In order to make sure nobody ever used ours I remember telling my Lewis gunner to take it apart as we went along the road in the darkness and chuck the pieces over the hedge, partly to amuse everybody but also make sure that nobody ever found them again. I'm sure the bits are still lying in the hedgerow somewhere.

There were also some horrifying moments. Lieutenant Gregory Blaxland watched as French cavalry appeared to assemble in a nearby field, until he saw their real purpose. 'They were shooting the horses one by one and at my distance from them it all seemed to be done so casually, with each horse patiently awaiting its turn.' Frank Farley of the Middlesex Regiment came across what he described as a

Hogarthian scene as a medium artillery regiment wrecked its equipment. 'Many of the gunners were obscenely drunk. . . . How they ever finished and got out, God alone knows.' Others had simply cracked under the strain. Stan Smith remembers a group of British soldiers running up and down the middle of a road firing their rifles into the air.

There was no shortage of bidders for unwanted clothing. Colonel James Birch, commanding the 2nd Bedfordshire and Hertfordshire Regiment, found Belgian refugees crowding round him 'like vultures' as he began to discard his kit, grabbing the clothes and oddments he flung at them. When he had to get rid of all the books he had purchased while stationed in France, Anthony Rhodes stashed them in a wardrobe with a note in French and German asking the new owner to treat them with care. The prudent General Montgomery left a box of personal papers 'and a very good lunch basket' at an abbey at Westvleteren in Belgium for safe keeping. They were bricked up and subsequently returned to Montgomery when he helped to liberate Belgium in September 1944.

The urgent need to fill the gap caused by the collapse of the Belgians led to a fierce row between the British and French commanders, Gort and Blanchard, on 28 May. Blanchard, Gort's superior, travelled to British command HQ where he was horrified to learn of Britain's unilateral decision to evacuate its army. Though he had been ordered to co-operate in a withdrawal, Blanchard's understanding had been that the bridgehead would be held 'with no thought of retreat'. In addition, said Blanchard, he had been told by General Prioux, now in command of the French 1st Army, that his men fighting in the area around Lille were tired and so he could not contemplate further withdrawal. Eventually, elements of Brooke's 2 Corps, a couple of divisions of General de la Laurencie's III Corps and parts of the French 7th Army were put together to plug the gap. Almost half the 1st Army was eventually cut off in the pocket around Lille. After resisting until 31 May, some thirty-five thousand French were taken prisoner – including Prioux, captured at his command post.

Those French formations which *were* moving back towards the Dunkirk perimeter had been allocated separate routes from the British, but in the confusion of retreat all became hopelessly intermingled, particularly in and around Poperinghe, where several of the roads to Dunkirk converged. John Matthew, the RASC troop-carrying major, was reduced to despair at the frustration he encountered as he attempted to do his job.

The French road discipline was absolutely nil, consequently every journey was a nightmare. They simply pushed their way through wherever they wanted to go, completely regardless of anyone else on the road. They cut into other convoys, double and treble banked, and time and again created complete paralysis of roads for miles around, making in daytime perfect targets for air attack and by night complete and utter chaos.

George Sutton, commanding 125 Brigade, had been issued careful plans for the withdrawal but complained that 'No power on earth could keep the hordes of mixed French troops from using any roads they felt inclined.'

At one stage near Poperinghe Colonel Graham Brooks's unit found itself among what Brooks claimed appeared to be the dregs of the French Army.

One panic-stricken major, trying to scramble past our column, ditched his car. Rushing up to Boots Brown's truck, he tried to pull the driver out of his seat, presumably in order to clamber in himself. When Boots shouted at him the major pulled his revolver; he was mad with terror. Bang went the *entente cordiale* and Boots slogged him hard on the jaw. . . .

A little further on the driver of a French lorry at the side of my truck kept honking his horn and screaming like a maniac at the driver in front to let him pass which, of course, was quite impossible. The Frenchman then went mad. Jamming his foot on the accelerator, he jumped his lorry forward full tilt at the tailboard of the truck in front. I jumped out and dealt with him; his eyes were wild, he was dribbling at the mouth and screaming oaths at everybody. However, the sight of my revolver had a calming influence and he behaved himself after that.

We came across a column of French lorries, engines still running, abandoned by their drivers right in the centre of the road. It was a pathetic sight, too, to see some French cavalrymen slide off their horses and jump into passing lorries, leaving their terrified mounts to fend for themselves. I must say I felt rather proud of my own countrymen that day. Not a sign of panic or bad discipline did I see among any British troops.

The gunnery lieutenant and former Cambridge languages student, Eric Loveluck, found a more diplomatic way to deal with demoralized French troops as he trudged towards Poperinghe.

A whole battalion lay in the ditches while their officers stalked apprehensively up and down the road. I spotted the colonel, saluted and advised him *inter alia* that, although some of us had lost a battle, we hadn't lost the war and that if they sat on their *culs* (slang for *derrières*) much longer they would all be in the bag, with all the deprivation that would mean. He was so delighted he invited me to address his battalion; I did so and rose to heights of passion undreamed of . . . spirit of Verdun etc., and finished by singing the first verse of '*La Marseillaise*'. This brought them to their feet and they rapidly joined in and cheered as we all marched off together towards Dunkirk.

The Sherwood Foresters colonel, Julian Wright, found his line of vehicles hopelessly mixed up with three other columns at Poperinghe, where he had fought in the First World War. 'The transport column must have been seven or eight miles long. One good bomb on the road would have dished the whole outfit. I cannot understand how or why we escaped,' said Wright, who harboured suspicions that the German High Command wanted to let them get away.

The anonymous officer who wrote a series of newspaper articles in 1950 about the experiences of the 5th Green Howards ten years earlier was also puzzled by the freedom from air attack in Poperinghe. 'We got through with nothing worse than some delay and the watery feeling round about where breakfast ought to have been that assails men trapped in their transports in an undefended town under an open sky of which the enemy had the undisputed mastery.'

Even the Coldstream Guards had problems keeping together in the confusion of Poperinghe. 'I began to doubt if we would ever get through individually, let alone as a fighting unit,' wrote Lieutenant James Langley. However, an alternative route through the town was arranged, with a group of Belgian Boy Scouts to show the way. 'Why and how a troop of Belgian Scouts was on parade in the swirling mass of men, guns and horses that choked the debris-littered streets of Poperinghe on that May afternoon is beyond my comprehension,' said Langley. The problems that the 1/7th Battalion of the Middlesex Regiment suffered were resolved by their intrepid commanding officer, Lieutenant Colonel B B Rackham. A 1914–18 veteran and inventor of the Rackham clutch, he stood in the main square in his greatcoat, directing the transport under his command down a side turning and away from the jams.

Unlike Julian Wright and his Sherwood Foresters, many British found themselves under regular assault from the air, still being carried out with impunity. Frederick Noon, a gunner with the 53rd Field Artillery, remembers the German planes actually dipping their wings, with the pilots waving from the cockpits at the unfortunates below them. Gregory Blaxland recalled that, on 28 May, 'German planes came over in larger number than I had ever seen. They just filled the sky without any attempt to fly in formation. . . . One big one, I think a Dornier, collapsed and crashed like a bird shot through the head, which at least proved that someone was firing at them with something larger than the Brens that chattered from our position.' Brigadier Merton Beckwith-Smith, commanding the 1st Guards Brigade, encouraged his soldiers to counter the dive bombers by standing up and shooting at them with a Bren gun from the shoulder. 'Take them high like a pheasant, give them plenty of lead,' Beckwith-Smith advised, promising £5 to any of his soldiers who downed one.

Though there was now a definite destination for the British, many of them remained confused about their role. Laurie Whitmarsh, of the 91st Field Regiment RA, complained, 'Retreating, upwards and backwards, was all so bewildering.' Contrary orders still plagued them, too. After destroying its guns and ditching the ammunition, Whitmarsh's battery was ordered to retrieve the shells. 'We had to fish for them in green ponds and take them to guns further up.' An indication of the peril in which the BEF suddenly found itself was Alf Hewitt's comment that 'no matter which way we were facing we seemed to be heading into the war. It was a nightmare.'

There was, however, the occasional morale-booster, even at a time like this. Gregory Blaxland's group of East Kents came across another company of the regiment who, in a counter-attack the previous evening, had captured three Germans, all of whom complained bitterly of the way they had been driven on and on without rest and without food. 'It was of interest to find that the foe were feeling as sorry for themselves as we for ourselves,' he noted. Bill Brodie's signals detachment was greatly cheered when, to the tune of 'Tipperary', an artillery unit marched past, footsore and dirty but proudly carrying their mascot, an Underground sign from the Angel station. 'We saluted our fellow Londoners,' said Brodie. Driver Bill Edwards also felt much better after a senior officer told his group, 'When you get home don't tell them how you ran away, tell them how well you fought.'

When his unit of the Manchester Regiment abandoned its vehicles ('You fight on your bloody feet from now on, see,' they were told by a regimental sergeant major), the medical officer Joe Patterson, still hanging on to Splinter, the spaniel he had rescued earlier in the retreat, was provided with four trucks in which to collect the wounded.

My job was to crawl along at walking pace behind our chaps. However, by the time I got to Bailleul I had lost touch with all our men. The town was in an appalling mess; absolutely shattered and burning in many places. We dodged through the centre of it, picking up one French soldier with a shattered leg at the crossroads. There were dead horses and bits and pieces all over the place. The hospital, with big red crosses all over the roof, was smashed to atoms. At last we got through the jam in Bailleul and joined a column of all-sorts, including tremendous numbers of French horse transport. The poor horses were done up, and some of them had horrible wounds. I had quite given up hope of making contact with the regiment and kept on towards Poperinghe. There, we found the same fearful destruction and traffic chaos. Always there were masses of French horse-drawn transport, holding everything up and every bomb crater was surrounded by shattered horses. At last we got through Poperinghe to the north. By now I had a following of some ten vehicles from the Manchesters. No one knew where to go or what to do next, as Poperinghe was our destination.

Patterson was told to head for Dunkirk with his wounded Frenchman but made desperately slow progress on the crammed roads. 'At last we came to a block so frantic I decided to pack in and walk. So we climbed out, wounded man and all on his stretcher, into the darkness and off we set in the howling, swirling, cursing jam of vehicles, horses, guns, ambulances and infantry.'

13

Massacre at Le Paradis

In these dark days the Prime Minister would be grateful if all his
colleagues in the Government, as well as important officials, would
maintain at high morale in their circles.

Winston Churchill, strictly confidential memo, 28 May

On 27 May, the first full day of Operation Dynamo, the Luftwaffe destroyed Dunkirk. On previous raids the bombs had been aimed at dock installations; now, from first light, successive waves of bombers, accompanied by fighter escorts, saturated the town with fifteen thousand explosive and thirty thousand incendiary devices. With Dunkirk's water supply already out of commission, the fires raged unchecked. The attackers, in some cases summoned from airfields inside Germany, had no need of navigation instruments. They simply headed towards the huge cloud of smoke rising from the port's oil tanks, set alight the previous day.

Because of the speed of their Army's advance, few German squadrons had managed to base themselves on former Allied aerodromes in France close to the fighting, so it was the RAF which generally found itself operating from bases closer to the aerial combat over Dunkirk. This was the first day the Spitfires and Hurricanes of Fighter Command had seen so many planes in the evacuation area and they took a heavy toll, particularly when they ran across unescorted bombers. One Luftwaffe Group alone had 23 Dornier bombers shot down, with the loss of 64 aircrew. In all, the British fighters claimed 38 'kills' for the loss of 14 of their own.

Field Marshal Albert Kesselring, commanding the Luftwaffe's Air Fleet Two, asserted (after the war) that he had complained vigorously about Göring's 'incomprehensible' offer to destroy the BEF without Army assistance.

He must have been sufficiently aware of the effect of almost three weeks of ceaseless operations on my airmen not to order an operation which could hardly be carried out successfully by fresh forces. . . . Nevertheless my misgivings led to no change. Our battered and gradually reinforced formations strained every nerve to attain their objective . . . the number of sorties flown by the overtired formations was higher than usual, with the natural result that the Spitfires steadily increased our losses.

In fact, having helped persuade Hitler to halt the Panzers on 24 May and let his airmen take care of Dunkirk, Göring failed to follow through. On 25 May the feared Stukas of General the Baron von Richthofen, the forty-four-year-old cousin of the famed Red Baron of the First World War, did not attack Dunkirk at all; and on the next day – even though the port's oil tanks went up in flames – the heaviest Luftwaffe concentrations were aimed at the struggles for Calais, Lille and Amiens. All this was remedied on 27 May. Two French ships, a freighter and a troop transport, were sunk in the harbour; a third of the remaining civilian population of three thousand was estimated to have been killed; and General Sir Ronald Adam, deputed by Gort to organize the defence of, and evacuation from, Dunkirk, reported on his arrival at the end of the air attack: 'What lorries were there were burning and the large masses of GHQ and other troops, mostly RASC, which were in the vicinity were completely disorganized.'

Late in the afternoon the destroyer *Wolfhound* sailed into the devastation of Dunkirk carrying Captain William Tennant, a desk man at the Admiralty in London who had volunteered for the job of organizing the lifting of troops as Senior Naval Officer ashore. Tennant brought with him a dozen officers and 160 ratings, plus communications staff. After escaping a series of air attacks without damage, *Wolfhound* delivered Tennant's group at about 6 p.m. and the SNO went ashore to contact the British army commanders in the town. 'The sight of Dunkirk gave one a rather hollow feeling in the pit of the stomach,' said Tennant. 'The Boche had been going for it pretty hard, there was not a pane of glass left anywhere and most of it was still unswept in the centre of the streets.'

Tennant, with the initials SNO cut out from the tinfoil of a cigarette packet and pasted to his tin helmet with sardine oil by one of his aides in order better to identify him in the turmoil, took swift stock of the appalling situation in the docks. Having decided that the beaches were the only possible evacuation point he urgently wired Ramsay in Dover: 'Please send every available craft to beaches east of Dunkirk immediately. Evacuation tomorrow night is problematical.'

Tennant spread his sailors along the beaches east of Dunkirk to act as police and stewards, and was soon receiving advice that the transfer of soldiers to ships offshore via rowing boats and small craft was a painfully slow process, especially when at low tide later that evening the Channel waters receded half a mile. With the docks unusable, Tennant found an alternative in two long piers which protected the dredged channel leading from the docks set deep in the town to the open sea. They became known as the West and East Moles. The West one, the shorter of the two, came out of Dunkirk's oil storage area and was built of stone. The East Mole, which would prove the pathway to safety for almost two hundred thousand British and French military personnel over the next week, stretched for just under a mile out to sea from the harbour entrance and was also easy of access from the beach. A concrete-based wooden boardwalk, with room for no more than four men to walk abreast along it, the East Mole was subject to a tide fall and rise of up to 16ft and the rip of these tides through the open substructure made berthing ships (not to mention loading men) a tricky proposition. But Tennant appreciated very early that it was preferable to the alternatives offered on the open beach. At 10.30 p.m. he signalled *Wolfhound*, now handling communications offshore, to send in a personnel ship to embark troops from the East Mole. The honour of being the first vessel to load from that historic place went to a ferry, *Queen of the Channel*, which was diverted from collecting soldiers from the beach at Malo-les-Bains, the resort just outside Dunkirk.

Just before dawn, she got away with just under a thousand troops. On the way home the ship's back was broken by a near-miss from bombs and she was lost. All aboard were rescued, however – and, more important, *Queen of the Channel* had shown that the East Mole could serve as the main avenue of escape. At 4.36 a.m. on 28 May a signal went to Ramsay in Dover requesting a switch of emphasis. Now Tennant wanted as many ships as possible, not off the beaches but alongside the Mole. Since the Belgian surrender had taken official effect half an hour earlier, they would be needed.

Until that surrender the southern and western wall of the corridor, where the 2nd Division was spread along a frontage of twenty miles on the La Bassée Canal facing the combined might of the newly unleashed Panzers and SS formations, had been the more likely to fragment. The lone British division was attacked on 27 May by the 3rd, 4th and 7th Panzer Divisions and a brigade of the 5th, as well as elements of the Totenkopf and Verfügungs SS. The 2nd Division's 6th Brigade, consisting of battalions of the Royal Welsh Fusiliers, Durham

Light Infantry and Royal Berkshires, was over-run and decimated, the remnants taking refuge in the Forest of Nieppe. The 4th Brigade (1st Royal Scots, 2nd Royal Norfolks and 8th Lancashire Fusiliers) had already been mauled on 26 May when the Germans managed to get across the canal, and at the assault's renewal next morning the BEF defenders found themselves hopelessly outmatched.

Eventually some ninety men, all that remained of the Norfolks, were surrounded at a farm in the ironically named hamlet of Le Paradis by the Totenkopf SS. When they surrendered they were kicked, beaten, insulted and finally led into a paddock, where two heavy machine guns opened up on them. Although troops moved in to finish off the wounded with bullet and bayonet two of the Norfolks, William O'Callaghan and Albert Pooley, survived the massacre despite being wounded in several places. They dragged themselves from the scene of horror and were tended by a local farmer's wife who arranged for them to be taken to a civilian hospital in Béthune where, following treatment, they were eventually made prisoners of war after the fall of France. Repatriated early because of his wounds, Pooley reported the massacre, to be greeted with disbelief by the Army. After the war he pursued the matter, returned to Le Paradis and gathered the evidence which brought to trial Fritz Knoechlein, commander of the Totenkopf's 2nd Infantry Regiment involved in the murders. Knoechlein, tried in Hamburg, was convicted and hanged in January 1949.

The remnants of the Royal Scots, who had resisted with equal stubbornness alongside the Royal Norfolks, came close to suffering the same fate. They had been lined up for execution until a humane German staff officer intervened. There were other instances of cruelty and murder, mainly of wounded British by SS troops still furious at their defeat near Arras and the rumours of ill-treatment of German prisoners from that battle.

The massacre which has attracted the most publicity in recent years is that of the 2nd Battalion Royal Warwickshires at Wormhout on 28 May by elements of the Leibstandarte SS Adolf Hitler Regiment. The Warwickshires, part of the 48th Division, had, like everyone else, attempted to hold off the Panzers and SS virtually bare-handed. One of their officers, Major Claude Chichester-Constable, a forty-seven-year-old who had won the Military Cross in the First World War and served four years in a prison camp, was killed as he walked towards German tanks waving a pistol.

As the Adolf Hitler regiment smashed its way towards Wormhout its commander, Josef 'Sepp' Dietrich, an influential and colourful

Nazi, showed an unexpected courtesy towards some of his British prisoners by presenting them with SS badges as souvenirs, while just down the road some of his soldiers were murdering a BEF chaplain, the Rev. Reginald Podmore.

On 28 May Dietrich celebrated his forty-eighth birthday in hair-raising fashion, pinned down in a ditch after his staff car had been destroyed by an anti-tank shell near Wormhout. The enraged SS, not knowing whether or not their beloved commander had been killed, reacted savagely. Many wounded and prisoners were shot out of hand and some ninety men, mainly from the Royal Warwickshires, were herded into a cramped barn between Esquelbec and Wormhout, guarded by a dozen Germans. When an officer, Captain J F Lynn-Allen, complained there was no room for the wounded to lie down one guard told him, in American-accented English, that there would be plenty where he was about to go and lobbed a grenade among the prisoners. More grenades were hurled, then the survivors of this horror were ordered out in groups of five and formally shot before the SS moved into the barn and attempted to finish off those still inside. Astonishingly, a handful of British lived to report it, and although attempts have been made in recent years to bring to trial the SS officer, Wilhelm Mohnke, alleged to have been responsible, nothing had been achieved by the time this book went to press.

The experiences of Arthur Baxter, a gunner in the 53rd Anti-Tank Regiment who was at Wormhout, illustrate the savagery of the SS in that battle. Baxter was under fire in a ditch with two companions named Adkins and Bowns when he caught sight of the enemy for the first time.

What a shock, they were just the other side of the road, about forty of them, SS troops, as tall as our own Guardsmen, camouflage dress, carrying light machine guns, rifles and bayonets, stick grenades, and a couple of half-track light tanks, and we could see their white insignia, the two lightning strike flashes on their helmets and tunic collars.

They covered us from across the road and then a small swine of a chap appeared who seemed to be an interpreter. I'd know him today if only I could cross his bloody path again. His nose was pushed back level with his face – Alf Garnett reminds me of him in some way . . . the shape of the face. He was middle-aged, with a short row of medal ribbons on his chest. He spoke some command to the chap in charge of the light tank and they drove across to the edge of this ditch and then drove up towards us. At one frightening stage we all thought they were going to put one of the tracks of the tank into the ditch and crush us to death.

The commander of the tank, who at this stage was leaning over the top of the turret, drew a revolver and ordered me to get up out of the ditch with Bowns and Adkins following, then five or six SS surrounded us. They stripped us of our jackets, steel helmets, our webbing, even our dog tags. We had just our trousers, vest, boots and socks left. And then it started: this swine with the flat nose wanted to know what unit we were with, where our HQ was, what other troops were in the area, how many guns and their positions, what tanks. All this was in perfect English from Flatnose.

Adkins replied that we were only allowed to state our name, rank and Army number. At this remark, and without any order from Flatnose, the SS chaps around us went mad. We were all three kicked, belted in the face, rifles jammed into our sides, then Bowns and myself were knocked to the ground and the boot was put in again, then they grabbed us by the hair and lifted us to our feet. I got belted in the right ear and one big sod gave me a full mouthful of snot straight into my face and in broken English said, 'You English bastard' and made a motion to throw his stick grenade. I remember thinking at that moment, 'Yes you cow, you do and you'll go with me. . . .'

Suddenly there was a hell of a commotion. A British Army truck with a canvas hood over the driving cab (I think we called them 15cwt officer trucks) came belting straight down the road towards the lot of us. This came to a stop about eight feet from where we were standing. The SS chaps covered it from the front. One of them had a light machine gun, the type with an outer jacket with air holes cut out of it which fitted over the barrel. I saw the passenger, who was an officer, raise his arms above his head, and the driver too. They started to edge their way out of the truck to surrender. When I saw what followed next I could hardly believe my own eyes – I stood rooted to the ground. Without any order given the SS trooper blasted the officer and the driver back into their seats. They were never given a chance to get out of their truck. The SS followed this up by cheering and handclapping. Then one chap went to the back of the truck and pulled out a jerry can full of petrol, splashed this over the bodies and over the truck, and then he put a match to it. To this day I can still smell the sweet sickly smell of burning flesh.

But this wasn't all. Whilst the truck burned another truck, a 30cwt Bedford, came tearing down the road from the same direction. Again bullets began to fly and this truck came to rest partly in the ditch and just at the rear of the 15cwt. Whoever was in the front of the cab must have been badly wounded or killed. Then about five SS went to the back of the truck and pulled out a Tommy. This chap must have had a watch chain hanging from his tunic pocket. I saw one SS reach out to his tunic pocket and the Tommy automatically pushed his hand away. The SS chap then placed a pistol at point blank range and shot him through the heart. The Tommy went down flat on his face, fell like a straight piece of timber. The SS chap turned him over on his side, took out the watch from his pocket, put the watch to his ear, found it still ticking and then started laughing and doing a little dance with the rest of his mates slapping him on the back, clapping and laughing their heads off.

As Baxter was marched away with four other prisoners he was convinced they were about to be executed, so he decided he might as well die making a bid for freedom. He plunged through a roadside gap in the hedge and, despite being wounded in the leg by a stick grenade hurled at him, managed to get away. However, his troubles were far from over. Treated by the medical officer of an artillery battery he stumbled across, he was loaded into an ambulance making for Dunkirk. 'During the night the driver of our ambulance and his co-driver got out and abandoned us, a full ambulance of wounded. To make matters worse there seemed no way of getting out of the back doors. All the chaps were shouting out for water.'

Next Baxter was lifted into a car driven by a French officer. 'As he moved off into the darkness I began to feel uneasy. I soon realized from his manner and speech that he was already three parts cut and had nearly consumed three-quarters of another bottle which he was drinking whilst trying to drive.' When they were held up in traffic Baxter persuaded the occupants of a Signals truck in front to rescue him. From there he was transferred into another ambulance and delivered to Dunkirk on 29 May, to be loaded aboard the hospital ship *Paris*.

Still his nightmare was not quite ended. As he hobbled towards the ship, orders were given to pull in the gangplank ready for departure. 'At this I tried to move faster, but tripped over and hit the ground,' said Baxter.

I tried to get up but couldn't. I remember smashing my fist into the ground in despair thinking I had gone through so much and now just a few yards from this ship and freedom the captain could not wait. But I guess Mother Luck was still with me, for suddenly I heard a voice shout out from a large service hatchway in the side of the ship and level with the quayside. This sailor dashed across a plank which was still stretched across from the hatchway to the quayside, picked me up in his arms as though I was a feather and then carried me up to the top deck.

Having been the last aboard, Baxter was first ashore at Newhaven and on to the waiting hospital train.

There were many others who discovered that injuries offered them no priority. When Tom Peck of the 2nd Royal Norfolks was wounded in the chest at Locon he was told to make his way back to battalion headquarters for treatment. 'But where was HQ?' said Peck. Eventually he got to Hazebrouck on foot, helping to pull more seriously wounded comrades in a farm cart. In Hazebrouck Peck was bandaged, issued with a large white tag certifying he was wounded and loaded on to an ancient French truck to be transported to Dunkirk. When it ran out of petrol Peck, this time in the company of French soldiers, walked again, via Poperinghe, to the newly established Dunkirk perimeter.

It was towards dusk and suddenly our group, now down to about nine, was challenged. We went through this outer perimeter of the Dunkirk defences and it didn't matter what mob you were in or what you were, they were collaring you for the defences. I was told to help man a machine gun.

'But I'm wounded,' I said. 'Can't you see my tag?'

They said, 'You can feed a belt, can't you?'

I was there about a day and a half before my wound started to get bad again. When this sergeant major came round I pointed out that I was bleeding like a pig. Since it was quiet on the perimeter he told me to go back and get it dressed by the medics. When I told them what had happened to me they said I had no business being on a gun, I was supposed to be in transit to Dunkirk. They gave me another dressing and I joined other stragglers making for the beach as best they could.

John Hammond of the 6th Lancashire Fusiliers, wounded in the left leg and right hand during the fighting on the Escaut, arrived in Dunkirk by ambulance at the height of an air raid. 'A bomb dropped in front of the ambulance, killing the driver and blasting my clothes and bandages off.' Eventually Hammond was put down on a stretcher in sight of the East Mole.

There I was, wearing only a watch and a dog tag, lying watching the Stukas, so I began to look out for more strays coming on to the beach. After a while I spotted one who was obviously a stretcher-bearer. I called him over and suggested if he could get me along the Mole he might be allowed to go aboard with me. I had observed that some priority was being given to the wounded. He agreed and, after wrapping my foot in some rags, got me up and we set off towards the Mole.

Arriving there we found, thankfully, that the Navy was in charge but that there was a great gap in the Mole, with some sailors trying desperately to hold a 'bridge' steady – just a couple of planks. This was the longest bridge I ever crossed. Then an officer came along and said he had room for two more but I could not see any boat until I looked down. I suppose the tide was out. A great big, hairy-chested sailor shouted 'Jump.' I didn't really jump, I just fell and he caught me. The moment we were aboard, the boat was under way, zig-zagging like mad. I was passed below and as quickly had my leg cleaned up and dressed. A young sailor brought me a slice of bread and a hot drink. He apologised for giving me dry bread! If I had been able I would have given him a medal.

With his RAOC workshops detachment in danger of being surrounded by Panzers near the Aa canal, Staff Sergeant Frank Hurrell and colleagues decided on a break-out by night. When they came under fire Hurrell threw himself into what he thought was a ditch but turned out to be, in his own words, 'a small quarry', severely damaging his right leg. Using his rifle as a crutch and with a piece of wood clamped between his teeth to help him bear the pain and to ease the craving for a cigarette, Hurrell limped into Bergues on the Dunkirk defensive perimeter. Here he had his injuries treated before, wearing a carpet slipper and using a stout cabbage stalk as a support, he walked the last eight miles to the coast with his mates.

A gunner, Paddy Boyd, rode into Dunkirk, first by horse and then aboard a bicycle, after his right foot was smashed in an air raid. His pals, Ernie Skelcher and Alfred Baldwin, took it in turns to carry him until they spotted a couple of stray French Army horses. Skelcher mounted one while Baldwin sat behind Boyd on the other, supporting him. On the approach to Poperinghe they became mixed up with a French horse-drawn artillery unit and when that was ordered to move, the two horses went with them. 'We had no bridles or saddles,' said Baldwin,

so there we were hanging on for dear life as we went through Poperinghe at full gallop. On the other side of the town we got left behind and were plodding along when the Stukas came over again. At the side of the road were some concrete drainpipes so we dived off the horses, Paddy with his foot in a hell of a state. We lay there until the raid was over and when we came out my poor old horse had had his leg blown off by a bomb, so I shot him where he lay.

We started off again trying to carry Paddy on our backs when we came to an *estaminet*. Outside was a mass of cycles. Inside, getting very drunk, was a mob of French soldiers. I didn't connect the two at the time. There were bicycles with wheels and Paddy with only one leg so I helped myself to a bike. Suddenly the French came chasing up the road wanting their bike back. Without a word of French I just pointed to Paddy's foot, covered in blood-soaked bandages, and they let us keep the bike. We carried on that way right into Dunkirk, pushing Paddy on the bike.

Before Wormhout fell, the medical colonel John McDonald reported from his casualty clearing station a story of 'stench and filth and gore' in the four days they were based there.

We admitted about nine hundred wounded, we fed them, operated upon a hundred men and buried nearly fifty. Then we evacuated all our patients to a hospital ship at Dunkirk. What calls most for remark was the courage and endurance of the men. I never heard a word of complaint. Perhaps the sight most distressing to me was the long queue of ambulances waiting to come in. Many of the plastered limbs were swarming with maggots and the stench was dreadful. Yet never a word of complaint.

Although the BEF continued to resist gallantly, considering the growing shortage of ammunition and food, the German advance lost much of its impetus on the south-western edge of the shrinking pocket with the withdrawal of the bulk of the Panzers. The decision was taken, according to the War Diary of Guderian's XIX Corps, 'in order to avoid further useless sacrifice after the severe casualties suffered'. So command of that sector of the German front passed, on 29 May, to a motorized corps at the moment of greatest British vulnerability. When a company of the 3rd Grenadier Guards, running low on ammunition, opened their remaining boxes they contained nothing more lethal than Very signal lights. On 28 May, Alfred Baldwin noted, his battery was firing smoke shells at German tanks 'because there was nothing else left'. Soon afterwards Baldwin's battery was ordered to destroy its guns before heading for Dunkirk. 'In the honoured artillery manner,' he said, 'you stick a shell in the breech and another one the wrong way round in the muzzle and blow the muzzle, but we didn't even have enough shells to do this. So the guns were dismantled, dial sights were smashed, pickaxes put through the tyres.'

Though rain and low cloud severely curtailed German air attack on 28 and 29 May the BEF continued to be hammered by highly accurate enemy artillery. Harry Dennis of the 1st East Surreys recalled, 'You had to admire their shooting, they were plumb on. We had these seven Bren gun-carriers in a wood with battalion HQ at Oudenaarde. We tried to get them out and as each one came out of the opening by the wood Jerry scored a direct hit.'

Such accuracy did not bother one brigadier in the fighting around Poperinghe. The signaller, Lawrence Vollans, was pressed into service to help an anti-tank gun at a farmhouse which soon came under shellfire.

We had been so intent looking to our front none of us noticed the arrival of the brigadier, a tall, imposing officer resplendent in cavalry boots and red tabs. Shells were still falling as he climbed a gate and strolled nonchalantly forward to higher ground before turning to address us. 'They're just whizz-bangs,' he said as yet another shell landed on a barn near us. 'Whizz-bangs are what we call them. Make a lot of noise and do damned little else.' As he strode off a third shell landed on the barn and in seconds the whole building was ablaze.

Frank Southall, the Royal Engineers sergeant, had cause to thank the less-than-efficient quality of one German shell. He was in a field with some dispersed transport when a despatch rider arrived with orders and left his motorcycle in Southall's care. 'I was unable to resist the chance to sit down and was astride the saddle when I heard a dull thud. About four feet away a shell had landed and not exploded. I dived for cover and in my haste to get off the motorbike I fell and twisted my ankle.' Southall enjoyed another 'life' next day when he cut his hand badly while attempting to open a tin of sardines with a knife.

Somebody said it wanted stitching and that there was a hospital in the next road, but when I saw the casualties they had to deal with I realized that my cut hand was miles down the list of priorities, so I wrapped it in a handkerchief and went back to the unit. I had only just joined the others when there was a loud explosion and we later found that a shell had landed on the hospital.

Non-combatants, too, were beginning to suffer, even though their privation was relative.

In Paris, the journalist Alexander Werth complained in his diary entry for 28 May, 'Slept badly, having had two omelettes, one at lunch and another at dinner. There was nothing else at the damned *bistrot* except rabbit entrails.' Omelettes would have been considered a luxury round Dunkirk, though Harry Dennis thought his luck was in when his unit of the East Surreys came across a farm where chickens were still running about. 'So after dark we lit fires inside the barn and boiled these chickens. When we'd finished we could have played football with them, they were so tough. They were just old roosters we had killed.'

The RASC driver Stan Smith was another who had to do without food in the last stages of the retreat. 'But hunger you could contend with,' he said. 'Thirst was the biggest problem.' He had shared only a tin of Carnation condensed milk with others in the previous thirty-six hours when he came across a bombed-out building which looked like a café. 'There were a few bottles still left on the shelves. We thought it was lemonade or something. A quick swig revealed it had been a barber's shop, not an *estaminet*. The bottles contained shampoo and hair oil.'

Toby Taylor, a second lieutenant in Dennis's battalion, recalled his delight when a fellow officer turned up bearing a crate of Cordon

Rouge. 'At least we could have a decent drink with whatever rations there were. But somehow champagne did not taste quite the same out of an enamel mug.'

Alcohol, in fact, seemed the one item not in short supply to many of the BEF as they withdrew. Eddie Foulkes, a forty-five-year-old corporal with a Royal Engineers construction company and a much-decorated veteran of 1914–18, was still celebrating an escape on the road to Dunkirk after being knocked down by a stampede of abandoned French cavalry horses when he was shocked to come across another distinctly unmilitary scene.

There was a group of soldiers around a campfire made from whisky and champagne cases. They were all drunk. When I warned them of the danger of air attack and suggested they come along with me only one responded. He carried a 14lb tin of Carr's biscuits under one arm and on the other a gas cape, over which he kept tripping. After a while I said, 'Look, drop your burdens and let's make haste.' He put his luggage down, took up a sparring posture and circled round me, saying, 'I'm Tug Wilson, middleweight champion of the north-east coast. If you want my biscuits you'll have to fight me for them.'

By the morning of Wednesday, 29 May, the hills of Cassel and Mont des Cats, which stood out as landmarks on the Flanders plain, had become the focus of resistance and the object of main German attention outside the Dunkirk perimeter, since they commanded views as far as the coast. The fortress town of Cassel, which stood astride the main road to Dunkirk, came to exercise an importance out of all proportion to its altitude of 544ft during three days of fighting for its possession, which eventually left the British forces there surrounded and forced to make their way out at night. Mont des Cats, described as 'a little pimple on which all the vehicles in the BEF seemed to have been piled', was crowned by a monastery, which had been a familiar landmark to troops in the First World War. Lieutenant Gregory Blaxland considered Mont des Cats 'a freak of nature that appeared to have been put there by a vengeful God specially to provide a magnet for every bomb and shell in an attacker's armoury'.

Both hills were so savagely shelled and dive-bombed that their defence eventually became out of the question. The retreating 44th Division, newly arrived and poorly organized, suffered heavily under the bombing of Mont des Cats and soon columns of men were streaming down the hillside and north towards Dunkirk.

'We were a rabble,' remembered Joe Catt of the 5th Royal Sussex.

Nobody had lined us up to march off, so I just left with the brothers Arthur and Harry Driver. Harry, who was a sergeant, had a map but couldn't make out where we were so we decided to follow the crowd in the end. When you realize the people you are supposed to obey don't know what they're doing, that's when you begin to get a bit worried. When one has been trained to jump at the sound of the sergeant's voice, can you begin to imagine the feeling of panic when officers ordered us to make our own way to Dunkirk? Most of us had no idea where it was, or even what it was.

Catt's bewilderment was shared by some officers. Lieutenant Blaxland, told to make for Dunkirk, had to ask whether it was in Belgium or France. However, directions were not necessary. Like Joe Catt, John Platt of the RAMC simply joined the mob of troops trekking along the road. 'It was like going to a football match, except that the mob took to the ditches from time to time as low-flying planes attacked.'

The gunnery officer who used the pseudonym 'Gunbuster' wrote that 'into this pancake of a land it seemed as if the whole of the BEF was pouring'. As they struggled into the pancake, those who had not already been ordered or persuaded to destroy their equipment and jettison belongings began to do so. The gunnery officer, Alan Bell Macdonald, was distraught at this wholesale abandonment. 'I had to leave Daddy's old Army bedroll behind and 90 per cent of my belongings.' The transport officer, John Matthew, recalled, 'Most of us changed into our best clothes with as many small articles of value in the pockets as possible.' Frank Southall, the Royal Engineers sergeant, came across a flurry of unexpected excitement when the flood of traffic towards the coast was interrupted by a lorry heading back in the direction of the fighting. When it was halted, the driver turned out to be an escaped German prisoner daringly attempting to get back to his own lines.

As he was marching his men towards Dunkirk, Graham Brooks was pulled up by a superior officer he decribed as 'an aged brass-hat, a typical base-wallah', who told Brooks 'Make them march properly.' The Welsh Guards had no need of such instructions after immobilizing their remaining Bren-gun carriers and setting off on foot for the coast eight miles away. 'We marched in Guardsmanlike fashion,' said Sergeant George Griffin. 'I don't wish to denigrate others but some of them were a shambles, lost souls. We marched in single file, in step, our weapons at the ready in case of aircraft. The poor blighters who were officerless from other units would tag along behind, a motley crew.'

When Bill Brodie's signals section was decanted from lorries at night into a field some way short of the beaches, he remembered,

There was not a star in the sky but the dull red glow of Dunkirk's burning oil tanks acted as a beacon and we marched resolutely towards this fix. Signalman Ritchie, who knew his Bible by heart, quoted 'And the Lord went before them by day in a pillar of cloud to lead them the way / And by night in a pillar of fire, to give them light'. He told us it was from Exodus and we thought the passage was apposite. Ritchie had been studying to be a Minister in one of the Nonconformist churches and he was quite convinced that God had sent the war to punish the French for their wicked ways.

George Sutton, commanding 125 Brigade, drew a vivid and bitter picture of those last few miles to Dunkirk:

The centre of the road was packed with traffic, British in every kind of lorry, truck and car, French on bicycles, horses, weird horse-drawn contraptions, gun teams and cars. . . . Looking back, it seems marvellous that the traffic moved at all. There was no attempt at direction or control, or keeping road discipline. Nobody seemed in a hurry and nobody seemed interested in anybody else. A lot of Frenchmen seemed very angry with one another or with anything, irrespective of nationality, that got in their way. They somehow managed to make themselves extremely annoying and to be far more in the way than the British, but it would be quite wrong to suggest that there was the least hint of panic or even of flight in their movements.

We went on, mile after mile through ditches and roadsides crammed with fully loaded, abandoned vehicles. Depression is too mild a word to use to describe the feelings of anyone who had served for years in an equipment-starved army. . . . We felt it a deep personal humiliation that it had come to this and now we fully realized that one of the great military disasters in our history was taking place.

Eventually Sutton abandoned his staff car and had to decide what to take with him on the march to the sea. He rescued a few documents, a map and some papers which he carried in a leather portfolio under his arm and set out along a footpath which wound in and out among flooded fields near Bergues.

We marched for some hours along this path and I was struck by the unchanging character of the British soldier who was this day exactly as he was in the last war, at his best when things are at their worst; tired as troops have rarely been tired, without food or drink, mostly separated from their own leaders with an extraordinarily vague future, they were cheerful and unperturbed. There was no sign of haste or even depression. They were shouting jokes, singing or whistling, sometimes playing mouth organs and sometimes ukeleles. Much guff has been written about the heroism of Dunkirk. There was no heroism here but the men were absolutely indomitable. They had, of course, not been defeated and most of us had not been allowed to fight it out. We felt a sense of disaster but my own feelings were that the army had been deserted rather than defeated. . . . I felt that if this was what it came to, then all the years of thought and time and trouble we had given to learning and teaching soldiering had been wasted. I felt I had been labouring under a delusion and that after all this was not my trade.

When he saw what the Allies had left behind on the road to Dunkirk, Hitler's Chief of Staff, Keitel, thought it presented 'the most devastating picture I have ever seen or thought possible'.

14

Y for Danger

I hope the Tommies are good swimmers.

Hermann Göring

William Tennant, the senior naval officer ashore at Dunkirk, continued to direct a stream of urgent requests to Dover for more rescue vessels. On 28 May he signalled: 'Unlimited numbers are falling back on this area and the situation will shortly be desperate', following up with the further message; 'Vessels urgently required.' While finding time to comment on the 'magnificent' sight of Dunkirk on fire ('the red blaze simply turned night into day') Tennant hammered away. 'Keep on sending any ships' was his request on 29 May.

Although privately convinced that he and his naval party would all end up dead or prisoners of war, Tennant maintained a bright front, reporting cheerfully to Dover: 'I am getting along splendidly here.' He had certainly got things under better control in Dunkirk itself and at the adjacent resort of Malo-les-Bains after twenty-four hours ashore, but there were alarming reports of panic and confusion further along the beach at Bray-Dunes. Having lost a cut of cards to decide who should take on this job two of his officers, Commander Hector Richardson and Captain Thomas Kerr, a fifty-two-year-old, set off with a party of fifteen to organize the evacuation of a reported five thousand troops on 28 May.

'It took us some time to get there by bomb-cratered roads and wrong turnings, so that it was getting on for dusk when we got our party down on to the beach,' said Kerr. 'Then we gave a gasp. Five thousand? Not a bit of it. There must have been twenty-five thousand at the very least.'

Having signalled urgently for ships, Kerr and Richardson got to work. They attempted to persuade the troops to move towards Dunkirk, where there was already a better embarkation rate. 'But the

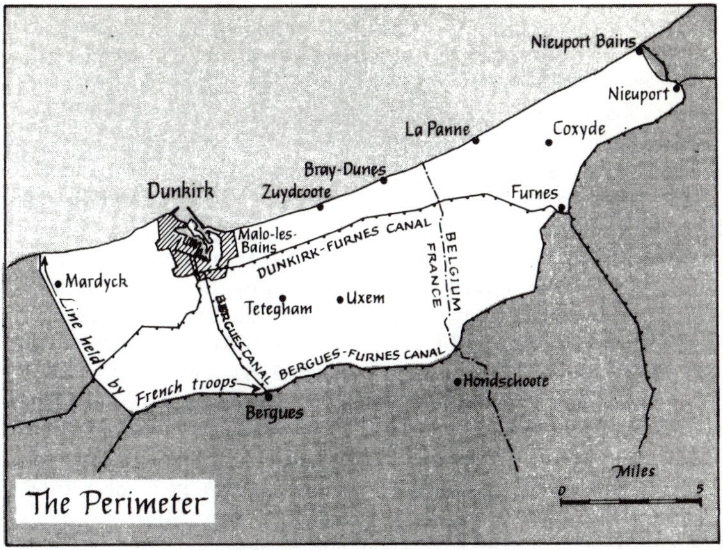
Nieuport Bains
Nieuport
La Panne
Coxyde
Bray-Dunes
Zuydcoote
Dunkirk
Furnes
Malo-les-Bains
DUNKIRK-FURNES CANAL
BELGIUM
FRANCE
Mardyck
Tetegham
Uxem
BERGUES CANAL
Line held by French troops
BERGUES-FURNES CANAL
Hondschoote
Bergues
Miles
0
5
The Perimeter

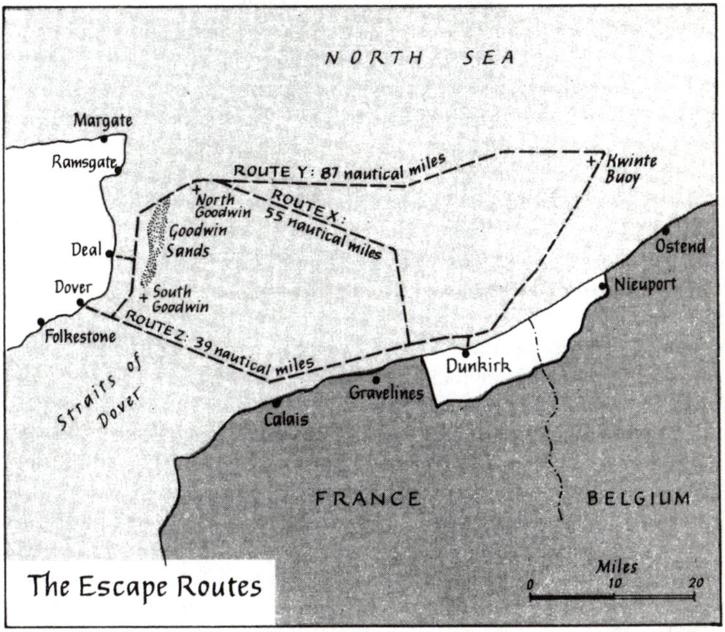
NORTH SEA
Margate
Ramsgate
ROUTE Y: 87 nautical miles
Kwinte Buoy
North Goodwin
ROUTE X: 55 nautical miles
Goodwin Sands
Deal
Ostend
Nieuport
Dover
South Goodwin
Folkestone
ROUTE Z: 39 nautical miles
Dunkirk
Straits of Dover
Gravelines
Calais
FRANCE
BELGIUM
Miles
0
10
20
The Escape Routes

sight of one little dinghy with two thousand men waiting to get into it was enough to make them hesitate about marching to Dunkirk,' said Kerr. 'What a terrible night that was, for we had got hold of the odds and ends of an army, not the fighting soldiers. There weren't any officers, and those who were there were useless, but by speech and promise of safety and the sight of our naval uniforms we got some order out of the rabble. Pathetic the faith in the Navy, but we did our best.'

Arnold Johnson was with what he described as 'an untidy group on the edge of the sand' in the darkness at La Panne, to the east of Bray, when a figure emerged from the shadows and told them, 'The Navy is in charge of this expedition.' Johnson recalled, 'My first reaction was incredible contentment. The Navy in charge! What a relief to escape from the confusion and chaos on the road to Ypres and find ourselves in the hands of the Navy.'

The Navy was doing its best to get to Dunkirk every light warship and vessel capable of carrying troops. They came by three routes, named simply X, Y and Z. The shortest was Z, thirty-nine sea miles and two hours' travel from Dover, but since it required running along the French coast from Calais to Dunkirk the danger in daylight from shore batteries was obvious. Route X, fifty-five nautical miles from Dover, went through a French-laid minefield which had to be cleared before it could be used, while the safest of the routes, Y, led north-east from Dunkirk to a point off the Belgian port of Ostend before turning sharply west to aim directly at Ramsgate. The problem with route Y was that it was eighty-seven miles long, more than twice the distance of route Z. In doubling the sailing time the lifting ability of the ships was halved.

Though the larger ferries and personnel ships were ordered to operate into Dunkirk via route Z only in the hours of darkness because of the batteries, the Navy and smaller vessels continued to serve the East Mole and beaches in the daylight hours during 28 May. At the Mole Commander Jack Clouston, a Canadian who had won the cut of cards and with it the 'easier' beach handling assignment, marshalled troops by megaphone, matching the flow to the availability of rescue craft. Already things were running smoothly there.

On the beaches there was still some way to go. The captain of the minesweeper *Gossamer* reported with astonishment: 'There appeared to be a large wood close to the shore but on approaching nearer this was seen to be a mass of troops on the sand.' The beach presented an extraordinary spectacle. Lieutenant Peter Hadley wrote:

As far as the eye could see it stretched away into the distance, the firm sand of the shore merging farther back into dunes where the surface was no more than a thin yellow powder interspersed with parched tussocks of coarse grass. And covering all this vast expanse, like some mighty antheap upturned by a giant's foot, were the remains of the British Expeditionary Force, some standing in black clusters at the water's edge, waiting for the boats that were to take them out to the two or three ships lying offshore, while others, whose turn had not yet come, or who were too exhausted to care whether it was their turn or not, lay huddled together in a disorderly multitude.

To Lieutenant Colonel Brian Horrocks the beaches presented a fearsome sight: 'Thousands and thousands of troops, like an immense, khaki-clad football crowd, straggling along.' When he breasted the final mound of rubble that littered the Dunkirk front and gazed at the scene Alan Bell Macdonald confessed, 'My heart, already in my stomach, sank to my boots.' Corporal Harry Calvert of the 149th Field Ambulance thought the beach looked like Blackpool on a Bank Holiday; similarly Tom Peck of the 2nd Norfolks, despite his chest wound, was reminded of a day out at Southend.

Many of the men were too tired to take in the historic scene properly. Having marched non-stop more than forty miles to get to Dunkirk, Alfred Baldwin helped himself to half a dozen blankets from an abandoned truck, made up a bed on the sand and went straight to sleep. The Welsh Guards sergeant, George Griffin, was also exhausted: 'I saw all these chaps snuggled down in their blankets and thought I would bed down with them until somebody told me they were corpses.' Griffin's strict Guards training cracked when he came across a French officer's abandoned bag. He stole a shirt from it to replace the one he was wearing, still soaked in the blood of the dead '17' Williams from the Bren gun-carrier action at Arras.

What struck Alfred Baldwin most about Dunkirk's beaches was 'the wonderful queues'. As the *Guardian's* television correspondent, Nancy Banks Smith, wrote in 1980, 'The touching thing about a film of the beaches in Dunkirk was that everyone was patiently queueing as if for half a pound of England.' Baldwin put this down to the sense of 'absolute security' generated by the sight of a line of destroyers out at sea. 'To see them out there made us certain that we would get off all right.'

John Carpenter, then a subaltern with the 50th Division, never noticed any lack of discipline on his section of the beach at Bray. 'My soldiers were extremely good, no panic,' he said. This despite the fact that, each platoon having been instructed to make its own plans for getting away, the arrival of daylight revealed not a ship in sight offshore. Undaunted, Carpenter spotted an abandoned lifeboat about three hundred yards out and dragged it inshore with the help of his sergeant. They loaded about sixty people into it and were picked up by a coaster.

Such discipline was by no means universal. Revolvers were frequently wielded – and sometimes fired – to halt panicky rushes swamping the boats attempting the laborious task of clearing the beaches. Bombardier Roy Lockett was in one sea queue which was warned by a naval officer that any man breaking ranks would be shot. 'At that moment a young lieutenant about a hundred yards in front of me broke ranks and rushed to board the ship. He was shot and fell. My mate said to me, "This is no place for us, let's get back to the sand." So we did.'

Stanley Nettle, an RNVR lieutenant and a member of Tennant's beach party, arrived at the eastern end of the rescue sector near the Belgian resort of La Panne. When a pair of ships' lifeboats appeared they were immediately swamped by over-eager British soldiers attempting to clamber in *en masse*. As a third boat came in, Nettle waded out alongside the troops shouting to them to wait until the craft got into shallower water.

But they took no notice. Then I drew my revolver and fired it into the water about three yards in front of the leading man. The effect was startling. They all stopped and I walked across to them waving my revolver to indicate that they should return to the shore. Here I pay tribute to the British soldier and the natural discipline of the Service. They accepted the orders and moved slowly back. Then I detailed two men to go out and tow the boat into shallow water so that the others could embark.

Just then a major appeared and asked what was happening. I told him I had seen two boats overturned and if this went on nobody would get away. Although he was senior to me in rank it was a naval operation and he asked me what I wanted. I said one embarkation point, the men in blocks of sixty with gaps in between to reduce casualties from aerial strafing, and the lines to go back to the sandhills. I also said it was sad to see so many rifles lying about the beach.

In no time at all there were two embarkation points on the sector and men were picking up rifles and cleaning them. The two men I had sent brought the boat in and I had it turned round with its head to seaward for the troops to embark over the stern. I asked for two of them to row it back and I would ensure that they stayed in and went back to the rescue ship, but I am afraid no one did and we had to rely on boats drifting in on the tide.

There were strict, and obvious, orders that no baggage was to be taken, so when I saw an Army officer and a sergeant each with two enormous bags I told them to chuck them away, but they said, 'We are the Field Cashier, sir, and this is the money.' Such devotion to duty deserved support, so I let them through and only hoped that they would receive due recognition at their HQ.

Despite the order he had received that no French troops were to be embarked by him, he recalled, 'quite a number of bedraggled French officers and men appeared and I had not the heart to turn them away'.

Eddie Foulkes of the Royal Engineers was less fortunate. He got to the head of one long column only to be told by an officer, 'You're not one of my lot. Bugger off.' The artilleryman Les Shorrock was another unfairly turned away. Clutching a broken attaché case full of military papers he had been ordered to carry back to England, Shorrock waited in line at Bray-Dunes.

Just as it would have been our rightful turn to board the next rowing boat an officer, with drawn revolver, leapt into the water and ordered our party back, stating we had jumped the queue. Quite understandably my party began to argue against this injustice. The officer threatened to shoot us. I think he meant it; so did the others. In despair, we left the water and tramped wearily up the crowded beach. It was at this point that I began to see little future in this operation.

Shorrock lost five years of liberty as a result of the officer's decision to send him back ashore.

While embarkation from the beaches remained painfully slow, things were going with a swing on the East Mole, thanks mainly to the destroyers. Though the last thing these ships were designed for was the carrying of large numbers of excess human beings, they performed marvellously. During the morning of 28 May alone, eleven of them filled up with troops. One, *Sabre*, made three round trips to Dover that day. Another, *Montrose*, set a record not only by bringing home twelve hundred men and twenty-eight stretcher cases but also somehow finding space to offer them tea and food. At one stage Commander Clouston and his megaphone were shifting as many as two thousand men an hour off the Mole. On the 28th a total of 18,527 soldiers were disembarked at British ports. Although it was still a question of bits and pieces, the army was starting to come home in meaningful numbers.

In the early hours of 29 May Les Boyce, an RASC driver, and Captain Basil Bartlett of the Field Security Police both found themselves aboard the destroyer *Grafton* as rescued soldiers, but under much different circumstances. Boyce had walked fifteen miles to the beach at Bray-Dunes with two friends after dumping their vehicles. For three days they waited on the beach, living on tinned potatoes and rum salvaged from abandoned lorries. 'While we were there, there was no discipline at all,' said Boyce. There were sergeant majors threatening to blow people's heads off and that sort of thing.' Eventually the trio decided to swim for it.

All we had on was our vests, PT shorts and boots, with rifles over our shoulders. We waded out and were picked up by a whaler off the *Grafton* about a quarter of a mile out and he put us aboard a Dutch cargo boat. We got in the aft hold. We had been there about twenty minutes when a Stuka dropped a bomb into the forward hold. She started to sink, so we had to get out of that and back into the sea again. Another whaler picked us up and this time put us on board the *Grafton*. By now it was getting on for eight o'clock at night.

As an officer, Bartlett found himself in command of his section of beach at Bray on 28 May, organizing the queues. Eventually his own turn came to be taken off and deposited on to the reassuring surroundings of *Grafton*. Because he had been so late getting on board the wardroom was filled with thirty-five other officers, so he was shown to the cabin belonging to the captain, Commander Charles Robinson, a decision which subsequently saved his life. 'A Maltese steward gave me sausage sandwiches and whisky and I began to feel like a human being again. . . . I went to sleep in a chair in front of the fire in the captain's cabin.'

Off Bray, too, that evening had been HMS *Wakeful*, a cramped, twenty-three-year-old destroyer which had seen better days. On the way over earlier, *Wakeful* had been attacked by nine bombers: a hole had been blown in the engine room and three ratings wounded. Warned that he might expect motor torpedo boats and submarines on his return journey via the long Route Y the captain, Commander Ralph Fisher, stowed all the 640 troops he had gathered (the result of eight laborious hours' loading) as low in the ship as possible for greater manoeuvrability in case of attack, and had all movable timber like mess tables and stools placed on deck for life-saving purposes before weighing anchor at 11 p.m.

Waiting that night near the Kwinte Whistle Buoy, off Ostend, where the British ships swung west for home, was a German torpedo boat, *Schnellboot S.30*, and forty-five minutes into 29 May along came a prime target, *Wakeful*. Fisher himself was on the bridge and saw the torpedoes, a pair of them about thirty yards apart, their tracks bright with phosphorescence. By swinging the ship hard to port Fisher managed to avoid the first torpedo but the second struck the forward boiler room. *Wakeful* broke in half and the two portions sank within fifteen seconds, leaving the bow and stern protruding above water. All the troops, except one who was on deck having a breather, were lost.

Captain Fisher floated clear off the bridge and into the most eventful night of his life. Some survivors from the crew were picked up by the minesweeper *Gossamer*, others – including Fisher – by the Scottish drifter *Comfort*. More ships closed on the flare-lit scene to see what they could do – the minesweeper *Lydd*, laden with troops, and *Grafton*, carrying some 860 of the BEF. Easing his rescue boat alongside the destroyer, Fisher shouted a warning that *Grafton* should get away quickly because of the danger of torpedoes. He was too late. Seconds afterwards *Grafton* was struck by two torpedoes fired by the German submarine *U.62*, operating in unusually shallow waters near the Kwinte Buoy. The first ripped through the wardroom, killing all the Army officers there. The second blew off *Grafton*'s stern. The little *Comfort* was swamped and, for the second time in rapid succession, Commander Fisher found himself overboard.

Les Boyce, saturated from wading off the beaches and asleep on an iron grille above *Grafton*'s engine room, was shaken awake by a sailor and asked, 'Can you pull an oar, Tommy?' Boyce found himself in a lifeboat collecting survivors from *Wakeful*. 'I suppose we got thirty or forty yards away when a couple of tin fish came through the water and hit the *Grafton*,' said Boyce. 'When I eventually got back on board the section of the deck where I had been lying was gone.'

Down in the captain's cabin Basil Bartlett stumbled around in the dark, trying to find the door of his unfamiliar room. 'The whole ship was trembling violently,' he said. 'The furniture appeared to be dancing about. There was a strong smell of petrol.' Wearing only a battledress top and pyjama trousers, Bartlett found his way to the upper deck, where a quick check revealed that he had lost three teeth.

The torpedoing of *Grafton* caused such panic among the soldiers aboard that they had to be calmed at gunpoint. There was also chaos among the ships on the scene. The drifter *Comfort*, engines jammed at full ahead and circling menacingly in the blackness while Commander Fisher was in the water hanging grimly on to a trailing rope, was mistaken for a German torpedo boat and fired on by both *Lydd* and *Grafton*, whose captain, Commander Robinson, was killed on the bridge in the wild exchange of fire. Several others died unnecessarily before *Lydd* rammed the luckless *Comfort* and cut her in half at the very moment when Commander Fisher was preparing to climb back aboard. Back into the sea went Fisher, where he swam around until he was picked up next morning.

Les Boyce, struck in the chest by two spent bullets during the firing, was the only one in *Grafton*'s lifeboat to get back to the mother ship, and for a while he wondered if he would see the night out. As *Grafton* steadily settled in the water orders were given to abandon ship. 'Everybody started singing "Abide with Me", sailors and soldiers together,' Boyce said. Eventually all were safely taken off by the railway steamer *Malines* ('The soldiers' behaviour was now all that could be desired,' reported Lieutenant Hugh McRea of *Grafton*) and the destroyer *Ivanhoe* which then shelled and sank the heavily listing *Grafton*.

Until this dire news reached Dynamo headquarters at Dover, Ramsay's fears for the BEF had begun to ease. So well had the embarkation from the East Mole gone on Tuesday the 28th that all available Royal Navy vessels were ordered there the following day to augment the personnel ships, a move which was to precipitate even greater disaster than the loss of *Wakeful* and *Grafton*. By mid-afternoon the Mole was jammed with shipping – the destroyers *Jaguar* and *Grenade*, six trawlers, the troopships *Fenella* and *Canterbury* and the paddle-wheel Thames pleasure boat *Crested Eagle*.

The first air raid of 29 May, a minor one by half a dozen bombers at 3.30 p.m., was beaten off with no damage and only a few casualties. Lieutenant Robin Bill, in charge of the detachment of six trawlers, had the thankless task of trying to persuade soldiers on to his tiny vessels during this attack, but their lack of enthusiasm had nothing to do with the raid. 'They were mostly unwilling to embark in what they considered fishing boats at first and made various excuses to try and get to the larger ships,' he reported.

The destroyer *Jaguar* completed loading and left harbour before the second air assault, another half-hearted affair dispersed by RAF fighters. It was the third attack, pressed home with much more determination from 6 p.m., which caused widespread damage and chaos. *Grenade* was struck at her moorings by a direct hit and near-miss so close that the force of its explosion lifted the destroyer's bridge personnel four feet into the air. The captain, Commander Richard Boyle, said, 'I personally noticed that I was level with the top of the screen at the back of the bridge before I commenced to fall.'

As Boyle's ship caught fire those of his crew who were still alive or had not been blown overboard stepped across to the trawler *Polly Johnson*, tied up immediately astern. Boyle himself waited until *Grenade* had been towed clear of the harbour before he walked off the deck, now awash, into the sea and was collected by another trawler. *Grenade* burned on for several hours before exploding.

Back at the Mole, the trawler *Calvi* had been hit and sunk at her berth, masts and funnel still protruding from the water and her ensign fluttering at the foremast. The Isle of Man Packet Company's *Fenella*, riddled by near-misses, also went down at her moorings. Below decks Mowbray Chandler of the Royal Artillery was sipping a welcome cup of cocoa after a day's wait to get on to the East Mole when he noticed that his rescue ship was doomed: a glance from the porthole showed that the jetty outside was rising. Tom Nolan of the Royal Signals and his two mates had just dumped their packs on *Fenella*'s covered deck and gone to clean up in the washroom when there was a terrific explosion. They went back to retrieve their packs and found them buried under lumps of concrete torn from the Mole. Chandler, Nolan and other British soldiers hastened back on to the jetty, together with a group of Luftwaffe prisoners being embarked in *Fenella*.

There was some panic. 'Men started climbing out of the ship into another and some attempted to run back towards the shore,' said Lieutenant Bill. 'At this time I was with the piermaster (Commander Clouston) and he instructed me to draw my revolver to quell the panic, load up with survivors and troops and get the ships out as quickly as possible.'

This was done. The paddle wheeler *Crested Eagle* pulled away with, among others, the German Air Force prisoners, Nolan, Chandler and survivors of the *Fenella*'s crew. Though heavily damaged, *Canterbury* also slipped her moorings with 1950 troops aboard. Still the Luftwaffe pressed home its attack. So heavily was *Jaguar* bombed as she headed away from Dunkirk that nine soldiers were killed and another, reduced to hysteria, committed suicide on the stokers' mess deck. Her engines damaged, *Jaguar* was drifting back on to the beaches until the destroyer *Express* towed her clear and transferred all the troops, leaving *Jaguar* to crawl back to Dover empty and so badly damaged that she took no further part in the evacuation. Nor did *Canterbury*.

At least those ships survived. Others were less fortunate on this disastrous evening. Only half the six hundred soldiers aboard were saved when the paddle minesweeper *Waverley* sank after being bombed, and *Crested Eagle* also lost half her load of six hundred when, struck by four bombs, she turned back ablaze and was beached near Bray-Dunes. Rather than burn to death, many troops leapt overboard before the paddle wheeler ran ashore, only to be machine gunned in the water. Edward Cordeaux, commander of the Thames Local Defence Flotilla which included the Eagle paddle boats, dived into the sea from the bridge of *Golden Eagle* to help rescue survivors and was eventually himself dragged from the water unconscious, an act of bravery which won this veteran of Jutland and the Dardanelles the DSO at the age of forty-six.

Both Mowbray Chandler and Tom Nolan made it safely back on to the beach. Chandler, both hands badly burned, was taken by ambulance to a collection point for the wounded at the Casino at Malo-les-Bains, thus finishing an eventful day only a few hundred yards from where he had started it. Nolan, too, came ashore a few yards from where he had spent the previous night. Having collected dry clothing from the profusion of discarded material on the beach he was soon dry again, if no nearer to England.

Next it was the turn of the minesweeper and former Isle of Wight ferry *Gracie Fields*, named after Britain's most popular singer. Homeward bound with eight hundred troops, she was struck amidships by a bomb and her engine room exploded, scalding to death many soldiers as well as crew. The commander of one of the rescue ships which managed the tricky task of taking off survivors while the stricken ship, its rudder jammed, sailed in a circle, reported 'terrible mortality and shambles aboard'. The list of losses for the day was appalling – fifteen British and four French ships. Also sunk were the personnel vessels *Normania*, *Lorinia* and *Mona's Queen*, but it was the damage inflicted on the Navy's destroyers which caused the deepest alarm. The Admiralty ordered the immediate withdrawal from Dynamo of all eight modern destroyers that Ramsay had left, leaving him with only fifteen older ships, considered expendable.

This dreadful blow came soon after Ramsay had been informed Dunkirk was blocked by sunken ships. It was only by the greatest good fortune that this had not, in fact, happened, but the faulty report only served to underline the wretchedness of this Wednesday, 29 May. All ships approaching Dunkirk were instructed not to attempt to enter harbour but to remain off the eastern beaches. So that night only four trawlers and a yacht went in to collect men from the East Mole. Just over fifty thousand were lifted that day from jetty and beaches, but another ten thousand could have been rescued had ships been available in the harbour.

That evening, on the BBC's Nine O'Clock News, came the first call for the Little Ships: 'The Admiralty want men experienced in marine internal combustion engines for service as enginemen in yachts or motor boats.'

Although the sand helped to cushion the effect of bombs and keep down the casualties, those on the beaches suffered terribly from the raids of the 29th. The artillery captain, Alan Bell Macdonald, recalled

Oh, the terror of those hours on the beach, lying flat on the sand listening to the shriek of the bombers and the crack of explosions. I can still see the hand of the person next to me one time. It was only a few inches from my face as we two lay prone. It twitched with nerves, the knuckles gleaming white as his hand clenched and unclenched, the fingers biting into his thigh.

Most of the anti-aircraft guns had been destroyed in the retreat to Dunkirk, so the BEF had little to aim at their tormentors except rifles and Bren guns. Incredibly, this popgun reply occasionally worked. Sergeant Jimmy Walsham's Royal Artillery detachment were tramping along the beach of Bray-Dunes when three planes coasted low overhead. 'With hope in their hearts the riflemen put up a curtain of bullets and a Bofors gun also opened up,' said Walsham. 'Great cheers went up when the left-hand engine of one plane burst into flames . . . it caused an argument as to who brought it down.'

Some on the beach dug deep foxholes, using helmets, bayonets or even enamel plates and steel helmets as trenching tools, to escape the blast. The unfortunate were smothered by the force of near-misses. Others took their own personal measures to avoid death. George Hill, a private in the Lincolnshire Regiment, lay flat on his face for more than an hour during one raid, not stirring, in the sincere belief that the Stukas might think him dead and not machine-gun him. The signaller, Lawrence Vollans, was confronted by a fighter at a height of fifty feet. 'It was dipping its wings as if trying to get us into its gunsights and at the last moment I dropped on to one knee, deceived into thinking that if I remained upright it would surely take my head with it.'

Paul Temme, pilot of a Messerschmitt 109, admitted, 'I hated Dunkirk. It was just unadulterated killing. The beaches were jammed full of soldiers. I went up and down at three hundred feet hose-piping.' Tom Bristow witnessed one such hose-piping as his group made for Dunkirk along the seafront.

A solitary plane put five bullets into the backs of one stretcher-bearer's legs as he lay face down on the sand. He could not now walk at all and we were unable to assist as we needed all our own strength to keep moving ourselves. The poor lad said, 'It don't half hurt' and the few around him looked down helplessly, then managed to get him up to the road and made him comfortable there, hoping he would be picked up by someone.

Having spent an exhausting night lugging wounded along the beach on stretchers to lay them out for greater safety around a Red Cross flag, Les Collis of the East Surrey Regiment was horrified when German planes strafed them. 'They gave these helpless chaps no immunity. They shot them up with tracers and, after all our efforts of the previous night, we had to watch them being killed before our eyes.'

As German pressure tightened on the perimeter the beaches came under shellfire, too. Lieutenant Gregory Blaxland's trench survived a near-miss from a shell but a neighbour was less fortunate.

A desperate, frantic cry came up from the beach: 'WATER! I WANT WATER. HELP!' It is a revealing test of courage to see who will be the first to break cover to give succour to the wounded. In this case it was a war-commissioned officer, Buckwell. By the time I dared move he was kneeling beside him, trying to comfort and restrain him. I did no more than stand and gape. The man lay on his back with a mere slit across his stomach, and he kept yelling and yelling for water, as if more in rage than pain. I despised him for making such a furious din, then he let out a gulp and his jaws snapped shut. He was quite obviously dead. I realized even then, deep down, that it was not the stricken gunner I despised, but myself. I had felt revolted by his agony and I shrank from touching him, even to feel his pulse to confirm he was dead.

The territorial gunner, Les Shorrock, who had been turned back at the head of a queue for boats and then awoke next morning to find all his companions had got away while he slept, was still clutching the briefcase of papers he had been ordered to carry back to England. Confessing 'a feeling of ultimate disaster' he approached a major, surrounded by the men of his regiment, sitting nearby on the beach.

I broached the possibility of perhaps being captured if the beaches were overrun and sought his advice. He perused the papers, sorting them into two piles, one of which he told me to burn, which I did then and there. The other pile he replaced in the battered case and told me to bury it in the sand, which I did. I felt a lot better having rid myself of my unwanted burden.

All this time the mayhem continued unabated, the Navy firing out from the sea, the bombers seeming to own the skies, plenty of noise. Suddenly a shell landed right in the group in front of me. The major leapt to his feet and shouted 'Don't run, stay down.' I was inexperienced, just 20 years of age. I decided to take my chance and run for the sandhills. I got to my feet and clearly recall running, falling flat as the shells whined over. I did this three or four times, when suddenly the next shell seemed to burst above me and I felt stunned. I tried to get on my feet, knowing there was something terribly wrong.

I looked down at my battledress tunic which was turning red with blood. I knew I had been hit and realized it was in the back. As I staggered forward, two soldiers rushed at me, getting me to the cover of the sandhills. They took off my tunic and as they did so I pulled out of my trouser pocket the emergency field dressing which was always impressed on us to retain for our own use. These gallant lads quickly bandaged my wound but one of them tore his own field dressing from his pocket to add to mine. I must have been still dazed, for I said to him, 'You're not supposed to use your dressing on my wound.'

Shorrock's injury was serious enough for him to be kept behind and operated on but others who were more mobile sometimes found that the successful boarding of a rescue ship was no guarantee of immediate safety. The Grenadier Guard, James Stevenson, with seven pieces of shrapnel in his left leg, made it on to a hospital ship, the name of which he could not remember.

I was lying on deck when Jerry bombed us. The blast of one bomb took the skin off my hands and face, set me alight and blew to pieces several of the men near me. I rolled over to the side of the ship and jumped into the sea because I was alight. I swam back to Dunkirk and as they pulled me out on the beach I remember hearing somebody say, 'Poor bastard.' My eyes and mouth had been stuck together by the blast wave and I could just about breathe through one nostril. I was taken to a French hospital until that was blown up too. I don't remember much more until I came to in a Dover hospital.

The RAOC sergeant, Frank Hurrell, who had limped into Dunkirk using a cabbage stalk as a walking stick, managed to insert himself into the queue on the Mole – not being given priority because he was not a stretcher case – and eventually got on board a warship. Like Stevenson, certain he was now safe, he found space for himself on deck.

I was about to make myself as comfortable as I could when bombs began to fall in and around the ships at the Mole and suddenly, I don't know how, I found myself in the sea, minus rifle, my equipment and my stick. Being in the sea didn't worry me, having learned to swim at a very early age. I got clear of the Mole area using the 'dog's paddle' and the sidestroke, with my gammy leg as a trailing leg. I made my way through floating debris, other swimmers and bodies and finally crawled up the beach a long, long way from the Mole.

After another night on the beach and a grandstand view of the raid of 29 May on the Mole, Hurrell was lifted off the beach that evening in a ship's boat and somehow negotiated the scrambling net hanging down the side of a destroyer. It hurt, but he didn't care. 'Having got this far, I wasn't going to complain now.'

For Private John Illman of the RASC and many others who spotted the opportunity, one quick way to safety lay in helping to carry a stretcher aboard ship. Illman noticed that whenever ambulances arrived at the beach there was a need for hands to help carry the wounded.

I said to my mate that when the next one came we'd grab hold of a stretcher and stick to it, whatever happened. We ran to the first ambulance and dragged this poor chap out. He was in a bad state, a head wound and one in his side. We carried him down to a rowing boat and when we got out to the *Royal Daffodil* we had to lift him up the side, which was a terrible job because we had to push him up. Two or three times I thought we had lost him but eventually we got him up and we went up with him.

Alfred Baldwin and Paddy Boyd, the wounded pal with whom he had shared a horse and then pushed on a French Army bicycle, had a slightly less difficult time in getting off the Mole. The last stretch, through the sand to the foot of the Mole itself, was the most arduous.

We couldn't get the bike through any more so I put Paddy on a fireman's lift across my shoulder to clamber over the rocks and he was moaning like buggery, not about the pain he must have been in but because I insisted on carrying this rifle I had found. I was determined I wasn't going to let it go. We got on to the land end of this Mole, shells dropping around, the noise was absolutely horrendous. The shout went up: 'Wounded and injured first.' I thought this qualified me, so I picked old Paddy up.
It was a very black night and with all this confusion I never felt any sense of fear. We got to this gap in the Mole, about ten feet across, bridged by a couple of planks. There was a naval chap at the land end of this plank. 'Take a run at it, mate,' he said, so I went back a few steps and I ran at these two planks. With the weight of one man they might have been all right but with two they were sagging badly by the time I got into the middle. I think I would have fallen off had it not been for the fact that there were a couple of Navy blokes at the far end. They grabbed me and dragged me on by my battledress. I ran and staggered on with Paddy on my back and I think I might have run right off the end of the Mole but there were a couple of officers there and they took Paddy off me. I went up the gangway and on to the boat and we sat on the deck.

It was *Maid of Orleans*, the same Channel ferry on which Baldwin had been transported to France. Next morning he was distinctly surprised to see, for the first time in his life, the white cliffs of Dover. Like many other members of the BEF, he had expected to be disembarked further down the French coast, re-equipped and sent into action again.

Although by 29 May the beaches had taken on a semblance of organization (at Bray-Dunes there was even a small wooden hut with the word 'EMBARKATION' chalked on its wall) many survivors recall only the confusion and lack of direction. Joe Catt, of the 5th Royal Sussex, said, 'According to our regimental history we had been rounded up and marched to the beach to wait for the boats. It didn't happen like that for us. We made our own way into the dunes, sat down, had a bit of a kip. There was drink knocking about, and food. Not a lot, but you didn't have to starve.'

Others did suffer terribly, from thirst as well as shortage of food. Sapper Jack Toomey, scrounging on the beach for water, could only lay hands on wine. 'I had a drink of *vin blanc* and had to sit down. I was as drunk as a lord. The last time I had had anything to eat was about three days off, and on an empty stomach the wine had a devastating effect.'

Water was one of the priority loads carried to Dunkirk by the ships to relieve hardship. The RASC driver, Stan Smith, who had almost drunk shampoo by mistake in the wrecked hairdresser's shop, remembers well his eventual reunion with drinking water. 'I was in a queue in the sea and somebody passed us a jerry can of water from the rescue boat. Unfortunately I was the last one to get any – there was just enough to wet my lips. So I turned the can upside down to show those behind there was no more. I was punched in the back.'

Sam Wright of the 5th Green Howards managed to buy a large tin of apricots from a shop which he found open in Dunkirk. It was his first food for sixty hours. Sapper Joe Hooker joined those looting bombed shops and to his joy came across a tin of sardines. Together with a packet of biscuits he had scrounged and a swig of two-day-old well water from his bottle, it made a memorable repast for a famished soldier. Signals sergeant Bill Brodie also found a shop still open, but there was little left by the time he arrived. 'A milling crowd round the small counter had demolished the stock. I counted myself lucky to be able to buy a small bottle of tomato juice, my first drink that day.' It came in handy to wash down French Army biscuits out of a tin date-stamped 1918. Told on the evening of 28 May that his group would not be embarked that night, Brodie recalled, 'All standards were now reduced to the primitive. Anyone who had food and drink was rich, and the fortunate who had found shelter were millionaires. I was awakened at 3 a.m. by the chattering of my own teeth.'

There was a touch of the primitive, too, about the behaviour of a French soldier who boarded *Royal Eagle*. Bill Richardson, a gunner aboard the ship, watched as French soldiers were offered tins of corned beef. 'Some of the tins had lost their key and I can remember this Frenchman, a giant of a feller, squeezing a tin and breaking it open with his bare hands.'

Military police lieutenant Harold Dibbens found himself on the wrong end of a revolver in an Allied dispute over food. Patrolling Dunkirk's streets with a group of seven volunteers, Dibbens came across a stack of cases of rations.

A French Army captain was hovering around and we had no sooner broken open one of the cases when he came alongside me and pushed the nozzle of his revolver into my ribs. I was not frightened but I was, however, angry. . . . He paid no attention when I pointed out the War Department markings on the boxes. In fact I gained the impression he wanted to shoot it out.

At that fraught moment a senior British officer came along and dispensed the judgement of Solomon by dividing the rations, half to the French officer and half to Dibbens for distribution to soldiers heading for the Mole. Satisfied, the two men shook hands and parted company.

The incident was only one example of the strained feeling between French and British. On the afternoon of 29 May Commander William Tennant signalled the disturbing news to Dover, 'The French staff at Dunkirk feel strongly that they are defending Dunkirk for us to evacuate, which is largely true.'

15

The Cracked Alliance

I think the English find it very hard to say nasty things to people.
They prefer to say nothing, so it was quite by accident we heard that
the BEF was leaving.

Jacques Mordal, French historian and former naval officer.

By Wednesday, 29 May the BEF, apart from a few stragglers, was inside the Dunkirk perimeter and preparing for its last stand, following a disastrous campaign of less than three weeks in which it had done nothing but retreat after the initial, heady rush forward to the Dyle Line. Perimeter duties were shared, by arrangement, with the French, who held the western side of the defences from the sea, along the Mardyck Canal, then swinging eastwards to the ancient walled town of Bergues, a distance of some eleven miles. From there, the British held the line of the Bergues–Furnes Canal, onwards to Nieuport in Belgium and thence by the line of the River Yser to the sea, about twenty-five miles in all.

The need to push the perimeter as far east as Nieuport was partly dictated by the fact that the undersea telephone cable to London, the sole remaining link with Britain, passed through the resort town of La Panne, with a special connection to the seaside villa formerly owned by King Albert of Belgium. This monarch's insistence on the link to keep him in touch with the London Stock Exchange whenever he was on holiday stood the BEF in good stead in those last, desperate days. General Sir Ronald Adam, in charge of evacuation arrangements, operated from the royal holiday home and on 29 May Gort's command headquarters moved there for a couple of days, too. Thus Gort, in the short time he was there, was able to talk freely to London but could not communicate with either the supreme military headquarters near Paris or even Dunkirk itself, a few miles down the coast.

The French, who in many cases had not been informed of the decision to jettison equipment before entering the perimeter, found it difficult anyway to agree to hand over the means to defend themselves in their own country, and when the rule was sometimes over-vigorously applied by British troops screening entry points, fights and shooting matches erupted. One French divisional commander, General Tesseire, complained to Admiral Jean-Marie Abrial, overall commander of the Dunkirk area, that his troops had only been permitted to cross into the British zone of defence on condition that they were disarmed. Tesseire's memorandum alleged:

An officer of my motor transport section was stopped by the English, who compelled him to leave his car and destroyed it, together with two trucks and two anti-tank weapons which were following . . . Furthermore, an officer of the division, having been given on the beach an authorization from a British officer to embark in a rowing boat, was thrown into four metres of water as soon as he arrived at the passenger ship. He owed his survival only to his excellence as a swimmer.

Lieutenant Charles Lenglart, commanding a group of French infantry, found his way into the perimeter blocked at a canal bridge by a British sentry who ordered them off in another direction. 'So we waited a bit, wondering what to do', Lenglart said.

Then we saw a tank arrive, with a car behind it. They stopped and a general got out, General Altmayer I think. So I told him we were supposed to go on but the British sentry had stopped us. The general thought a bit, then got back into his car. The tank commander lowered his turret and aimed it at the British sentry. And that's how we crossed the bridge.

When the French 38th Division moved unexpectedly into the perimeter from Belgium, its transport blocked the vital road link between La Panne and Dunkirk until General Adam ordered the vehicles to be bulldozed into ditches and flooded fields. Colonel Lionel Westropp, commanding the 8th King's Own Royal Regiment who were guarding a perimeter bridge, decided to send all except British troops down a side road because the area behind him was congested, a course of action to which refugees and other Allied troops did not take kindly. 'As they came nearer we shouted "Allez à droite" but the crowd growled and came on.' So Westropp and one of his officers, Captain Bob Everett, fired just over their heads. 'Without further ado the poor devils turned down the side road,' said Westropp. 'We then sorted out the British soldiers and allowed them over the bridge.'

It was at the eastward end that the perimeter was in greatest danger following the capitulation of the Belgians. When he learned of this, General Adam sent out a staff officer to reconnoitre the Belgian countryside on 28 May. He found no sign of advancing Germans but made fortunate contact with a troop of the 12th Lancers, whose armoured cars occupied Nieuport that morning, just in time to thwart an enemy motorcycle patrol's planned move into the town. All British troops, whatever their status, were rushed in to help fill the gap before the Germans could exploit it.

Brigadier Arthur Clifton, of the 2nd Armoured Reconnaissance Brigade, was ordered to organize a defence line from the sea, through Nieuport and on to Furnes. He had under his command at that time three light tanks, one armoured car, one anti-tank rifle, one Bren gun and eight riflemen with which to achieve this. On the spot he came across two hundred Royal Artillerymen with rifles, fifty mixed Royal Engineers and RASC personnel and four 18-pounder guns under the command of Lieutenant Colonel W R Brazier of the 53rd Medium Regiment RA. Brazier, with twenty-five officers and two hundred men of his regiment behind him, was anxious about the reported presence in the area of German tanks since he had nothing available to halt them, short of 'making ugly faces at them'. Small parties of infantry were sent to help out but, Clifton reported, 'they were very tired and very hungry so I ordered them to rest for the time being'.

Another six lorryloads of infantry turned up that evening, also tired, hungry and bewildered. They were pulled round by a pep talk from Clifton, who nevertheless had to send a third of the new arrivals off to the evacuation beaches when he found they had no weapons. During the night an artillery regiment with its full complement of two dozen 25-pounders arrived, though the gunners were reduced to shooting by eye with the aid of maps since their instruments had been destroyed. By next morning the 12th Brigade, Nieuport's designated defence, was also in position. The moment of danger had passed.

The German Army's failure to seize the chance was understandable. They, too, were exhausted and short of ammunition. The Wehrmacht's 256th Division had been required to spring forward from east of Bruges, forty miles from Nieuport, outflank the French 60th Division stranded near Zeebrugge by the Belgian collapse and – supreme irony – then face delays caused by the flood of refugees initiated by its own advance. By the morning of the 30th, however, the Germans were ready. 'We came under continuous shelling, the heaviest we had had,' said Alf Hewitt of the South Lancashires, part of the 12th Brigade. 'We were really hammered and lost quite a lot of men.'

As the Germans massed for an attempt to cross the Yser that evening behind the shell barrage, Hewitt suddenly heard the sound of aircraft engines behind him. 'By that time we were fed up with being attacked from the air so we got really panicky as they flew low over our heads. But they were RAF planes and right before our eyes they gave Jerry a real pasting. That was the only time I saw the RAF in action, but it really worked. The Germans broke and ran.' The attackers were eighteen RAF Blenheim bombers and six Fleet Air Arm Albacores, and the happy coincidence of their arrival had the British troops on their feet cheering, exhaustion forgotten.

The main area of British-held perimeter, the Furnes Canal, was the most difficult to defend. The existence of farm buildings and houses along the banks afforded plenty of cover, and although the flooding of fields had been enough to deter a commital of Panzers it had been far from fully effective. Some parts were under three feet of water, others hardly damp. There was, too, the serious problem of shortage of guns and ammunition. Of the BEF's sixteen heavy and medium artillery regiments, only the 59th Medium remained operational. The others had complied with orders and spiked their guns. Even so, German attempts to rush the canal and get across in rubber boats were beaten off with heavy casualties, so they swiftly resorted to forms of subterfuge already familiar in the campaign. Brigadier Clifton reported that 'machine gunners advanced between horses and cattle or adopted various disguises, even dressing as nuns'.

Harry Dennis, the CO's chauffeur of the 1st Battalion East Surreys, watched one such attack come in at Furnes.

There was this column of French horse-drawn artillery retreating towards the canal where we were dug in. Eventually they arrived right in front of us and we shouted that they couldn't get across the canal. One of the French drivers was making strange signals to us. Suddenly we realized what it was. Jerry had captured them and was creeping up on the other side of the column hanging on to the wagons. I have never seen a bigger slaughter of horseflesh than that afternoon. We just mowed the column down. They were only the width of the canal away.

It was at Furnes that Dennis came across another example of the German efficiency that he found so admirable.

We shot a German officer across the canal and saw he had a map case. When it got dark we went out and collected it. The maps he had inside just left you speechless. They even had planks marked across the ditches. It was so well done when you compare what our officers had. That was the difference between being prepared for war and not. Why the hell did we go to war if we weren't prepared?

One of the most exposed parts of the Bergues–Furnes Canal was allotted to the 2nd Coldstream Guards, who had ample time to prepare themselves. Looting of abandoned lorries brought rewards in the way of weaponry and food, and Lieutenant James Langley was much cheered by the fact that his company, by now reduced to thirty-seven men, mustered twelve Brens, three Lewis guns, one anti-tank rifle, thirty thousand rounds of small arms ammunition and twenty-two grenades. Langley turned a canalside cottage into a fortress. There were two Bren gun nests in the attic, with two buckets of water for cooling the gun barrels as well as keeping the wine and beer chilled. The kitchen was equally well equipped, being stacked with tins of bully beef, milk, vegetables and stew, in addition to luxuries such as marmalade and Wiltshire bacon. Langley's company commander, Major Angus McQuorquodale, was so impressed with the set-up that he added a bottle of whisky and two of sherry to the haul. 'So we were well supplied with the necessities of life,' said Langley. They settled down to await the enemy's arrival.

The French C-in-C, Weygand, wrote after the war, 'Dunkirk, it must regretfully be admitted, was the first rift in the lute of Franco-British relations.' That rift had been spotted as early as 27 May when Major General Sir Edward Spears, Churchill's emissary to the French government, noted, 'For the first time I sensed a break in the relationships between the two nations, no more perceptible than a crack in crystal, but going right through, irreparably. We were no longer one.'

What Weygand called, quite rightly, 'the increasingly bad relations and complete lack of understanding that existed between the British and ourselves' was dramatically highlighted by the meeting between Abrial, the admiral in charge of Dunkirk's defence, and Gort on 29 May. Having taken over King Albert's former holiday home at La Panne as his headquarters, the British commander travelled into Dunkirk to call on Abrial at his steel and concrete bunker, Bastion 32, in the harbour area. That very day, on the Channel telephone link, Gort and the CIGS, Sir John Dill, had discussed mounting French criticism about the British abandoning them. Gort said he was prepared to embark Allied troops with 'mutual co-operation', but urged that the French should take their share in providing naval facilities (ignoring the fact that the main French naval strength was based by arrangement in the Mediterranean) before pointing out, 'My instructions are that the safety of the BEF is the primary consideration. Every Frenchman embarked is in place of one Englishman.'

As he greeted Abrial, Gort had no idea that the French commander, whose troglodyte habits in his bunker endowed him, in the opinion of Spears, 'with the confidence and aggressiveness of a rhinoceros and similarly limited vision', did not even know about the full evacuation. The admiral was astonished to hear Gort's breezy plans for lifting the BEF back home. He had understood that the British were merely embarking rear units to clear space for the establishment of a permanent fighting bridgehead around Dunkirk. Both commanders sought immediate clarification from their governments, Gort the more easily by going back to his direct link at La Panne. The answer they received was identical, since Churchill had by then rushed a note to Spears ordering him to inform the French of the scale of the evacuation: from now on embarkation and the defence of the perimeter should be carried out as joint operations. This was bitter news for Gort's staff, who criticized what they saw as political interference, but it was overdue.

A prime example of the sort of indignity inflicted on the French was the case of General Champon, head of the French mission to King Leopold. Following the Belgian capitulation, Champon and his staff, just over a hundred strong, made their way to La Panne to seek evacuation under the authorization of the Allied commander in northern France, General Georges. Gort wanted to know why they could not be rescued by a French destroyer and the discussion bounced back and forth for thirty-six hours before the wretched general and his mission were finally taken off on the evening of 30 May.

It was to help resolve this sort of problem that the Admiralty decided to give Tennant, the Senior Naval Officer ashore at Dunkirk, more help. The choice was Rear-Admiral Frederic Wake-Walker, a fifty-two-year-old whose last sea-going command had been the battleship *Revenge*. In order that he should not appear to be superseding Tennant, Wake-Walker was given responsibility for everything afloat at Dunkirk, including the armada of small craft then being assembled. Offered the job on his return to the Admiralty from lunch on 29 May, Wake-Walker was on his way by 4 p.m., prudently halting in Canterbury to load up with chocolate and cigarettes, though his briefing from the First Sea Lord, Admiral of the Fleet Sir Dudley Pound, was not calculated to smooth existing prejudices against Britain's Allies. The French, said Sir Dudley, did not seem to be pulling their weight over the evacuation. Wake-Walker was told, 'Refuse them embarkation if British troops are ready to embark.'

He sailed at 8 p.m. in the destroyer *Esk* with an eighty-strong reinforcement beach party, and in a whirlwind twenty-four hours after his arrival off the French coast established what must rate as a record for any navy by managing to fly his admiral's flag from six different ships as he darted ashore for meetings and patrolled the shoreline assessing the situation. An urgent request to Ramsay secured the restoration of all available destroyers for rescue work, but the most memorable occasion of that hectic first day was dinner with Gort at his La Panne headquarters on the evening of 30 May.

By then Gort, who had planned to hang on in France until the very end, had been ordered by Churchill to nominate another commander of the BEF and come home. 'It would be a needless triumph to the enemy to capture you when only a small force remained under your orders,' said the Prime Minister. Although reluctant himself to depart, Gort was wisely shipping out the commanders who would form the nucleus of Britain's new army. His Chief of Staff, General Henry Pownall, and his personal aide, Lord Munster, left on the evening of the 29th, and on the 30th it was the turn of General Brooke. After a lunch of chicken and asparagus conjured from nowhere by his aide, Captain Barney Charlesworth, Brooke handed over his 2 Corps to Montgomery. ('This surprised me,' Monty confessed, 'as I was the junior major-general in the corps.') As he did so Brooke, known as a cold man, broke down and wept. Also renowned for his sartorial excellence, Brooke discarded his smart, brand-new Huntsman breeches and heavy Norwegian boots in favour of slacks and shoes for his departure from the beach ('Ready for any swimming contest,' he explained) but in the event he did not even get wet. The faithful Charlesworth carried him on his back to a ship's boat, while Brooke's despatch rider promptly donned his chief's abandoned clothing and got home safely wearing it.

Half an hour after Brooke's exit a whaler deposited Wake-Walker in the surf at La Panne and the admiral, who was met on the beach by the indefatigable Tennant, headed for his meeting with Gort saturated to the waist.

I found Lord Gort and his staff about to have dinner and he insisted on my joining them. He was charming and seemed very cheerful and unperturbed and glad to see me. . . . I shall not easily forget that meal. For one thing my trousers and seat were very wet and it seemed to be so strange to be sitting there sharing the Commander-in-Chief's last bottle of champagne and looking out across the beach to the sea. There were eight or nine of us, including Tennant and myself. I forget what we ate, except that the final dish was fruit salad from a tin and I felt that my extra mouth was robbing the others of their share.

And so they sat, this evening of 30 May, on the brink of the greatest disaster in British military history, sipping champagne and spooning tinned fruit as if it were just another social gathering of the Phoney War.

The dishes cleared, the leaders got down to business. Wake-Walker received the firm impression that Gort, having fallen back to the coast, now felt that the Navy, whose responsibility it was to get them off, was not making much of an effort to do so. The admiral stressed the difficulties involved and the dependence on fine weather for beach evacuation, only for Gort's Deputy Chief of Staff, Brigadier Sir Oliver Leese, to criticize 'the ineptitude of the Navy'. 'I could not let that pass,' said Wake-Walker, 'and told him he had no business or justification to talk like that.'

When Wake-Walker left Gort about 10 p.m. Tennant asked if a boat had been told to wait for him, but the reply was that boats were too precious to be kept hanging around, even for an admiral, at this stage of the evacuation. So, coming across some men of the 12th Lancers attempting to float pontoons, Wake-Walker persuaded eight of them to paddle him out to the destroyer *Worcester*, his flagship of the moment, lying offshore.

I placed four on each side and told them to wade out with it and get in when I told them. They got in two by two until only my Flag Lieutenant and I were still wading at the stern with the water well over our knees. Finally we got in together and I started the soldiers paddling by numbers, rather like a racing boat's crew. They soon picked it up but I noticed there was already a good deal of water in the boat. The freeboard was about three inches and the wavelets were washing up to my stern as I sat on the gunwale. So we all got out and returned to the beach with our boat and emptied it. Tennant and Brigadier Leese had been standing all this time watching and as we came ashore I could not resist the temptation of saying to the latter, 'Another example of naval ineptitude.'

Reluctantly I had to reduce my crew by two and off we went again. This time things went all right and the soldiers, settling down in fine style, soon brought us to the *Worcester*.

Back at the villa Gort's remaining HQ staff despatched a late-night situation report to the War Office. The six British divisions still in the bridgehead were being thinned out and it was expected that the eastern (Belgian) end should be clear by the following night, 31 May. Half an hour later, at a minute to midnight, Dill rang Gort with the urgent news that the Prime Minister was insisting, not on a fair total of French being evacuated with the BEF, but on equal numbers. Churchill followed Dill on to the phone to confirm the order.

The timing of Churchill's comments was made clear next day when he flew to Paris for a session of the Allied Supreme War Council. The

British Premier opened the meeting with a brisk and optimistic summation of the evacuation's progress. As he gave the latest figures, Weygand interrupted, 'But how many French? The French are being left behind.' Churchill's emissary, Spears, was present and described Weygand's voice as 'high, querulous and aggressive'. Reynaud was the next to tackle Churchill on this theme in what Spears termed 'friendly but insistent fashion'. Of the 220,000 British 150,000 had already been evacuated, said the French Prime Minister, whereas of 200,000 Frenchmen only 15,000 had been taken off. Such statistics, he felt, could provoke extreme reaction among the public in his country. Something must be done to increase the proportion of French to British.

The more Churchill was pressed, the more he conceded on a matter which clearly embarrassed him. It was one of the rare moments in that harrowing month when Weygand must have been satisfied. He considered Churchill a producer of fine speeches but a maker of promises he could not keep. As proof of Britain's determination for (belated) fair play, Churchill announced that that day, 31 May, had been laid down as one when the French would have absolute priority over the British in the matter of embarkation. Then, when it was proposed at the meeting that the British in the perimeter should evacuate ahead of the French, Churchill was on his feet at once.

'In his execrable French', reported Spears, 'he shouted "Nong, Partage – bras dessus, bras dessous." The gesture he made, effectively camouflaging his accent, conveyed better than words that he wished the French and British soldiers to leave Dunkirk arm in arm.'

Quite carried away by now, Churchill went on to propose that the remaining British would even form the final rearguard, saying he would not accept further sacrifices from his Allies. This caused consternation among his military advisers at the meeting, who included the CIGS, Dill, and the final wording was quietly amended, in the telegram of instruction sent to Abrial in Dunkirk, to announce: 'British troops will remain behind as long as possible.'

Quite coincidentally, another vital conference was taking place simultaneously in Dunkirk between Abrial and the new British commander, Major General the Hon. Harold Alexander. The news of his appointment as Gort's successor that morning had been stunning. The C-in-C summoned the commanders of his army's two remaining corps, Lieutenant General Michael Barker of 1 Corps and the newly appointed Montgomery of 2 Corps, at 6 p.m. on 30 May to tell them of his recall. Gort said that since 2 Corps would be evacuated first, Barker would be the senior officer to remain in command, at which there was some rather strained humour about Barker (whose nickname was 'Bubbles') being fated to be entertained in a castle on the Rhine. Though he probably recognized that he was being declared expendable Barker was happy enough, closing the meeting with the comment, 'Right, now I know where I am.'

This was far from the case. The choice was not one with which Montgomery agreed and he decided to say so.

I stayed behind when the others had left and asked Gort if I could have a word with him in private. I then said it was my view that Barker was in an unfit state to be left in final command; what was needed was a calm and clear brain, and that given reasonable luck such a man might well get 1st Corps away, with no need for *anyone* to surrender. He had such a man in Alexander, who was commanding the 1st Division in Barker's Corps. He should send Barker back to England at once and put Alexander in command of the 1st Corps. I knew Gort very well; so I spoke very plainly and insisted that this was the right course to take.

Gort never made public his reasons for snubbing Barker so spectacularly (a decision which reduced that general to tears when the news was broken, by Alexander of all people), but the passion of Montgomery's advice must have made its impression. Alexander got the job on the morning of 31 May and Brigadier Cyrus Greenslade, a member of Gort's HQ staff and a long-standing friend of the C-in-C's, was present when Gort told the new commander, 'Alex, go over there and pick up the receiver and you will find the man waiting to speak to you is Anthony Eden. Think well before you speak because what you say will be recorded in history.' Alexander was also told by the War Office on behalf of the CIGS, Dill, then on his way to Paris with Churchill, that his duty was to hold the Dunkirk area as long as possible, provided the safety of the BEF was not imperilled, a factor which was also stressed personally to Alexander by Gort.

It was with this instruction very much in mind that Alexander set off for his meeting with Abrial, inevitably in the admiral's deep bunker. The fact that he was dealing with a sailor puzzled Alexander deeply, particularly since there were by now several well-qualified French generals in the area. Abrial had originally been appointed in expectation of an invasion from the sea. That the danger had materialized from another direction altogether was a paradox perfectly acceptable to the French.

The argument which erupted at the meeting was an inevitable one, the French maintaining that the British should continue to defend the perimeter, Alexander insisting that he was under orders to disengage before the night was out. This conflicted with a letter which Abrial had extracted from Gort promising the BEF's continuing participation in the defence of Dunkirk. If the British persisted with their plan to withdraw, Abrial threatened to close the port and stop them.

When Abrial then suggested Gort should be contacted to find out which version of his instructions was to be followed, he was further astonished to be told that the British commander had already left. Like many other things Abrial was hearing from the British, this was not true. Gort spent the afternoon at his headquarters in La Panne, due to be closed down that evening as part of the shortening of the perimeter, sorting through his belongings and snipping off the VC and other medal ribbons from the spare uniforms he was leaving behind so that they should not make souvenirs and propaganda for the enemy.

The arrangements were that Gort and his staff would leave at 6 p.m. on 31 May. Wake-Walker planned to evacuate the GHQ personnel aboard the destroyer *Keith*, but four motor torpedo boats had also set off from Dover that afternoon for the purpose. The signal informing Wake-Walker of this never reached him.

As they walked on to the beach at La Panne, Brigadier Greenslade recalled,

Gort took hold of my arm and said quietly, 'Cyrus, to think I brought you from India to lead you into this.' He then climbed on to a temporary pier and got into a small boat and was rowed out, whereas we went further down the sands and were finally signalled to wade out to a whaler which couldn't get any closer. We waded out up to our chests and were pulled into the boat and transferred to *Keith*.

While Gort's staff finished up on *Keith* the C-in-C boarded a minesweeper, *Hebe*, which astonishingly hung around for several hours to pick up troops being ferried from the beach. Eventually a frantic signal reached Wake-Walker: London wanted to know where Gort had got to. Wake-Walker admitted later, 'I had not realized the anxiety of the government to have him safe and sound at home but felt he would sooner the ship helped to bring off more men rather than that he should land a few hours earlier in England.' It was a severe miscalculation on the admiral's part. Perhaps Gort might have felt that way, but a deeply worried British government did not agree.

Even Gort had clearly become a little restless by nightfall, transferring from *Hebe* into a small launch in an attempt to join his staff on *Keith* and find out why he was still off La Panne. The launch eventually found the destroyer, and Gort and Brigadier Leese were promptly embarked in a motor torpedo boat which landed them at 6.20 the following morning in Dover; here Gort caught the next train to London, an audience with the King and oblivion.

According to Admiralty statistics, Gort was one of 61,557 landed in UK ports on 1 June. By then, of course, the news was out about Dunkirk and the hype was flowing. (The previous day's *Daily Mirror* had suggested that BEF stood for 'Bravery, Endurance, Fortitude'.) The same statistics show the huge build-up in numbers of French troops disembarked in the United Kingdom. On 28 May the total is shown as 'nil'. By the 29th it was 655, on the 30th 8616, on the 31st 14,874 and on 1 June, for the first time, French outnumbered British with a count of 35,013. These figures do not tally with those available in the excellent war museum in Dunkirk, which gives the totals of French troops lifted for the same five days (possibly to French ports as well as British) as 1527 on 28 May, building to 20,826 on 31 May, slightly more than the 1 June figure of 19,769.

Whatever the discrepancies, the French complaints were having an effect. However, there was no chance they would persuade the British to dally in Dunkirk. Alexander went straight back to GHQ at La Panne from his meeting with Abrial and, although close-down was imminent, he managed to get a call through to London, telling Eden of his differences with the French. Within an hour Eden rang back to tell him, 'You should withdraw your forces as rapidly as possible on a 50-50 basis with the French Army, aiming at completion by night of 1/2 June. You should inform the French of this definite instruction.'

Alexander did so. Abrial had pointed out to his government that the British were abandoning the defence of Dunkirk, but all they could do was pass on the complaint to London, reminding the British of the decision reached in Paris that very afternoon. It was no good. The British were determined to go and, with no other option, Abrial eventually fell in with their plans.

The last day of May 1940 passed quietly, like so many others before it, in the Maginot Line. An historian of the Line wrote that 'the men were happy to come out into the sunshine and talk of the ordinary things of life. In the stillness of the countryside war seemed very far away.'

Around the Dunkirk perimeter, too, there had been a comparative lull, so much so that some of the German staff officers worried that the momentum had gone out of the victory surge. With the emphasis now on Plan Red – the push on Paris – Colonel Rolf Wuthmann, Operations Officer of von Kluge's 4th Army at the French-held western end of the defence line, complained on 30 May, 'There is an impression here that nothing is happening today, that no one is any longer interested in Dunkirk', while von Kluge's Chief of Staff, Kurt Brennecke, warned, 'We do not want to find these men, freshly equipped, in front of us again later.' But the final German push was about to be unified under the command of General Georg von Kuechler of the 18th Army. From 2 a.m. on 31 May he would be in charge of ten divisions for the assault that would shove the British and French into the sea. That offensive was timed to go in on 1 June, despite the fact that there were clear signs of the British abandoning the eastern end of the line on the night of 31 May anyway.

The six divisions allotted to assault the British-held sector had all been hard used during the past three weeks, but it was a moot point whether it was more exhausting to advance than to retreat. At least the German soldiers had the exhilaration of conquest. When Lieutenant Colonel James Birch called a meeting of his company commanders of the 2nd Bedfordshire and Hertfordshire Regiment for evacuation orders, he recalled, 'It was an unforgettable sight. Not one of us seemed able to keep awake. I believe I slapped Senior to keep him awake and promptly fell asleep myself. The doctor (Bell) said we took it in turns to say something but were asleep before the other replied.'

As part of the thinning out process among the perimeter defenders, Toby Taylor of the 1st East Surreys was put in charge of an assorted group of non-essential personnel with orders to oversee their evacuation. While issuing instructions about this, Taylor's battalion commander, Lieutenant Colonel Peter Boxshall, was so exhausted that Taylor found his speech difficult to follow. 'Though I was occasionally nodding off myself he kept falling asleep and with a thud banging his head on the table in front of him,' said Taylor, who found what he termed 'a strange bunch' assembled as his flock – 'signallers with no equipment, drivers with no vehicles, cooks, the walking wounded, all the odd bods who could no longer take an active part in any future battle. I collected together about forty NCOs and men.'

They set off through a night made hideous by saturation shelling before the German assault of the following morning. Harry Dennis, Colonel Boxshall's driver, was taking one of the battalion's company commanders, Major Bousfield, from Coxyde along the coast road to La Panne when a shell landed in front of the car. 'It was like hitting a brick wall,' said Dennis.

When I came to the steering wheel had gone, blood was pouring out of my right hand, the thumb was hanging off and Bousfield, next to me, was slumped over. One of the other officers in the car put my thumb back in position and bound it up. They put Bousfield and me on a truck and told them to take us on to La Panne. At a field dressing station at the edge of the beach there an RAMC officer told me to make my own way on to the shore and get away. By that time Bousfield was dead.

Dennis passed out on the sand, was picked up by sailors and put aboard the minesweeper *Albany* which docked at Sheerness. In the ambulance *en route* to Dartford Hospital Dennis noticed a tag on his clothes. He turned it round to read the one-word message: 'Amputation'. But the hand was operated on, and saved, by a German surgeon who had been interned at the outbreak of war but released to work at Dartford.

On that night of 31 May the news was passed to the South Lancashires at Nieuport – withdrawal again. Transport had been laid on for this particular retreat into La Panne, and as they pulled away from the line Alf Hewitt thought the sound of heavy German shells passing overhead reminded him of tramcars going round a corner.

Away we went along the coastal route, which was under continuous shellfire. I don't know how we got through because the lorries had to keep stopping and starting, negotiating shell holes, going off into the country and coming back on to the road. About an hour before dawn we arrived at La Panne and as we went to form ranks in the main street the shells were crashing into the buildings around us. We were so packed in that street that, though some of the shells were landing fifty yards from me, packed bodies were taking the blast. I was just lucky. Then somebody shouted, 'Every man for himself, make for the beach.'

As we headed towards the beach there was a small side turning. Some people had been blown through the railings which had gone through them like a mesh through cheese. The gutters were literally running with blood. At this turning I found myself next to a mate, name of Jim Welch, who came from Stoke and joined up with me. We heard a voice shouting 'Jim' and we saw two figures sitting in the middle of the road. One was a mate of ours, also from Stoke, name of George Barnes, who was a batman. His officer, Lieutenant Watts, had been badly wounded in the leg and Barnes had helped him to get to the coast. We went to give them assistance when one of these tramcar shells whistled in. We flung ourselves into a shop doorway and the shell landed right where they were. All that was left was a crater in the road.

We rushed straight across the promenade, on to the beach, and kept on running into the sea. We waded in until it was up to our waists. We had been on our feet for three weeks. That cold sea on our feet was a marvellous feeling in the dark. There we were, standing in the sea, enjoying a paddle and cooling off. We didn't want to come out, the shells didn't seem to be reaching us.

An RAOC private, Frank Farley, attached to the Middlesex Regiment was in the centre of La Panne after the German artillery barrage lifted early on the morning of Saturday, 1 June and the sheltering troops were ordered to make for the beach.

Men promptly sallied forth and commenced running up the street. Numbers of buildings were well ablaze and also several vehicles, including ambulances. Debris was scattered far and wide and a number of motionless figures, some hopelessly mangled, lay along the gutters and pavements.

Beyond the crossroads was a broad boulevard, with a bandstand at its seaward end, opening across the esplanade on to the beach. There were no railings, simply a short step down from the paving on to the sand; and here all was darkness in contrast to the blaze left behind. As the torrent of boots abruptly encountered soft sand the illusion of silence was created, and one felt suddenly removed from the turmoil of La Panne.

Who my immediate companions were at that particular moment I did not know. We numbered about five. Whatever individual thoughts may have been concerning the renewed danger ahead, they were brutally terminated by the arrival of a salvo directly upon us. The nearest explosion was mere yards away, to my right front. At that moment we happened to be passing a small covered van, stranded in the sand to our immediate left. One fact which I have never fully understood about that very close one is that I was hardly aware of any bang. On the contrary, my recollection is of something seen and felt but scarcely heard, an orange flash and blast, a choking burst of sand and smoke and, simultaneously, the sound of splinters rending the panelling of the van. Instinctively I dropped, realizing even in doing so that this time it was too late, but felt no impact or pain, and promptly scrambled to my feet. Those with me at that moment were not so fortunate. To my right and left lay three still figures; a fourth, propped on one hand, spoke. His voice carried an entreating note of despair which still rings with the same clarity on the conscience. 'Help me, help me,' was all he said, face indistinguishable except in outline in the darkness, a stranger whose voice has ever since accused – because I slogged on without pause. Those were the orders.

Dawn on 1 June was a misty one for those holding the line of the Bergues–Furnes Canal, a day when the fourth Victoria Cross of the campaign was won. Its recipient was Captain Harold Ervine-Andrews of the 1st Battalion East Lancashires Regiment. The early German assault carried them across the water and the flank of the East Lancashires was in danger of being turned until Ervine-Andrews, accompanied by a handful of volunteers, occupied a barn. Their combined firepower halted the advance and Ervine-Andrews was said in his citation to have claimed seventeen of the enemy with his rifle and 'many, many more with a Bren gun' until the barn was set ablaze and destroyed. He held on until 4.30 p.m. before successfully extracting the eight survivors of his company.

There were numberless other deeds of bravery that day as the Germans strove to break into the perimeter defences. When the junction between the Green Howards and Durham Light Infantry began to cave in it was restored by the appearance of Major Will Lacy, a former Scarborough bank manager and commander of the Green Howards' A Company, stalking across the open fields and directing a counter-attack with his walking stick.

As the mist lifted that day Lieutenant James Langley and his Coldstream Guards manning the fortified cottage by the canal were treated to the astonishing sight of some hundred Germans standing unconcernedly in groups at a distance of six hundred yards. The resultant slaughter, Langley confessed, made him slightly sick. It also brought heavy retribution, but not before Langley had managed to enjoy a glass of sherry from their well-stocked kitchen with three other Guards officers, none of whom survived the next twenty-four hours. Serious problems began when the Germans occupied a house on the opposite bank of the canal and opened up on their tormentors.

'There was a most frightful crash and a great wave of heat, dust and debris knocked me over,' said Langley.

A shell had burst on the roof. There was a long silence and I heard a small voice saying 'I've been hit' which I suddenly realized was mine. . . . No pain, just a useless left arm, which looked very silly, and blood all over my battledress. A stretcher-bearer arrived and put a field dressing on my arm, removed my watch, which he later sent to my parents in England, and bandaged my head. I remembered being half carried, half helped down from the loft and some time later being put into a wheelbarrow. Later, splints made out of a broken wooden box were tied round my arm, I was put into an ambulance, then off we went to the beaches. No pain, only a terrible thirst. I shouted for water but nobody heard me over the noise of the engine.

For what seemed like hours we bumped along, continually stopping and starting. The man above me must have been bleeding badly as the blood began to drip on my face and I had to keep wiping it off with the edge of my blanket.

When the ambulance reached the shore Langley was approached by a man in blue naval overcoat who asked if he could get off his stretcher. When Langley said he did not think so, the man told him, 'Well, I am very sorry, we cannot take you. Your stretcher would occupy the places of four men. Orders are only those who can stand or sit up.'

'I said nothing,' Langley wrote of that crushing moment. 'I was just too damned tired to sit up, stand up or argue.'

16

Little Ships, Few Planes

Our great-grandchildren, when they learn how we began this war by snatching glory out of defeat and then swept on to victory, may also learn how the little holiday steamers made an excursion to hell and came back glorious.

J B Priestley

The Little Ships are an integral part of the legend of Dunkirk, the miracle of evacuation. Much has been written, filmed and broadcast of their deeds and no better summary in their praise exists than Priestley's comment above. They are rightly accorded capital letters, these small vessels, manned by civilians as well as naval crews, which grew to be the Little Ships of Dunkirk. No matter that their contribution was not especially significant in the numbers of troops rescued (the personnel craft, ferries and destroyers did the bulk of that); they helped to carry crucial supplies of ammunition, food and drink to the beaches, brought home as many men as they could and, above all, cheered a British public in urgent need of such a morale-boosting tale of heroism.

They came in their hundreds as word went out that there was an army in need of rescue. The removal firm, Pickfords, despatched its lighters built for the trade between Solent ports and the Isle of Wight, while the London County Council sent its garbage-carrying hopper barges. Off to sea, for the first time, went the London Fire Brigade's tender *Massey Shaw* (whose huge water cannon, resembling a gun, almost caused her to be mistaken for a German warship by a British destroyer). There was *Count Dracula*, formerly a German admiral's launch, scuttled at Scapa Flow after the First World War but raised years afterwards; and the pioneer aviator Tommy Sopwith's racing yacht *Endeavour*. There were eleven *Skylark*s, nine Port of London tugs all called *Sun* with different numerals, cockle boats, drifters, pleasure boats, river cruisers – ordinary little boats belonging to ordinary (and sometimes extraordinary) people. They were called *Ben* and *Lucy*, *John* and *Norah*, *Girl Gladys* and *Boy Roy*, *Yorkshire Lass* and *Young Nun*, *Pudge*, *Cabby* and *Dumpling*. There were, too, names which could only belong to England: *Elizabeth* and *Nelson*.

An Admiralty report paid fulsome tribute to this makeshift fleet.

From all around the compass they came. From up the river, along the coast, from the yachting harbours, the pleasure beaches, naval ports and fishing towns – anything that would float, move under its own power and collect a dozen men or so from the beaches where they waited. The first assembly was typical of the whole of this miniature armada. A dozen or so motor yachts from 20ft to 50ft in length, nicely equipped and smartly maintained by proud individual owners; a cluster of cheap 'conversion jobs', mainly the work of amateur craftsmen who had set to work in their spare time to convert a ship's lifeboat or any old half-discarded hull into a cabin cruiser of sorts for weekend trips on the quiet waters of up-river reaches; half a dozen Thames river launches resembling nothing so much as the upper decks of elongated motor buses with their rows of slatted seats.

One of these river launches was the *Marchioness*, still in service as a pleasure cruiser until it was sunk with heavy loss of life in the Thames collision tragedy of 1989.

Such was the urgency that, when the call came, some boats were requisitioned without their owners' permission or even knowledge. The boat-building firm Tough Bros of Teddington were appointed agents for the collection of small craft along the Thames by the Ministry of Shipping. Douglas Tough, accompanied by a naval officer, scoured the upper reaches of the river in search of likely boats. If they saw one they put a crew aboard and took it. One owner, hearing that his vessel was being removed, complained to the police who pursued it to Teddington Lock before discovering what was happening. More than a hundred private boats were assembled at Tough's yard and prepared for the rigours of a Channel crossing. Next they were sailed down-river to Sheerness where their temporary crews were supposed to hand them over to naval personnel. By this stage of the evacuation the Royal Navy and its men were in heavy demand, so many civilians simply sailed on to Dunkirk and into history. Civilians like Harry Hastings, landlord of the Gloucester Arms in Kingston-upon-Thames, who abandoned the beer pumps and took his boat *Tigris I* off to its second war. The vessel, which had served in the First World War before being converted by Tough's in 1933, took off about 800 from the beaches before being disabled and abandoned. Two days later it was sighted off the Goodwins with 90 French troops aboard and still very much afloat. After being towed to Ramsgate *Tigris* was returned upriver to Teddington but was so badly damaged that she ended life as a houseboat.

The arrival of such ships coincided with a time of great need. They helped to compensate for the severe losses suffered among the original whalers, cutters and warships' boats in the earlier part of the evacuation, either through enemy intervention or because rescued troops had abandoned the boats which had brought them to the sanctuary of a larger ship rather than ensuring that they were ferried back to shore for further use.

The Admiralty was inundated with offers from would-be volunteers. Half a dozen women, all experts in boats, wanted to help but a naval spokesman told the *London Evening News*, 'We rather shrank from letting them go.' Undeterred, one of them rang again next day to apply once more, this time adopting an unsuccessfully gruff voice. When she was again turned down and asked why, she was told, 'Your sex is against you.' To which, the *News* told its readers, she replied, 'Blast my sex'.

If sex proved a barrier, age did not. Pensioners and elderly office workers crewed boats alongside teenagers. Aboard the Thames tug *Sun 12* was Albert Barnes, a fourteen-year-old galley boy, who recalled, 'I was making tea – they kept me down below as much as possible – but I didn't realize how serious it was, coming straight from school and right into the thick of it like that.'

Most of the early sailings set off without so much as a pistol between them. 'Even a record of the "1812 Overture" would have been better than nothing,' said one volunteer. Some even lacked compasses – not that one was really needed. 'We had a course to steer but we didn't need to use it,' recalled Bob Hilton. 'It was like Piccadilly Circus over there.' Sailing in the opposite direction did not always prove so simple. 'We had no charts or compass but trusted to our sense of direction,' reported Able Seaman P T Sullivan aboard the motor boat *Silver Queen*. 'Halfway over we found a soldier's compass and used that. Then we sighted land and, thinking it was Ramsgate or some other port, turned towards it and got about half a mile off when the Germans opened fire.' *Silver Queen* had been sailing into Calais. Despite being hit twice she managed to get away and next time succeeded in finding Ramsgate, where her load of French troops was safely disembarked before she foundered at the dockside.

Reliance on a faulty compass aboard the motor boat *Swallow* also led William Williams, a Royal Navy sub-lieutenant, into what could have been fatal error when he went ashore at night in search of Allied soldiers to rescue.

After about a quarter of a mile I saw two men silhouetted against the glow of a distant blaze. I approached to within a few yards and hailed them. I heard one of them say 'Lieber Gott' and they turned around and commenced to shoot at me. By this time I had come to the conclusion that I was in enemy territory, so I hid behind a dune and shot back.

Fortunately it was a very dark night and the Germans could not see me properly, while I could see their outlines quite well. I shot the one on the right twice and he fell without a sound. The other one screamed when I fired two bullets at him and he dropped whatever he was carrying and then fell and lay still. By this time I heard nearby shouts so, deeming discretion to be the better part of valour, I ran at top speed back to the boat and my ship was under way at her full six knots within less than five minutes.

The Admiralty report on the participation of the Little Ships stressed the good fortune with the elements ('beautiful yachting weather, hardly a chop on the water, half the small craft could never have made the crossing otherwise'). Even so, many of them, laid up since the previous summer, broke down and never got to France. Others, being towed across the Channel for this very reason, found their planks less durable than tow ropes and lost their gunwales. There were, too, hazards aplenty on the journey, both real and imagined, even for the larger civilian craft. The crew of the converted Thames paddle wheeler *Golden Eagle* spent a desperate few minutes one dark night fending off with boathooks what they thought were mines. They turned out to be oil drums. A look-out on the excursion steamer *New Prince of Wales* excitedly reported a periscope, but it was only the mast of a sunken ship. Having narrowly escaped being run down by a British destroyer which mistook her for a German torpedo boat, the same ship was also fired on when she pulled alongside a French cargo boat to ask, *'Où est l'armée britannique?'*

The *New Prince of Wales* was one of many Little Ships which did not survive Dunkirk. She was taken inshore under shelling at Bray-Dunes on 31 May by her commanding officer, Sub-Lieutenant Peter Bennett RN, despite being almost out of fuel and with engines malfunctioning. A shell exploded alongside, killing two of Bennett's crew and wounding two more. Hit in the nose, hip and foot, blinded by blood and unable to see the extent of the damage, Bennett asked for a report on his ship's condition and was told she was sinking. After ordering the burning of charts and papers, Bennett and his survivors transferred to the motor launch *Triton* where, sight now restored in one eye, he took over the wheel, thus freeing *Triton*'s commanding officer, Lieutenant Robert Irving, to carry on collecting military personnel swimming around the boat. 'After about forty-five minutes, the launch being loaded to full capacity, we went alongside HMS *Mosquito*,' said Bennett. 'I was given a morphia injection and remember nothing further until arrival in Dover.'

When they rescued Bennett, *Triton*'s crew of six had been working the beaches non-stop for the best part of two days. Irving was grateful for the extra hands provided by Bennett's men since one of his own crew had already fallen overboard from exhaustion, the coxswain who was replaced by the wounded Bennett was 'sleeping on his feet on and off' according to Irving, and two others 'lay down and stood up as strength permitted'. *Triton* had to be abandoned off Bray-Dunes with a rope tangled round her screw and her stem and stern badly damaged by shellfire. Taken aboard the yacht *Galatea*, where he slumped on the deck 'stupefied with exhaustion', Irving reported: 'It was about 1840 31st May 1940 when my activities ceased. I had been on my feet from 0700 29th May in a small craft and the only food eaten from 2000 29th May to that time was one tin of herrings, one tin of bully beef and two slices of bread, also four cups of tea without sugar. We simply had not time to eat.'

Constant Nymph was also kept busy collecting troops, for which her owner, B A Smith, was grateful. 'Being deaf and having a lot to do prevented my noticing the bombing much.' William Attwaters, master of the hopper barge *Foremost 102*, was also grateful that he did not have time to speculate about what was going on all around. 'We had our work cut out lugging half-drowned men to safety. We had about three hundred aboard. I put one wounded man in my cabin and the next time I went to the cabin there were two in my bunk, clothes and boots on, wet through, and six on the floor. They were in every bunk and space in the ship, dead beat.'

The art of squeezing people into boats came easy to Charles Lightoller, a sixty-six-year-old who raised chickens in Hertfordshire and kept a 58-foot power cruiser called *Sundowner* moored at Burnham-on-Crouch. Lightoller had been second officer on the *Titanic*, where his coolness had saved many lives on that night in 1912. Brushing aside official suggestions that *Sundowner* should be sailed to Dunkirk by a naval crew, Lightoller took along his son Roger and an eighteen-year-old Sea Scout as crew and packed a treacle tart made by his wife for the journey. While loading troops from the Mole, Lightoller also took on board Charles Jerram, a pre-war yachting friend and now a naval officer whose own Little Ship, a 40-footer and one of the many

Skylarks, had gone down. On the return trip Jerram helped Lightoller eat the treacle tart. 'Though it was so brittle it broke like china, it was really excellent as it was the first food I had had for thirty-six hours,' Jerram said. When *Sundowner* docked at Ramsgate the fifty soldiers on deck were disembarked, to be followed by another seventy-five who had been crammed down below. 'Strewth, mate,' an astonished bystander asked Lightoller, 'where did you put them?'

The true value of the Little Ships at shunting small numbers to huge benefit is encapsulated in the precise report of Lieutenant C W Read RNR, in command of the 35-foot motor launch *Bonny Heather*:

Made 7 complete return trips to Dunkirk Beaches. Average number soldiers carried 60 = approx. 420 soldiers. Made 10 trips from Mole at Dunkirk to transports lying off, under shrapnel = 600 soldiers.

Rescued chief Steward and 39 soldiers from water ex S/S *Scotia* and bombed whilst doing so.

On last return journey was caught in parachute flares, bombed and then machine-gunned, but escaped without damage owing to speed and quickness on helm.

Service finished at 5 p.m. on 4th June. Estimated number of soldiers handled in launch:

Dunkirk Beaches to Ramsgate 420/450
Dunkirk Mole to Transports 600/650
Rescued from S/S *Scotia* 40

The achievements of the Little Ships, or indeed the extent of the emergency, were not fully appreciated by everybody. In January of the following year A G Lacey of Margate, whose boat had been removed from the harbour there 'under protest and without my permission', complained to the Admiralty that he had only just learned of its whereabouts since its removal. In November 1940 the Admiralty wrote to a solicitor, Malcolm Borg, about commandeered yachts belonging to his client B M Bailey: 'The removal of Mr Bailey's vessels was urgently necessary as a matter of military defence and unfortunately time did not permit of prior inquiry. These vessels, however, now lie at Mr Bailey's disposition. In the special circumstances, and as a matter of grace, My Lords would be prepared to bear reasonable expenses of removal of these yachts.'

The month of May had almost passed before any of the Little Ships saw action, but many of the other civilian-manned larger vessels, such as ferries and passenger steamers, had by then been exposed to death on a handful of occasions and the strain was beginning to tell. As the evacuation extended night by night into June, with no prospect of an immediate break, there was a flare-up of rebellion and refusal to risk again the maelstrom on the other side of the Channel. As early as 28 May the captain of the Southern Rail Channel steamer *Canterbury* refused to sail, saying that he and his crew were worn out after two trips to Dunkirk. In this, as in all subsequent cases, swift action was taken. When a medical officer reported the captain unfit he was replaced and a new crew put aboard.

There were rebellions aboard the ferries *Malines*, *Ben-my-Chree* and *Tynwald* in the early hours of 2 June at Folkestone. Armed naval parties were put aboard. The crew of *Ben-my-Chree* attempted to walk off after shouting and demonstrating that they had had enough, while those aboard *Tynwald* contented themselves with abusing naval sentries. The master of *Malines*, George Mallory, took his ship off the Dunkirk run by his own decision and then defied orders by leaving Folkestone to sail back to his home port, Southampton. Mallory explained:

Seven of our consorts were sunk in the vicinity and the weakening morale of my crew was badly shaken. The wireless operator, purser, three engineers and several other hands were already in a state of nervous debility and unfit for duty, while many of the crew were not to be depended upon in an emergency. I considered that the odds against a successful prosecution of another voyage were too enormous and the outcome too unprofitable to risk the ship.

When the skipper of *Ben-my-Chree* received a written request to sail he wrote back, 'I beg to state that after our experience in Dunkirk yesterday my answer is No.'*

There was trouble, too, among the vessels of the Royal National Lifeboat Institution after they had been called up on the afternoon of 30 May. 'Buller' Griggs, coxswain of the Hythe lifeboat *Viscountess Wakefield*, refused to accept instructions that he should run his boat ashore at Dunkirk, load it with troops and then float off with the high tide. The 14-ton vessel was too heavy for that, he claimed. Griggs also sought assurances in writing about family pensions in case of death, and when this was turned down he refused to go, a refusal which was shared by the crews of the Walmer and Dungeness boats. While this argument was raging the Ramsgate lifeboat, *Prudential*, and the one from Margate, *Lord Southborough*, were already lifting soldiers from the beaches.

The Royal Navy promptly took over the three rebel lifeboats, gave

*Secret files on the hearings into these refusals to sail still remained closed at the Public Record Office in 1990.

their crews railway vouchers and sent them home. As further lifeboats arrived at Dover in answer to the appeal their bewildered crews found the boats taken away from them by armed naval parties. The Navy needed boats and wanted no more argument. In the event, only one of the nineteen lifeboats which served at Dunkirk was lost. That was the Hythe boat, which had to be abandoned when it ran aground and stuck fast, just as 'Buller' Griggs had forecast. Griggs and his brother Richard, the motor mechanic on *Viscountess Wakefield*, were both dismissed from the service three weeks later after an RNLI inquiry found that 'failure to perform their duty at a time of great national emergency reflects discredit on the lifeboat service and can in no way be excused'. Buller, a First World War Royal Navy man who had been in charge of the Hythe boat for twenty years and was the holder of the RNLI's silver medal for gallantry, went back to fishing and made good his comment that he was 'no coward' by rescuing two airmen from a ditched British bomber two months later.

Much of the trouble with the crews of ferries and other large ships stemmed from the disasters of 1 June, a day on which the Luftwaffe sank thirty-one ships and seriously damaged eleven others. On the bridge of the destroyer *Keith*, Rear-Admiral Wake-Walker had watched the dawn of this particular Saturday through mist and low clouds ('I hailed these conditions with relief'), but the weather did not last. The dispersal of cloud cover coincided with the arrival of swarms of German aircraft which were able to inflict destruction at leisure in the lengthy intervals between RAF patrols over the evacuation. *Keith*, with the bulk of the BEF headquarters staff still aboard, was one of the victims. The destroyer expended all her anti-aircraft ammunition beating off the first attack and was defenceless when a second raid wrecked the engine room and holed the ship below the waterline. Since the bridge was crowded with people lying or crouching, Wake-Walker could only find room 'to bend a bit' and had a grandstand view as the bombs which destroyed *Keith* were released. 'It was an odd sensation waiting for the explosions and knowing that you could do nothing.'

Since he could no longer do his job in the stricken vessel, Wake-Walker transferred to a motor torpedo boat and was rapidly followed overboard by the crew and those lifted from the beaches. Brigadier Cyrus Greenslade, the ex-Indian Army man, went on deck to find it only a foot above water level.

I remember having read about being sucked down with the ship and tried to get as far as possible from it, but when she did go down the water was so shallow that she settled with the top of her mast still sticking out of the water. The whole sea around one was dotted with bobbing heads. It sounds theatrical and not to be expected, but everyone in the water started singing the popular music hall song 'Roll Out the Barrel'.

On this, the first day that the modern destroyers were recalled to Dunkirk, *Havant* and *Basilisk* were also sunk and *Worcester*, *Ivanhoe* and *Vivacious* damaged. Once again Ramsay ordered the suspension of daylight evacuation. The Stukas had done their work well.

The damage inflicted on ships and humans on 1 June increased the bitterness against the RAF. Alan Deere, a Spitfire pilot with 54 Squadron who was shot down fifteen miles from Dunkirk but managed to steal a bicycle, get back to the beaches and be embarked on a destroyer, was greeted with stony silence when he was taken into the ship's wardroom.

'Why so friendly?' he asked the Army officers massed there. 'What have the RAF done?'

'That's just it,' answered one. 'What *have* they done?'

Bill Murdoch, the only member of a Blenheim bomber to escape when it was shot down, also suffered antagonism at the sight of his uniform as he made his way painfully back to the Dunkirk perimeter. 'Where's your bloody aeroplane?' was a question he was asked many times. 'I had neither the time nor inclination to explain several times a day that my aircraft had been shot down and my two colleagues killed,' he recalled.

That the RAF lost the air war over Dunkirk and subsequently won the Battle of Britain was due to the miserliness of Air Marshal Sir Hugh Dowding, C-in-C of Fighter Command, with his warplanes, particularly Spitfires. Dowding argued relentlessly throughout May for the retention of a minimum fighter strength in Britain. On 15 May he warned the War Cabinet: 'If the present rate of wastage continues for another fortnight we shall not have a single Hurricane left in France or this country.' Next day he was hammering at the Air Ministry: 'If the Home Defence Force is drained away in desperate attempts to remedy the situation in France, defeat in France will involve the final, complete and irremediable defeat of this country.' His letter was laid before the Chiefs of Staff by his superior, Marshal of the Royal Air Force Sir Cyril Newall, with the supporting comment: 'I do not believe that to throw in a few more squadrons whose loss might vitally weaken the fighter line at home would make the difference between victory and defeat in France.' So Dowding won his private war – thus, as he said, 'converting a desperate into a serious situation'; but it had been a demanding time for this shy man nicknamed 'Stuffy', who later referred to 'the atmosphere of devastating strain when I was fighting the Germans and the French and the Cabinet and the Air Ministry and now and again the Navy for good measure'. He might also have mentioned the Army.

For the Dunkirk evacuation Dowding had some two hundred serviceable fighters to provide air cover for the beachhead. In order to prevent piecemeal destruction of small groups, the British fighter patrols were made larger and operated less frequently, thus risking empty skies over Dunkirk. The consequences of this policy were felt on 27 May and 1 June, the days when the Royal Navy and BEF suffered most heavily from the air. Larger patrols did not noticeably cut British losses, either. In five sorties between 24 and 28 May, 92 Squadron lost two pilots killed, three prisoners of war and one badly wounded. A E 'Titch' Havercroft, then a sergeant pilot with 92 Squadron, still feels his colleagues were lost to little purpose. 'How much better 92 might have done during the Battle of Britain had these men been available,' he said. 'All the efforts of Fighter Command could not have reversed the predicament of the BEF, nor could it have been expected to do so.'

In the nine days of Operation Dynamo the RAF lost 145 planes, 99 of them from Fighter Command. Of these, 42 were the treasured Spitfires. Afterwards, Churchill claimed the RAF had inflicted four-fold destruction on the Luftwaffe, but the true total of German losses in the same conflict was 132.

The fact that it was the RAF which suffered most over Dunkirk could be explained in part by the admission of many British soldiers and sailors that they blazed away at every plane they saw, whatever its markings – though, as Spitfires and Hurricanes attacked each other on more than one occasion, lack of skill at aircraft recognition was not confined to those at ground level. George Banham, a gunner on the Thames paddle wheeler *Golden Eagle*, said, 'Every time a Hurricane or Spitfire came low over the beach we opened fire because we had heard some had been captured by the Germans and were firing on the squaddies on the beach.' Even Admiral Wake-Walker admitted,

Our ships nearly always opened fire indiscriminately on low-flying fighters, though more often than not they were Spitfires. As this kept happening I hoisted 6 Flag – 'Cease fire' – and blew the siren to draw attention and try and stop the firing. In spite of this I can remember our own machine-gun aft in *Keith* firing away regardless of the 'cease fire' gong; once started firing they could hear nothing.

The signals sergeant Bill Brodie watched an anti-aircraft battery near the beach neatly shoot the nose, and then the tail, off a bomber. 'Congratulations were cut short when it was found to be an RAF Blenheim,' said Brodie, 'but as the artillery sergeant at the guns said, "He didn't oughter have been there."' Any pilot lucky enough to bale out also had to endure pot shots as he parachuted to earth or into the sea. One RAF flier drifted safely through such fire and when hauled aboard a ship told his rescuers, 'What bloody poor shots. No wonder we're losing the war.'

Such was the crisis of confidence between soldiers and airmen that on 1 June the CIGS, Dill, issued a confidential memo on the subject:

Many officers and men have come back from France with a strong feeling that had they only received a greater measure of close support from the RAF they could have achieved more and suffered less. This feeling in the circumstances is probably inevitable, but it would be grossly unfair to the RAF if it were translated into statements that the RAF had in any way failed the Army during the recent operations. The RAF have gone all out, and what their fighters have achieved has been limited only by distance and the numbers of aircraft available.

Important lessons have been learnt about the co-operation which the Army needs from aircraft and we shall profit by these lessons. Meanwhile, criticism of the RAF, in many cases based only on local knowledge, is not only unjust but also prejudicial to the interests of the Army. It is important that this criticism should be checked and you and all other officers should do all you can to check it. The less formally this is done the more effective it is likely to be.

To those who had been on the receiving end, such soothing words were of little use. Lieutenant Peter Hadley recalled: 'To lie helpless in a trench or ditch while enemy aircraft do what they like overhead is one of the most demoralizing ordeals that a soldier can face. "Where is our Air Force?" we asked ourselves all the time, with a savage fury.'

17

'Allez Bloody Vite'

We were beyond caring. Too tired, too hungry, too thirsty, too shattered, too frustrated. Call it what you will, we had had enough.

Laurie Whitmarsh, 91st Field Regiment

It is understandable that Captain William Tennant tended to regard every day he spent ashore in Dunkirk either as the final one on which evacuation would be possible or his last one as a free man. As early as 30 May he was signalling to Dover that Dunkirk would be untenable by the following morning. He told Wake-Walker on 1 June, 'Tomorrow we'll either be back in London, in a German prison or done for', and next morning he said to Tom Willy, who had been seconded – much against his will – to the naval rearguard as despatch rider, 'I don't think we are going to get away.' As Tennant wrote later, when safely delivered back to Britain, 'One was always expecting the Boche to arrive down the sands from La Panne with his MT. We had an awful scare one night when one of our own tracked vehicles came down the beach. We took this fellow for the advance guard of the German tanks we had expected for so long.' At least Tennant would have made a neatly turned out prisoner. With no change of collar from the one in which he had left his desk at the Admiralty, he decided to turn it inside out after three days and reflected, 'It looked quite smart.'

Every day the perimeter endured, every day Tennant remained a free man, the total of soldiers saved continued to soar. On both 29 and 30 May the number landed at British ports exceeded fifty thousand. On 31 May and 1 June it climbed beyond sixty thousand. As Churchill's instructions were implemented, the number of French taken off escalated dramatically. On 31 May 14,874 were put ashore in England. Next day it more than doubled, to 35,013, and thereafter Frenchmen predominated in the rescue ships – sometimes to the chagrin of naval personnel and volunteers who had made the hazardous Channel crossing in the expectation of lifting 'our boys' back home to Britain. They simply did not care about the French. G D Olivier, skipper of the motor yacht *Marsayru*, lifted more than four hundred Frenchmen from the beaches in three days. 'To our bitter disappointment we could find no British,' he reported. 'Others were luckier.' Lieutenant J N Wise RNVR filled the hold of his converted Dutch boat HMS *Pascholl* with French 'because not a Tommy was to be had'. Wise had expected to be able to cram five hundred soldiers into his vessel but managed no more than three hundred 'as the Frog insisted on embarking with his bed, kitchen range etc.'.

The slighting reference to 'Frogs' occurs frequently in reports on Operation Dynamo and the memoirs or diaries of BEF personnel. Lieutenant James Hill of the Royal Fusiliers complained that 'much to my fury the Frogs were looting everything and had pinched my washing kit'. Hill also considered French troops on the beach

a very serious problem as they were in no sort of order and merely jammed up the embarkation of our own troops. Although undoubtedly certain sections of the French Army must have put up a good show, the rabble we saw, who had thrown down their arms, was an absolute eye-opener and gave me little confidence in their fighting ability. The fault appeared to be entirely that they were badly led.

When Sub-Lieutenant Bill Hewett of the minesweeper HMS *Sutton* went ashore in the ship's whaler in search of soldiers to save, 'three tough-looking fellows came rushing towards me bellowing in what I presumed to be French, so I pulled out my revolver, waved it at them and told them to "*Allez* bloody *vite*", which fortunately they did'. Hewett was subsequently awarded the DSC for bravery in the evacuation, but won no medals for diplomacy on that particular occasion. Sub-Lieutenant A. Carew Hunt, in command of the Dutch eel boat *Johanna*, waded ashore in an attempt to persuade French troops to make their own way to his vessel moored a hundred yards offshore because of shallow water. 'I summoned my limited store of French and with cries of "*En avant mes héros*" and "*Courage mes enfants*" I tried to tempt them into the water.' When that failed he, too, brandished his revolver. After he had managed to get some aboard, Carew-Hunt reported, 'By far the worst experience of Dunkirk was being kissed on both cheeks by a large number of grateful *poilus*.'

Another RNVR Sub-Lieutenant, Michael Solomon, who acted as an interpreter on the East Mole, pointed out that when Frenchmen heard the word '*allez*' shouted at them 'they naturally considered this nothing more than an insult.' He also dismissed criticism of French conduct: 'On all occasions I came in contact with the French on the jetty and elsewhere their conduct was excellent. If anything their discipline was too good, as they did their best to embark as a complete regiment or unit, being most disappointed if they were forced to separate.' This tendency was noted in Ramsay's report on Dynamo: 'French troops were either demoralized and had to be controlled by force or were so rigidly bound by discipline and tradition that they would not embark, except by complete formation under their own officers.'

On occasion, this adherence to discipline was over-rigid. Lieutenant Commander H G Boys-Smith, attempting to load two motor launches, *Kestrel* and *Grouse*, failed to persuade any of the estimated two thousand French on his section of the beach to leave because their unit was not complete. Lieutenant Commander Charles Jerram was puzzled when his offer to move a French unit met with no response. 'They held a meeting, the outcome of which was a brief note saying that as they had eaten ten minutes previously they were unable to enter the water to come to my boat. Perhaps, on reflection, they did not want to leave their native soil.'

Lieutenant John Anderson, captain of the minesweeper *Duchess of Fife*, ran across a decided reluctance on the part of French soldiers to leave their own soil or, more accurately, their jetty when he moored alongside the East Mole.

The pier was stiff with French troops. They took my lines and then refused to come aboard. One of my men got one by the leg and hauled him down the brow but no others would follow. Accordingly I climbed the brow and harangued them in a strange language. As is my custom, I happened to be wearing a beret and at the sight of the familiar headgear some twenty-five of them followed me down the brow. Again there was a hold-up and, going on the bridge, I hailed to enquire if there was a British officer within hearing.

At the third hail a man forced himself to the rail and replied, 'Don't be so windy, what do you want?'

I replied, 'Damn you, sir, I am not windy or I would not be here. Are there any British troops on the quay?'

He replied that there were not, that these 'yellow bellies' would not board and that I might as well let go my ropes and clear.

Eventually Anderson found some British troops further up the Mole, loaded them and set off for Ramsgate with 550 men aboard.

French bitterness at their plight boiled over aboard *Royal Eagle*. 'I saw the French accusing some Belgians of letting the Germans through,' said Bill Richardson of the 36th Searchlight Unit which was helping to man the vessel. 'They started kicking and punching these Belgians, threatening to chuck them back in the water, so the British officers had to draw their revolvers and threaten to shoot them if they didn't stop.'

When his North African division reached the beaches, the French officer Denis Barlone learned that only 1250 of its original strength of 18,000 remained. They were embarked, without acrimony or reluctance, from the West Mole in the early hours of 31 May. Less than twenty-four hours later, via Dover and Plymouth, Barlone was on his way back to Cherbourg and the war, trans-shipped like so many of his countrymen.

Among the jetsam of the beaches were personal items and souvenirs which men had lugged to the water's edge, only to abandon when the time came to swim for it. The Sherwood Foresters major, Julian Wright, threw away his fleece-lined coat 'which I had stuck to like grim death all the time'. Some had to be parted forcibly from their treasures. S L Rhodda watched a row between one of his Signals officers and a naval beachmaster.

Our officer was a big bloke, so was his batman, who had full marching order on. On top of his pack was the officer's carry-all and in each hand he was carrying a big officer's valise. Talk about a donkey's load. A Navy officer wearing a battered blue raincoat ordered the batman to get rid of all the unnecessary kit. When the Signals officer stopped the batman, the naval officer tugged back one sleeve of his raincoat showing layered gold rings of rank on his uniform. Deflation of Signals officer. The dumping of his kit ensued. You must realize that whilst this was going on we were being bombed and shelled. As soon as the kit was dumped a nearby AA gun crew tore into it, exchanging their shirts for his clean ones and scoffing tins of food from the valises.

Soon afterwards, from his rescue ship, Rhodda saw the AA pit take a direct hit.

The medical officer Joe Patterson succeeded in slipping his dog Splinter aboard the destroyer *Intrepid* ('Very irregular,' he conceded) but many dogs had to be shot on the beaches or in Dunkirk when their new owners were refused permission to take them along. Some found this task too much, leaving the animals to roam the seafront, as did occasional French artillery men who lacked the resolve to kill the horses which had pulled their guns.

Having survived the shells on the beach at La Panne, Frank Farley opted to swim to rescue vessels offshore.

First, I was careful to transfer into my small pack a number of selectively looted items of gold and silver. Then, abandoning all else save identity discs and rifle, I stripped and took to the water. I pondered the weight of the small pack around my neck, perhaps three and a half pounds, and whether, after all, it was wise to attempt to swim with it. But greed prevailed.

Eventually his swim became a struggle against drowning, the pack was slipped off and allowed to sink and Farley was pulled into a whaler from the minesweeper *Halcyon*. He would, after all, be home for his twentieth birthday.

When the time came to swim for it, those who thought carefully about what was involved were the ones who survived. The Grenadier Guards warrant officer, Harold Foster, was heading along the beach towards Dunkirk ('though I didn't see much future there') when a ship lying about six hundred yards offshore sent over a loudhailer message that it would wait for those willing to try to swim.

I knew I could reach it if I kept my head. Dozens set out and many drowned because they underestimated the distance and attempted to carry too much. Taking off all my equipment and boots, I retained my steel hat and my pistol. I had learned that for a time at least my battledress would keep a certain amount of air inside, which would help. Thoughts of the Silver Medallion Life Saving tests I had passed while at the Army School of Physical Training passed through my mind and so I slowly swam out to the ship.

Foster made it. So did Rob Smith, a sergeant major in the RAOC, who had swum for England against France. Smith, a Yorkshireman from Pontefract, did the journey – a mile in his case – wearing shirt and trousers and had enough strength left at the end to appreciate that the vessel which pulled him from the sea was *Yorkshire Lass*.

To the RASC pals, Arnold Johnson and Arnold Foster, the embarkation at La Panne went smoothly. 'We saw no beachmaster or organization engaged in supervising embarkation but everybody played it by ear,' said Johnson. Steadily the queues dwindled until Johnson decided it was time to say goodbye to the beach. The two Arnolds removed their boots and hung them round their necks, then rolled up their trousers. Johnson recalled

Holding up the bottom of my greatcoat I waded out through the breaking surf with Arnold close behind. For a brief moment I was back in my childhood taking my first paddle in the sea. The sailors must have thought us a couple of calm ones after hauling troops aboard with their clothing needlessly saturated. The lifeboats had come in close so we only had to wade up to our knees before scrambling over the side. Like the beach behind us, the boat was almost empty and the sea was very calm. On the trip back to the ship [the destroyer *Greyhound*] I dried my feet and slipped on my socks and boots. To me, boarding *Greyhound* was the most hazardous part of the exercise. Weighed down with rifle on one shoulder, haversack on the other, gas mask strapped to my chest, a greatcoat and a waterproof cape, to ascend successfully a swinging rope ladder over the sea festooned like an over-decorated Christmas tree was nothing short of a miracle. This to me was the miracle of Dunkirk.

Those who insisted on wading or swimming any great distance with all their equipment (as many did) were soon in trouble. Joe Catt of the 5th Royal Sussex was perched on the gunwale of a rowing boat with his pals, the brothers Harry and Arthur Driver, when he heard an urgent croak from the water.

Looking round, we saw the top of a head, complete with side cap and RAOC badge and, believe it or not, the top flap of a large pack. We grabbed hold of him by the arms but we couldn't lift him as he was waterlogged. Arthur cut the straps of his webbing and managed to get him half aboard, the other half having to remain in the drink. No more room in the boat! After he had finished spluttering he rounded on the three of us in good old Army English, informing us that we would have to pay for his lost kit! I often wonder what happened to the twit.

Aboard *Royal Eagle* Bill Richardson helplessly watched a slow-motion horror as overburdened men disappeared trying to reach safety.

One of the great tragedies of Dunkirk was that the soldiers had been ordered to retain their arms. I saw lots of men drowned wearing overcoats and packs. They were wading out up to their necks with all this gear and carrying rifles over their heads. I screamed to them to chuck their overcoats away, to throw away their rifles, do anything, save themselves. I watched them pulled over backwards by the tide and drowned, lots and lots of them. What's an overcoat and a rifle? What was important was for them to get back – it was another soldier.

Richardson was a non-swimmer, so he determined that if *Royal Eagle* was sunk at Dunkirk he would shoot himself. 'I wanted it over quick.'

Don Ellingworth's skills as a motorcyclist did not extend to boat engines, as he discovered when he boarded a Broads cruiser abandoned on the beach. He and his companions managed to get the engine started but it cut out again about four miles offshore. Thinking it was out of petrol they poured in the contents of some cans, only to discover that they had refuelled the boat with drinking water. 'So we sat out there wallowing. In the distance we saw a little square on the horizon. We thought it was Jerry [this was 3 June and Ellingworth was among the last British to get away]. It turned out to be an infantry landing craft, the first I had ever seen, full of French soldiers. They offered to give us a tow.' The barge pulled them straight through a minefield and safely into Ramsgate.

The personnel ship *Killarney* collected an enterprising trio, one French and two Belgian soldiers, who had made their getaway in some style. Aboard their makeshift raft, constructed from an old door and pieces of wood, the men had stacked six demi-johns of wine and two tins of biscuits. Lieutenant Peter Hadley, in charge of a rowing boat in which nobody had the slightest idea how to row, stood in the centre shouting 'In, out – rather like John Snagge broadcasting a running commentary on the Boat Race'. David Strangeways, an officer in the Duke of Wellington's Regiment and a keen sailor, decided the best way off the beaches was self-help. When he spotted an empty Thames sailing barge offshore he swam out to it, followed by the men of his company. Steering a course by a school atlas he found aboard, Strangeways set off 'in the general direction of England'. When the barge came under air attack he sent all the others below and impersonated a fisherman. 'We were not hit and thereafter it was a pleasant sail and we all enjoyed ourselves.' Strangeways was particularly proud that, clad only in a bath mat while his uniform dried, he came alongside at Dover without even brushing the paintwork, though he had never before set foot on a Thames barge.

Out of the increasingly desperate situation on the beaches at La Panne and Bray-Dunes was conceived an idea which aided the escape of an estimated twenty-nine thousand troops. Although the weather was, for the most part, good and the seas calm, an occasional shift or increase in wind speed could rough up the water in minutes, causing boats working the beaches to broach and capsize. The problems of getting overloaded boats off the sand also contributed to a frustratingly slow rate of embarkation. What was needed was jetties where the boats could load rapidly from deep water. Since none existed on this bleak, exposed stretch of coast the answer was to build them and, if a pun can be permitted, the perfect vehicle was at hand in the cemeteries of abandoned lorries just off the beaches. Thus were born the lorry jetties. The credit for this improvised escape route goes to a military police lieutenant and former Scotland Yard detective, Harold Dibbens. On 30 May it proved such a winner that within twenty-four hours there were ten of these makeshift, but perfectly workable, piers in operation.

Henry Cornwell, one of a party of fifteen Royal Engineers from 250 Field Company, helped to construct the first lorry jetty out of abandoned three-ton trucks.

Some fifteen lorries were driven or manhandled through the soft sand and positioned – while the tide was out – nose to tail on the hard sand, thus enabling dinghies and other small craft to be loaded from either side. To anchor the jetty all tyres were punctured, generally by firing bullets through them, and when this was completed the backs of the lorries were filled with sand. The walkway was made up of decking panels and the gaps between the roofs were covered by planks 'borrowed' from a timber yard not far from the jetty site.

The engineers, under the command of Lieutenant John Bennett, a peacetime lecturer at Cambridge, and supervised by Dibbens's 102 Provost Company, had to stand at times, covered in oil and grease, linking arms to hold the jetty together until lashings could be fashioned to repair any breaks. So well did they do their job that, having been promised first use of the pier as a reward for their labours, they were ordered to stay behind on maintenance duty. Cornwell recalled:

No one envied us our job – if, in fact, any of the chaps who walked over the tops of the lorries ever thought about us – and it was no consolation to us to see other soldiers jumping into the small boats on their way home. We had a billet in the cellar of a building near the beach where we could get our heads down but with all the stuff that was being slung at us we felt, for some strange reason, safer in the open. Food and fresh water were almost non-existent, except that which was scrounged or confiscated by Lieutenant Bennett. Because of this we were not only hungry when we finished our stint, we felt half-starved and desperately tired when we were told to return to our hazardous, miserable and wet job.

Between us we covered about sixty hours of continuous duty – up to late Saturday, 1 June – when we were relieved by another team of sappers. At long last it was our turn to walk across the jetty and get ourselves ferried out to a paddle steamer, *Princess Elizabeth*. We were more jittery on the ship than the beach, probably a nervous reaction following so many days and nights of almost continuous air and land attacks.

Even those who made brief use of the jetties were required to help in their maintenance. When the time came for the 3rd Division Signals to go to the boats S L Rhodda recalled:

Someone handed each of us a sandbag with orders to fill it and we clambered into a truck driven into the sea. Ahead were more trucks, nose to tail, and tied along them a double line of planks and a rope handrail. Up on the planks and carrying a full sandbag we shuffled along. At the end was a naval petty officer who ordered us to throw the sandbags into the trucks to hold them down in the gently heaving sea. He was waving, of all things, a Thomson sub-machine gun of the kind so often seen in the 1930's gangster films and shouting, 'Anyone panicking gets this.' There were odd bodies around the lorry pier but I don't know if he was the culprit.

The lorry jetties were an idea which had come only just in time. By the evening of 31 May the beach at La Panne was under shellfire controlled by an observation balloon hovering over Nieuport and was becoming too dangerous to use. Lieutenant Commander J N McClelland, the naval beachmaster in that area, realized that by dawn the British withdrawal would have left La Panne in no man's land, so he urged commanders of formations falling back on to the beach and expecting evacuation from the jetties to take their troops westward to the marginally less dangerous area around Dunkirk. While doing so, McClelland reported, 'I was twice knocked down by HE bursts, one splinter smashing the box signalling lantern I was carrying and another slightly injuring my left ankle.'

McClelland limped off in the direction of Bray-Dunes, walking along the edge of the water to avoid the shelling as much as possible and shooing stray soldiers ahead of him. Eventually he made out the shape of three ships at anchor. Told that attempts to attract their attention had met with no success, the wounded McClelland swam out to the nearest, the minesweeper *Gossamer*, and urged the captain to warn Dover that the rescue should now be concentrated around Dunkirk. Then, this courageous man reported, 'Being very exhausted and unable to walk because of my left ankle, which had recovered from its numbness, I regret to state that I remained in *Gossamer* as I felt that I should be more of a hindrance than a help if I returned ashore.'

Those who could find transport for the trek west to Dunkirk were the fortunate few. For most it was an exhausting stumble along the sands, the final indignity in a bewildering three weeks. A natural instinct to quicken the pace when salvation lay in sight ('I could only just hobble by this time but two hundred yards from the Mole I took the lead in a final burst,' said Major Julian Wright) was boosted by actions such as that of Tennant's assistant, Commander Guy Maund, who positioned himself at the entrance to the Mole on the night of 30 May with a loud-hailer and told the troops: 'Remember your pals,

boys. The quicker you get on board the more of them will be saved.'
Thus cajoled and encouraged, they doubled along the walkway to the
waiting ships, the atmosphere of cinema and bus queues abandoned
at the very last.

After immobilizing their trucks in Furnes, Tom Bristow and his
companions had set off for the beach at La Panne in high spirits. 'It
was no more than a mile and a half, just half an hour's walk, then we'd
get on a boat and by the time the sun was shining brightly we should
be having the sleep of our lives in England.' But they arrived to find
the beach empty, and were told evacuation had ceased and that they
should make their way to Dunkirk as best they could. While searching
for a serviceable lorry among the litter of abandoned vehicles they
came across a dead horse lying on its back, legs in the air. 'Some
French soldiers came along and one produced a knife, carved a slice of
meat from the horse's rump and began to eat the steak held in his
hand. It almost made me retch,' said Bristow. They managed to get a
lift in a lorry until it was halted by military police and they were
ordered to walk the remaining seven miles into Dunkirk.

We slouched off to the beach and began mooching along the sandy shore,
but the tired men trudging along in twos or threes or individually did not
please the sergeant-major and he ordered 'Fall in.' Having got us into two
lines he gave the order 'Quick March.' How ludicrous: most were at the
limit of their endurance. Marching on sand added to the effort needed
and the very thought of seven miles took all the heart from them. . . .

Further progress was made in a sort of trance. The dead soldiers lying
about were ignored, but for a short time I was fascinated by the bodies at
the water's edge which were doing a macabre dance, the gentle incoming
wave floating them in and when the wave receded the bodies left high
and dry rolled back down the sand into the water, where they were lifted
and deposited once more up on the sand. At first I thought they were
French colonial troops, their faces a dirty greyish brown colour, and many
of them quite bloated. It was some time before I realized they were our
own men who had died by drowning. It was a grisly sight but we had seen
so much dead and mutilated human flesh in the last twenty days that,
except for a slight shudder, we were unaffected.

The sea was covered with twenty-packets of Player's cigarettes still in
their cellophane wrapping, but nobody was interested enough to get a
packet and see if the contents were dry.

None of us had any idea how far we had walked in our meanderings,
and it was the sound of gunfire that made us look up. The leading
elements of our group were over half a mile in front and were passing
some seaside resort, decked out with the usual holiday attractions but not
having any crowds to enjoy them. It reminded me of a cowboy film I had

seen in which there was a town that had died when the gold in the nearby hills had been exhausted. On one of the amusements we read 'MALO-LES-BAINS'.

Stepping out a bit livelier we set our goal on joining the rest. Up front we could see the East Mole and two ships lying against the other side of it, and this gave us renewed strength. Soon the ordeal would be over.

The signaller Lawrence Vollans, still lugging the 36lb weight of a Boyes anti-tank rifle, recalled those last exhausting miles. 'Somehow we kept going over the soft sand; kept going when our legs felt like lead and our shoulders ached and bodies and minds were numb.' At last Vollans made his way along the Mole and was directed on to the Channel steamer *St Helier*. On the stern deck a seaman was helping the troops aboard. 'When it came to my turn I handed him the anti-tank rifle first. ''What's this?' he asked, grasping it by the barrel. ''It's a Boyes anti-tank rifle,'' I replied. ''You won't be needing that any more,'' he said, and promptly dropped it into the sea.'

18

'Is Anyone There?'

Those Frenchmen were fine fellows; they deliberately stayed behind while the rest of the BEF got out.

Sub-Lieutenant Bill Hewett, HMS *Sutton*

Churchill's promises notwithstanding, it was the French who bore the brunt of the fighting round Dunkirk in the final forty-eight hours. As Hitler's Chief of Staff, Keitel, pointed out, the British were able to embark the whole of what remained of their expeditionary force 'thanks largely to the gallant stand made by the French who fought us to the finish there'.

On the night of 1 June what was left of the British rearguard withdrew behind shorter lines prepared and manned by French troops. 'We did not altogether like the sound of that,' admitted an officer in the 5th Green Howards. 'Yet they were first-class troops as it turned out. They held the fort, as did all the French throughout those final days. We said a good deal and thought a lot more about the behaviour of some French at Dunkirk harbour but they, in the last resort, made our getaway possible.'

The intention had been that the British should be pulled out on that night, and indeed many did get away among the contingents of French who now dominated the evacuation. However, by the morning of 2 June it was evident that the ships would have to come over again to take off more of both nationalities. At the edge of town that day was established a token British perimeter of some two dozen anti-aircraft and anti-tank guns; but the main line, three miles further inland, was defended doggedly by the French who surprised, and drove back, the occasional German penetration, permitting Alexander to report that, apart from the shelling and bombing, 'the British troops were not interfered with'.

Alexander, dispelling gloom, exuding confidence, showing he was

219

at one with his men by munching an apple as he made his round, yet quick to snap off a return salute to anyone alert enough to offer him one, was (as Montgomery had forecast) the ideal commander for such desperate circumstances. When he toured the perimeter by car under shellfire, Alexander admonished his driver, Corporal Wells, for going too fast, telling him, 'They'll get you, Wells, whether you drive fast or slow. Better not add another hazard.'

Inside the battered town in the last few days there was still a surprising amount of life. Having failed to get aboard the last boat of that night, Alan Bell Macdonald – 'weary, utterly hungry and scared' – determined to find a bed in Dunkirk. He was lucky enough to be offered one, albeit above ground in the area under shellfire. He recalled:

Slept soundly till six, only two hours but enough. I felt refreshed and walked downstairs to find an officers' mess in progress, a French one. I added myself quietly to it and had hot coffee and a good breakfast. Then, glory of glories, I got a can of hot water to shave in and clean my teeth, that put me right back to normal. I went down to the beach and found the rest, who immediately demanded to know where I'd been and how I was shaved.

There were also evident in Dunkirk soldiers of both nationalities who had given up the ghost and taken to the bottle. Anthony Rhodes came across two British who pointed out where there was lots of 'wonderful champagne' as they stood swaying and hiccuping, while Julian Wright saw French soldiers 'helping themselves to anything they could lay hands on, but chiefly wine'. Rhodes spent one night in the crowded and smelly cellar ('that musty, military smell, so much part of an army') of a house that had clearly belonged to a well-to-do citizen of Dunkirk. 'Its foie gras and champagne formed our staple food and drink. We did our best to dissuade the men from drinking too much champagne but our entreaties had little effect; the cat-calls and babbling of the drunkards soon formed a curious and rather sinister accompaniment to the shrieks, whistles and bangs that went on outside.'

Such unreality was not confined to cellars. When Second Lieutenant Toby Taylor arrived in Dunkirk with the collection of 'odds and sods' from the 1st East Surreys entrusted into his care he was told to go to the beach near the entrance to the Mole and await instructions.

As we had nothing to occupy our time I sent for some rather attractive deck chairs piled against the sea wall. With these we made a large circle in the sand and sat in comfort in the warm sunshine as though it was

Brighton or Margate at holiday time, although the billowing oily smoke still filling the sky, burning houses and dead French soldiers soon made us forget all thoughts of sunny days on an English beach. Would we ever see home again?

On the promenade some soldiers were enjoying themselves in brightly coloured pedal cars which they must have found in a funfair. In and out of the wrecked vehicles they pedalled, racing each other as best they could. The British soldier can always make light of his difficulties and a bit of relaxation certainly did not come amiss.

Private Pettit, getting bored, left his deck chair to go in search of food but he returned shortly afterwards with the news that our abandoned battalion transport was parked not far away and was there anything I wanted? I told him to collect my pre-war service dress, cap and Sam Browne belt. He was soon back, also bringing for some reason my portable gramophone. I stripped off my filthy, stained battledress, threw away my steel helmet and put on the correct uniform for an occasion such as this. Adjusting my sling I settled back into my deck chair.

My shoulder was by now quite sore so I thought I would also wander off to see if I could find a Field Dressing Station anywhere. I could not, but in one of the main streets I found a sweet shop, of all things, open and bought several bars of that rather nice French milk chocolate – the kind that is wrapped in pale blue paper. The shopkeeper was quite happy to do business, which was a godsend because we were all now rather hungry. On the way back I noticed a barber's shop, and stepping over the rubble went in and asked in my best French for a haircut. This did not seem to take the barber aback and he was quite happy to be of service to a now smartly dressed English officer. As I sat down in the chair I saw my face in his mirror. It was the first time I had looked at it for some weeks. It was dirty, streaked with sweat and lined like that of an old man – and I was only twenty-two.

Arriving back at the deck chairs I distributed the chocolate, but the men were now getting a bit fed up. No orders had arrived, so could they dump their rifles? No. Could they go and try to scrounge some food? No. Could Private Kelly now throw away the heavy Boyes anti-tank rifle? No. We were still part of the regiment and we did not abandon our weapons unless correctly ordered to do so.

In the evening an RAMC officer came running up to us and asked who we were. On being told, he explained that he was to collect all the walking wounded he could find. At last I had received an order – and had a shrapnel wound to go with it. He told me there was a hospital ship (*St Andrew*) just about to leave. We did not need a second asking, so I handed over to the senior unwounded NCO and those of us who could ran with the doctor towards the Mole. I was soon way behind and as it was now quite dark, getting a bit lost.

Eventually I reached the beginning of the Mole and could see at the far end the gleaming and brilliantly lit hospital ship. The whole length of the

Mole seemed entirely blocked with wreckage, tangled wire and other debris. There were more dead French soldiers and, strangely enough, dead mules. It was an obstacle race made more difficult with one arm in a sling.

When I was about fifty yards away from the ship I could see that it was no longer moored: it was already *en route* to the UK! I now forgot the obstacles and entanglements blocking my way. Soon I could see that the *St Andrew* was about six feet clear, all ropes cast off and the engines churning up water. I noticed a sailor by the rail, presumably watching to see if everything was clear. Seeing me he shouted 'Jump', and jump I did. I caught the rail with my good hand, hung for a moment, then with a heave he pulled me over the rail and on to the deck. A few more seconds and that jump would not have been possible. I would either have been in the sea or helplessly watching the ship steam away.

This good sailor took me to a stairway leading down to one of the wards and the sight I now saw before me was quite incredible. If I had just left outside an accurate representation of hell, then this was certainly heaven – a clean, bright, shining hospital ward, with immaculate nurses in starched uniforms standing by neat beds with white linen sheets. Calm efficiency now took over and soon I was between those clean white sheets and in a deep sleep.

Taylor's fond memories of finally getting onto a ship are shared by many. Julian Wright recalled how, on boarding the *Malines*, 'I went down below into the saloon and there discovered my officers drinking beer. I joined them and the great war outside was soon forgotten. In fact we all felt perfectly safe with a roof over our heads.'

Brigadier George Sutton's joy at getting aboard another former ferry, the *Canterbury*, and finding food for sale was tempered when he had to lend English money to colleagues as the ship's stewards would not accept French currency. 'I thought this refusal the final stupidity.'

Aboard the minesweeper *Glen Gower* an officer noted that, with BEF officers' uniforms being dried in the engine room, 'the wardroom presented the appearance of a Roman feast, with military officers garbed in togas from the curtains and girded with an under-garment of blanket round the waist'. The Rev. Ted Brabyn's diary registered the following warm reception aboard the destroyer *Malcolm*.

Greeted kindly, self sent to the captain's cabin and men to the crew's quarters, washed, changed (I'd hung on grimly to my pack which contained a clean change, though rather damp), ate some egg sandwiches and drank a glass of whisky and soda so kindly brought to me at the captain's orders. . . . Never was a prayer more heartfelt than the one 'Thank God we've got a Navy.'

Once in the hands of the Navy, many simply did not want to know about further involvement. The bombardier Eric Manley noted of his rescue ship, 'The wounded seem to need constant attention but few of us have the spirit to pay them much heed.' Tom Bristow was among the hundreds crowded below decks on the destroyer *Harvester* when a hatch was opened.

'Anyone down there know how to use a Bren gun?' asked the face. No one would admit ever having seen one. He asked again but got no volunteer. 'All right,' he shouted angrily, 'If any of you remember what a Bren gun is, come up on deck.' There must have been over a thousand men below – how could it be possible that not one of them knew how to use a Bren? And yet it could be. I drove a Bren carrying-truck but had never handled the weapon, and no one had bothered to show me how to load it.

Because of the state of the ships which collected them, others had no choice but to become involved in the dramas of the voyage home. As their paddle steamer limped into Ramsgate, Joe Catt and others were all asked to gather on one side of the deck to help tilt the ship over. When he disembarked, Catt saw why. 'There was this flaming great hole near the waterline on the other side. We heard he had done several journeys like that.'

After several hours spent ferrying people from a lorry jetty, culminating in a capsize, a soaked Frank Southall thought his problems were over when he was loaded on to the destroyer *Ivanhoe*.

I was given hot cocoa with rum and went sound asleep. I woke up once, heard the engines throbbing and thought, 'At last, we're bound for Blighty.' In the twenty-one days we had been on the run I worked out I only had a total of twenty-four hours' sleep until this night.

At eight next morning, 1 June, Southall awoke. He was now dry and the ship was stationary – in England he thought. 'I went on deck and to my dismay we were anchored off Dunkirk.'

Ivanhoe was so badly damaged in the savage air assaults of that morning that the order was given to abandon ship. Southall was put in charge of thirty-two soldiers who were left behind in the confusion, and they were set to work with the few sailors remaining on board to try to get the destroyer back to England under tow by the tug *Persia*. 'The method of steering the destroyer was by verbal instruction from the captain on the bridge, relayed by sailors at strategic points until the order reached the sailors who were manually operating the gear working the rudder,' said Southall. 'It was a truly remarkable performance.'

The soldiers' job was to stretch a watertight skin over a hole at the waterline and keep it in position during the cross-Channel trip, on which the tow rope broke three times and *Ivanhoe* again came under air attack. As the ship was still taking in water, lifejackets were issued and the situation became so critical, said Southall, 'that eventually we were all told to leave the skin and move as far astern as possible to try and lift the bows out of the water'. *Ivanhoe* made it back to England – just.

Making it back to England was something few of the BEF doubted once they had got as far as the beaches or the Mole. But the driver Bill Edwards, an optimist who had taken shelter behind a plywood tea chest during an air attack on the beaches, narrowly escaped becoming a casualty through the carelessness of a fellow soldier as he prepared to embark. 'The Essex Regiment were passing through in front of us and one of them fired his rifle by mistake. The bullet hit the ground in front of me, struck the man next to me in the stomach, went through the arm of another and then hit a third man. It was terrible to see that sort of thing happen right beside you at that point.'

The First World War veteran, Colonel Lionel Westropp, having managed to get his ill-trained Territorials of the King's Own Rifle Regiment as far as the beach, also faced unexpected and unnecessary danger as he rested in celebration of his achievement.

A soldier was playing about with a French hand grenade. He was standing just in front of us and the maddening imbecile had thrown it along the sand, run after it, thrown it into the sea and retrieved it. This was piling on the agony with a vengeance. On top of all the dangers from the enemy we were now likely to be blown up by one of our own side.

I shouted at him to put it down quietly before it went off. He replied that he did not see why he should! The sight of him standing there without arms and equipment, together with his insolent reply and the idiocy of his conduct was, although he did not know it, about to release the frustration, nay fury, which had been mounting since the battalion was formed in such a wretched manner – and not only since then, but since before the war because of the antics of the British people.

No doubt to his extreme surprise, I arose and seized the creature by his coat collar and shook him as a dog shakes a rat, until his teeth rattled and his coat burst at the seams. I then picked him up and hurled him away from me on to the sand, following his departure with a notable kick to the bottom. I then told two NCOs to chase him out of my sight before I put a bullet into him, which they did with pleasure and alacrity. Of course, to strike or shake a private is a court-martial offence, but at that time and place I do not suppose I even thought of it and, if I did, I did not care. I sat down feeling mentally much restored and in better humour.

Despite the circumstances there was humour available at the Chapeau Rouge, the rambling Victorian house in the Dunkirk suburb of Rosendaele which had been converted for hospital use by the 12th Casualty Clearing Station of the RAMC, who set themselves up there on 25 May. Three days later the orderlies and doctors were warned they would probably all be taken prisoner the next day. 'Next morning nobody had turned up to capture us, so we carried on,' said one of the male nurses, Len Wilson.

The wounded continued to pour in, until at one stage there were more than eight hundred. They overflowed into the extensive grounds of the Chapeau Rouge, where the departed owner's valet and his wife made a huge Red Cross flag which was laid on the lawn. It was struck squarely the next day by a bomb or shell.

Shifting those of the wounded who were considered well enough to risk the journey was a problem, since many of the ambulance drivers simply boarded the rescue ships with their passengers. Len Wilson recalled, 'Ambulancemen who had done one run to the beach or the Mole with wounded were given rum if they returned. It was to give them courage and the incentive to go back on another run.'

By 1 June, with the number of regular drivers down to two and the evacuation due to close down, the decision was taken to transfer that night all the remaining wounded who could safely be moved, together with nursing staff and doctors. Since there were some three hundred too ill to go, staff had to be provided to care for them in the ratio of one doctor per hundred patients and one orderly for every ten wounded. So a draw was organized, with all names going into a steel helmet. The agreement was that the first names out of the hat would be the first to leave. Wilson remembered: 'As the first name came out a bomb landed alongside the hospital and knocked us all over the place. When we got up again somebody said, "What was that first name again?" It was Wilson, me.'

Major Philip Newman, the chief surgeon, suffered exactly the opposite luck. His name was the last to be drawn of the seventeen doctors. The Catholic padre at the hospital, Father Cockie O'Shea, gave Newman his crucifix and told him, 'This will see you home.' Newman then prepared himself for what was to come by seeking out a wounded German airman in the hospital and learning a few useful phrases with which to greet his captors, such as 'Red Cross' and 'Don't shoot.'

On 2 June there was an unexpected reprieve for more of the wounded at the Chapeau Rouge. An RAMC major managed to get hold of three lorries, and those who had been left behind in the clearance of the previous day were told that, if they could get themselves into the vehicles, they might get away that night after all since the close-down of Dynamo had been extended for twenty-four hours. At dusk the hospital's semi-ambulant made for the lorries with all manner of improvised devices. One man had even constructed a pair of uneven crutches out of a coal hammer and garden rake. Altogether another hundred managed to board the trucks, get down to the Mole and on to a destroyer, *Sabre*, whose captain, Commander Brian Dean, reported: 'Most of them collapsed on arrival on board and over fifty had to be hoisted out on stretchers at Dover. Their courage was magnificent and I never heard a complaint or hardly ever a groan.'

Lieutenant James Langley, whose arm was shattered too badly for him to leave, did not like the heat or the smell inside the hospital, so he asked to be moved outside to await the arrival of the enemy on 3 June. Their proximity was announced by a salvo of shells which fell on the lawn and deposited the main doors of the hospital at the foot of Langley's stretcher without harming him. Next morning an orderly told Langley the Germans were at the gate, so the wounded Guards officer had his stretcher carried down the driveway to meet them, remembering at the last moment to push the booklet he had been reading, *Fifty Filthy Facts About Hitler*, down his pyjama leg.

'If we were exhausted, so were the Germans,' wrote Langley of his capture. 'The small section which wended its way up the drive was reeling with fatigue. Caked with dust, two of them sank to the ground as they halted by the stretcher.' Langley requested water and a cigarette and was given both. When he asked the section leader what he wanted in return, the German soldier said 'Marmalade'. At that moment Langley knew he was safe from execution.

Les Shorrock, wounded in the back on the beach, was carried into the nearby sanatorium at Zuydcoote to await treatment.

The whole floor was covered by wounded men on stretchers. I was placed face down on a stretcher to await my turn to be taken into the operating room, which was a makeshift one. I thought to myself that if there was ever a hell on earth I had probably found it. I saw two elderly Sisters of Mercy hurrying about the room comforting the wounded, and one had tears streaming down her face. I felt so sorry for her that she should have to endure this horror also.

As I tried to swivel my head round to see the whole of the room I saw a French priest, dressed in full religious clothes with a purple sash around his neck and a crucifix suspended also. He was, I thought, a Roman Catholic father. I am, of course, C of E. He was very calm. He approached many stretchers and made the sign of the cross over those lying on them. I became apprehensive as he worked his way towards me. Straining my neck until it ached I saw the slow, deliberate sign of the cross placed over me, from the shadow afforded by the light. I called out, 'No, no, not me, not me.'

The priest moved to the front of my stretcher, smiled, not understanding my outburst, patted my head gently and moved on. He must know, I thought, he can perhaps see the state of my wound. . . . So this was it. After all this.

Shorrock passed out, came to briefly as he was being lifted on to the operating table and awoke fully in bed – to find, to his pain, that he had been deposited on his wounded back. Shorrock survived that mistake, and also escaped shelling of the sanatorium which destroyed the neighbouring ward. Then came quiet. 'It could mean only one thing – that it was all over. I looked out of the window and saw, with very mixed feelings, a middle-aged German soldier slowly riding along on a bicycle. I knew we were now prisoners of war.'

The hospital ships *Worthing* and *Paris* were despatched on 2 June in a bid to collect Dunkirk's remaining wounded, and a message was broadcast in clear announcing their planned departure. *Worthing* was attacked by a dozen planes and turned back; *Paris*, badly damaged by shelling and engines out of commission, sank ten miles off the French coast. At five that Sunday afternoon the all-out effort began for what was planned to be the final lift of troops that night. The rescue armada comprised thirteen personnel vessels, eleven destroyers, fourteen minesweepers, nine drifters and a large number of tugs towing small boats.

A couple of hours earlier Tennant had reported from Dunkirk: 'French still maintain front line. . . . In port no movement. Present situation hopeful.' So hopeful, in fact, that Tennant decided he would, after all, see England again. He sent out the despatch rider Tom Willy to summon the remaining British officers on inner perimeter duty to a meeting to announce withdrawal that night. So, for the last time, Willy had to run the gauntlet of the gates leading from Bastion 32.

I used to dread it. There was a great big French *matelot* on guard there with a .45 revolver, drunk as a saint. He used to stop me every time and poke this thing into my chest, cocked, and ask for my identification. That man frightened the life out of me.

That evening we collected as many walking wounded as we could, plus half a dozen blinded men, and marched down this road to the Mole. It was like a Sunday afternoon stroll down to Southend pier, simple as that.

The destroyer *Sabre* came alongside and we jumped aboard. I was surprised to see one or two people throwing their rifles into the water. I could never understand that. I kept all my gear.

At 10.50 p.m. Tennant loaded the last of his naval party on to a motor torpedo boat, and before leaving radioed Ramsay: 'Operation complete. Returning to Dover', a message which was subsequently shortened for posterity by some gifted report-compiler to 'BEF evacuated,' one of the most triumphant messages in Royal Navy history.

At about the same time Alexander prepared to take his leave, too. While the destroyer *Venomous*, loading troops at the Mole, was ordered to wait for the British commander, Alexander toured the darkened beaches in a motor boat with a megaphone enquiring, rather like Madame Arcati in *Blithe Spirit*, 'Is anyone there?' Though the question was posed in English and French there was no reply. There were, in fact, thousands of French troops 'there'. There was one German, too: First Lieutenant von Oelhaven, a Luftwaffe squadron commander whose Junkers 88 had been shot down by Spitfires. The captured pilot was being led off the beach on a lorry jetty when, in the confusion of an air raid, he leapt into the water and hid under one of the trucks for thirty-six agonizing hours until friendly German faces appeared.

Faces friendly to the other side were notable by their absence that night on the Mole, and soon after midnight a frustrated Wake-Walker signalled to Dover, 'Plenty of ships, cannot get troops.' It was, he felt,

a most disappointing night; for some reason the flow of French troops stopped for some hours. One report said they were held up to make a counter-attack, but to us there with ships waiting to be filled and no one appearing it was most exasperating. Even when the French did come it was almost impossible to get them to the ships at the end of the pier. They all wanted to get into the first one they came to, and the pier was so narrow that they then blocked the way to any ship beyond. One ship lay three and a half hours at the end berth waiting for men. I had to send back empty two personnel ships, three destroyers and several fleet sweepers.

Aboard the destroyer *Codrington*, Able Seaman Dave Holder was peering down the Mole.

It was all silent and eerie after the noise we had experienced, nothing moving. Suddenly this little squaddie, about five foot tall, came running down the jetty, jumping over the holes and with rifle and bayonet at the high port. Pointing his rifle at us, he asked in broad Scots, 'German or British?' When we assured him we were British he gave a wave back along the jetty and two or three hundred other Scottish soldiers came running.

When the Thames paddle wheeler *Golden Eagle* came alongside the Mole at 2.40 a.m. only one soldier, a French colonial, could be persuaded to go aboard. 'On our way home we opened a tin of bacon for him and cooked it with beans but he wouldn't have any,' said George Banham. 'When we insisted, he produced his paybook showing his religion which considered pork taboo.'

The Navy had expected to lift more than forty thousand on the night of 2–3 June. Instead, the total was well below thirty thousand, and this night of setbacks concluded on a further sour note when one of the blockships taken to Dunkirk to be scuttléd in the harbour entrance was swung around by the tide as she was blown up and failed to achieve the purpose intended.

There was relief and satisfaction, as the ships headed home in the early light of 3 June, that the job was at last over. However, the French government and Army did not consider the task completed, and in a strongly worded protest to London said their rearguard deserved to be rescued. Churchill agreed, and sent a message to Reynaud and Weygand: 'We are coming back for your men tonight. Please ensure that all facilities are used promptly. For three hours last night many ships waited idly at great risk and danger.'

The order to send his ships in once more was complied with reluctantly by Ramsay. At 10 a.m. on 3 June he signalled to his Dynamo command:

I hoped and believed that last night would see us through but the French who were covering the retirement of the British rearguard had to repel a strong German attack and so were unable to send their troops to the pier in time to be embarked. We cannot leave our Allies in the lurch and I call on all officers and men detailed for further evacuation tonight to let the world see that we never let down our Ally.

Wake-Walker received the news in Ramsay's office with the promise that this really would be the end. 'Each night had been thought to be the last, and then each day the ships had been asked for one more effort. By this time many of the commanding officers and men were at the limit of their endurance.'

Ramsay did not feel he could order ships to make even one more run, and told the Admiralty as much. So a signal was made asking who would be prepared to go. A heartening number said yes – ten transports, six destroyers, eight minesweepers, four paddle steamers, two corvettes, ten drifters and, as ever, a host of small craft anxious to help. The destroyer *Malcolm* had been planning a celebration party that night. Instead, the officers set off on their eighth trip to Dunkirk wearing dinner jackets and bow ties. They were in cheerful mood, too, aboard another destroyer, *Whitshed*. The ship's harmonica band was playing as the ship set sail at 7 p.m. They were accompanied, in a motor torpedo boat flying an admiral's flag made from striped dish-cloths, by the unflagging Wake-Walker, who had lost half a stone in weight over the previous week.

This time there were plenty of troops to be lifted – almost 28,000. By the time the destroyers *Express* and *Shikari* cast off soon after 3 a.m. on 4 June, the last British warships to leave Dunkirk, the sound of German machine guns could clearly be heard in the streets of the town.

The light was growing and the harbour was empty, save for two more blockships brought over in an attempt (again not wholly suc-cessful) to complete the job unfinished the previous night, as Wake-Walker took one last look round before speeding back to Dover. On the passage it was foggy, but by now they knew the way.

Lieutenant John Cameron, commander of *MTB 107*, the torpedo boat which had escorted the blockships from England, toured the harbour for a final time at dawn; his was the last British vessel to leave. 'The whole scene was filled with a sense of finality and death,' he said. 'The curtain was ringing down on a great tragedy.'

19

The Last Act

We went back to Dunkirk one summer and were asked by a bunch of young Germans why we were celebrating. 'It was a bad defeat for you, wasn't it?' they said. I told 'em we're the only bastards who can turn defeat into a victory.

Harry Dennis, East Surrey Regiment

Soon after first light on Tuesday, 4 June all resistance in Dunkirk ceased, most of the French rearguard being out of ammunition by now in any case. General Beaufrère, the senior officer remaining in the town, made his way to the battered town hall, where he donned his gold-leafed *képi* to lend a little dignity to the ceremony in which he surrendered some forty thousand troops, the overwhelming majority of them his own countrymen.

The BEF lost in France 68,111 men killed, wounded, missing or taken prisoner, a total which included some eight thousand men of the 51st Highland Division which had been doing a stint in the Maginot Line when the Germans struck. Cut off from the main BEF force by the Panzer thrust, the 51st was eventually committed to the Allied forces defending the line of the Somme against the southward assault towards Paris. Trapped with its back to the sea just west of Dieppe by another of Rommel's lightning Panzer surges, and waiting in vain for ships to provide a lift from the small harbour of St Valéry-en-Caux, the bulk of this Scottish division was forced to surrender on 12 June.

The British loss of equipment in the Flanders campaign was all but total: 63,879 vehicles, 2472 guns, 76,000 tons of ammunition and almost half a million tons of stores and supplies. However, there remained approximately one hundred thousand British soldiers, mainly base and organizational personnel, in the large part of France free of the enemy after Dunkirk's fall, and despite a daily worsening of the situation (the Germans got across the River Somme on 9 June, Italy came into the war on Germany's side on 10 June) Churchill determined to rebuild the BEF for the ongoing struggle in France. The newly knighted Lieutenant General Sir Alan Brooke was appointed commander and as early as 7 June another Scottish division, the 52nd Lowland, began to arrive in Cherbourg, due to be followed by the 1st Canadian and 3rd British divisions.

But the house of cards was collapsing. On 10 June the French government fled Paris and set up in Tours. Churchill flew to France on 11 June to urge on Reynaud a house-by-house defence of their capital. It was too late. That same night Weygand declared Paris an open city, and its abandonment shattered what little French morale remained. As German troops marched unopposed into Paris on the morning of 14 June (and the French government relocated again, this time to Bordeaux) Brooke was meeting Weygand at his new military headquarters in Briare, on the upper reaches of the Loire. The French commander, wizened, tired and now looking his age, told Brooke that 'the French Army had ceased to be able to offer organized resistance and was disintegrating'.

Brooke contacted Dill at once and, to his relief, was told to evacuate, though that evening he had to resist, successfully, a demand from Churchill that the newly arrived 52nd Division should remain in France as a token of British support. The Canadians, who had just disembarked, were turned round and shipped out again from Brest, while the 52nd Division went home from Cherbourg, together with the base organizations which totalled 65,000 at Nantes, 20,000 at Rennes and 7000 at Le Mans.

The evacuations from Cherbourg, St Malo and Brest were achieved without loss but there remained one final, horrendous blow to be suffered by the BEF. On 17 June the 20,000-ton Cunard liner *Lancastria* lay off St Nazaire taking aboard some nine thousand British servicemen, including RAF and naval personnel. While awaiting orders to sail the liner was struck by a single bomb and sank in twenty minutes, with the loss of more than half those in her. That one bomb caused the death of more than twice the estimated two thousand victims of all the Luftwaffe attacks on shipping off Dunkirk.

When he received the grim news Churchill forbade its publication, saying, 'The newspapers have got quite enough disaster for today at least.' Churchill admitted in his post-war memoirs, 'I had intended to release the news a few days later but events crowded upon us so black and so quickly that I forgot to lift the ban, and it was some time before the knowledge of the horror became public.'

The end was imminent for France. As the German Army occupied Paris Reynaud sent an urgent appeal to President Franklin Roosevelt that, unless the United States would agree to enter the war, his own country would very shortly be out of it. Apart from the fact that he was facing a presidential election in less than five months no politician, not even one as favourably inclined towards the Allied cause as Roosevelt, could have dragged America into the war in June 1940. Having staked everything on his telegram to the American President, Reynaud resigned when his plea was rejected on 16 June and proposed that his deputy, Marshal Pétain, replace him.

The eighty-four-year-old Pétain, who was described by De Gaulle as suffering from 'senility, pessimism and ambition, a fatal combination', wasted no time either accepting power or seeking an armistice, a move which was greeted with widespread relief in France. In the early hours of 21 June the French delegation, led by General Charles Huntziger, arrived in Paris without any knowledge of where the armistice was to be signed. They were driven fifty miles north to Compiègne, where in November 1918 the defeated Germans had formally surrendered.

The shocked French were now required by Hitler to suffer maximum humiliation for that ceremony years ealier. The same railway coach in which the First World War peace treaty had been signed was wheeled out of a nearby museum for the occasion, with the triumphant Hitler watching. The agreement was finally signed the following evening, 22 June, with the ceasefire to take effect at 1.30 a.m. on 25 June. Hitler's Chief of Staff, Keitel, who supervised the signing, reported that it was followed by a brief celebration in the dining room of the Führer's headquarters, where a military tattoo was succeeded by the hymn 'Now Thank We All Our God'.

At the moment the ceasefire came into force the Maginot Line still stood unconquered. Colonel Schwartz, commander of the Hagenau fortified sector, complained, 'We still dispose of sufficient means to sustain a siege of several weeks, the enemy not having succeeded at any point in breaking the defensive system. We are laying down our arms solely on the order of the French High Command.'

When the war began Hitler had expected the cost of France's overthrow would be a million German lives. In six weeks the task had been accomplished at a loss of 27,074 dead, 18,384 missing and 111,034 wounded, an overall total not much more than a third of Germany's casualties in one battle, Verdun, in the First World War.

Because of confusion and the speed of collapse, no precise figures were ever produced for French losses. They were estimated at 90,000 dead, 200,000 wounded and 1,900,000 prisoners. In addition Belgium suffered 23,350 casualties and Holland 9779.

Between 10 May and the fall of France the RAF lost 959 aircraft. Of these, 453 were fighters (386 Hurricanes, 67 Spitfires). Many Hurricanes were destroyed when they were caught on the ground or had to be abandoned by their repair crews as the German advance rolled over their airfields in France. The RAF lost 1382 personnel, including 915 aircrew killed, wounded or captured. Of these, 534 were pilots, a worrying number with the Battle of Britain looming.

German air losses between 10 May and 20 June, at first estimated to be around two thousand aircraft by the British, in fact totalled 1279 – including 522 bombers and 300 fighters. Because of the destruction of records French losses could not be counted officially, but were estimated at 757 planes.

Allied shipping losses were severe. Of the 50 destroyers taking part in Dynamo, nine were sunk (six of them British) and 28 damaged. Six troop-carrying ships of the 29 involved were lost and most of the others suffered damage. According to the Dunkirk war museum statistics, 647 British and 301 French ships and boats participated in the evacuation, of which 137 (102 British, 35 French) were sunk. In addition 75 British and 32 French vessels suffered damage. Warship sinkings are given as 37 British and 35 French.

Even after the signing of the armistice, the evacuation of Allied troops continued from southern French ports. The official total for the period *after* Dunkirk was 191,870, of whom 144,171 were British. When added to the Dunkirk figure, the total of rescued was 558,001, and 368,857 of those were British. There would, after all, be enough trained men to dispute any invasion of Britain, even if they lacked proper equipment.

Addressing some of the returned troops at Aldershot on 2 June, Anthony Eden promised that tanks and guns would be forthcoming for the vigorous prosecution of the war. Never again, he said, would British troops go into battle ill equipped. 'He was hooted down,' said Frank Farley of the Middlesex Regiment.

It was understandable that the Secretary of State for War should find himself booed. Despite the heartening warmth of their welcome back to Britain, the nerves, morale and confidence of many were in shreds. The sound of aeroplane engines, in particular, caused much distress. When three Spitfires roared low over his head along the seafront at Bournemouth, where he had been sent to be re-equipped, Jack Toomey threw himself flat on his face. 'I just couldn't help it,' he said. Joe Catt's Royal Sussex Regiment were put into camp close to the Rolls Royce factory in Derbyshire, where one morning a test was run on some aero engines. 'It was just as if somebody had pulled a rope – everybody got up and started running. You could have sworn it was Stukas coming down.' Even Captain Basil Bartlett, temporarily detained in a lunatic asylum converted into a hospital, twitched when a diesel lorry droned up the hill outside 'making a noise like a German bomber'.

There were also occasional indignities to be suffered. Reg Phillips, a pre-war policeman, found himself billeted in a prison at Usk on his return from France. 'We were three to a cell, had to stay there forty-eight hours and rest, they wouldn't let us out,' he said. 'But we didn't mind, since we hadn't had any kip for a week.' Bill Brodie and others at a transit camp at Chiseldon fell foul of a commandant who told them that just because they had been to France did not mean they knew everything about soldiering and proceeded to put them through roll calls, rifle drills 'and all the pinpricks to irritate us he could devise'.

But Lieutenant Peter Hadley spoke for many with the comment, 'Gradually our sense of values was restored to us, and what had been an all-too-present nightmare became no more than a memory – a memory vivid and unforgettable, of great events in which, however unpleasant they were, I feel glad (and a little proud) to have played a part.'

Certainly Germany had cause to rue the escape of these men, and in particular the brightest generals such as Montgomery of Alamein and Alexander of Tunis, who were to engineer the defeat and accept the surrender of so many of the enemy in the years ahead.

For Gort, who got his soldiers back to the beaches, and Ramsay, who lifted them home, there were contrasting fortunes. Gort never again commanded an army. First he was assigned to the defence of Gibraltar and then, in 1942, made Governor-General of Malta at a critical time in that island's history. His career ended as High Commissioner of Palestine and Trans-Jordan in 1945 and he died on 31 March 1946, aged only fifty-nine. Ramsay went on to mastermind the naval side of the landings in Normandy in June 1944, but did not live to see the Allied victory towards which he had contributed so much. He was killed in an air crash on his way to a meeting with Montgomery in Brussels.

Few outside the British Isles expected Britain to resist Hitler for long. Having seen what the German armies had done to his own forces, Weygand prophesied: 'In three weeks' time England's neck will be wrung like a chicken's' (bringing forth the famous Churchillian reply: 'Some chicken! Some neck!'). And the Duke of Windsor let slip to an American diplomat in Madrid his opinion that 'the most important thing now is to end the war before thousands more are killed or maimed to save the faces of a few politicians'.

After the fall of France Hitler was confident that Britain would want to seek peace terms. In a Reichstag speech on 19 July he said, 'I feel it to be my duty to appeal once more to common sense in Great Britain. . . . I consider myself in a position to make this appeal since I am not the vanquished begging favours but the victor speaking in the name of reason. I can see no reason why this war must go on.' Three days before uttering those words – just in case – Hitler had issued the directive for the invasion of Britain. So much for 'reason'.

Churchill, of course, made many stirring and scathing speeches about Germany's man of reason, but nothing better typified Britain's new attitude than these words by the writer Margery Allingham:

In those weeks in May and June I think 99 per cent of English folk found their souls, and whatever else it may have been it was a glorious and triumphant experience. If you have lived half your life's span without a passionate belief in anything, the bald discovery that you would honestly and in cold blood rather die when it came to it than be bossed about by a Nazi, then that is something to have lived for.

What Britain had unearthed was the Dunkirk spirit, of which Nicholas Harman said, in a BBC TV programme on Dunkirk in 1980, 'Dunkirk is more than just a piece of military history; it's a slogan, a catchword, a particularly British rallying cry for muddling your way out of disaster with a stiff upper lip and a strong cup of tea.'

Into the mosaic of victory
I lay a pattern piece
My only son
Into thy hands.

Tribute on the gravestone of Private D R Harris, aged twenty-one, of the Worcestershire Regiment, killed 27 May 1940, in the British military cemetery at Dunkirk.

Source Notes

IWM	Imperial War Museum, London	ADM	Admiralty Files
PRO	Public Record Office, Kew Bridge	CAB	Cabinet papers
INT	Interview or correspondence with author	WO	War Office Files

CHAPTER 1: The Routed Heroes

'Nail in the coffin of the Beast', *E. Kent Times*, 8 June 1940; 'I wasn't looking forward . . .' Lt. Gen. Sir Brian Horrocks, *A Full Life* p. 91; 'If anybody had even smiled . . .' George Griffin INT; 'More moved than I can say . . .', Memoirs of Maj. J E Matthew, File 86/3/1 IWM; 'And we cried, I'll tell you', Laurie Whitmarsh INT; Military police anecdote, T J Bristow, Ms *A Private View*, File 83/4/1 IWM; 'Ashamed to be in the BEF', S A Nettle (ed.) *'Dunkirk – Old Men Remember'*, p. 54; Mason-Macfarlane's statement, Bernard Gray, *War Reporter*, p. 120; 'Authoritative circles in Paris . . .', *London Evening News*, 29 May 1940; The return home stories, *Daily Express, Daily Mail, News Chronicle, Daily Mirror, Daily Telegraph, Times*, (all 31 May, 1940); 'They looked clean and smart', *Daily Telegraph*, 3 June 1940; 'Getting dressed I was aware . . .', Capt. Harold Foster memoirs PP/Mcr/174 IWM; The French farmer's trousers, Robert Jackson, *Dunkirk*, p. 209; Hurrell's fur coat, Frank Hurrell private MS, *Dunkirk and Return*, 88/4/1 IWM; 'Good luck old man', *Isle of Thanet Gazette*, 7 June 1940; The dogs of Dunkirk, Arthur Moss and Elizabeth Kirby, *Animals Were There*, p. 113, *Dover Express*, 21 June 1940; 'The French were subjected . . .', *Sheerness Times* 7 June 1940; 'Most of us came off . . .', Tom Peck INT; 'Two chaps picked me up', John Hammond INT; 'Sister, ring the Ministry', W C Brodie MBE, Ms *Too Little Too Late*, 83/48/1/ IWM; 'Day and night for a week now . . .', The *Times*, 3 June 1940; 'Food, fruit and chocolates . . .', Diary of Col. J R McDonald 72/54/1 IWM; 'All the way up to London . . .', Joe Catt INT; 'What's Yours, Poilu?', *London Evening News*, 5 June 1940; 'It was terribly hot . . .', Mrs I. Phillips memoirs 80/6/1 IWM; 'The heat, added to the sweat . . .', Mrs. J. Cole diary 81/33/1 IWM; 'It was about 8am . . .', Spr. J R Toomey letter P. 474 IWM; 'But not the Guards, oh no', George Griffin INT; Gort's return, The *Times*, 3 June 1940; Brooke's return, Sir Arthur Bryant, *Turn of the Tide* p. 156; Worthington nods off, Walter Lord, *The Miracle of Dunkirk* p. 278; Driving charge dismissed, *E. Kent Times*, 15 June 1940; The French in Bournemouth, *Bournemouth Times*, 7 June 1940, Norman Longmate *How We Lived Then* p. 104; Inundated with free drinks, diary of T J Bristow 83/4/1 IWM; The ten-shilling notes, *Daily Mirror*, 6 June 1940; 'Good old Navy', Capt. Thomas Kerr letter 75/99/2 IWM; 'Where have you been?', J H Patterson diary IWM; 'Some enterprising Herbert . . .', Alfred Baldwin INT; Montgomery irritated, Alun Chalfont *Montgomery of Alamein* p. 115; 'Wars are not

Pillar of Fire

won by evacuations', Winston S. Churchill, *The Second World War Vol. II Their Finest Hour* p. 103; 'Even though large tracts . . .' *ibid* p. 104; 'And if they do come . . .', Richard Collier *1940: The World in Flames* p. 91; 'Never has any generation . . .', *London Evening News* 1 June 1940; Prisoners of war attacked, Ray Cole, Les Boyce INT; Hitler's proclamation, The *Times* 6 June 1940; 'There is no real elation . . .' William Shirer, *Berlin Diary* pp. 308, 310; 'Personally, I feel happier. . .' Noel Barber, *The Week France Fell* p. 293; 'Far from being alarmed . . .' Herbert Agar, *Britain Alone* p. 65; 'Thank God we're now alone', Collier *op. cit.* p. 124; 'Taking the job on ourselves', Margery Allingham, *The Oaken Heart* p. 215; 'Gayer and more serene', Agar *op. cit.* p. 99.

CHAPTER 2: The Day War Broke Out
'I was sitting quietly . . .', Nettle *op. cit.* p. 102; Harry Dennis's call-up, Dennis INT; 'That Sunday, just before eleven. . .' Don Ellingworth INT; Peeling potatoes while listening, F. Palmer Cook, Ms *Bless 'Em All* 81/44/1 IWM; 'After the first shock . . .' L H Vollans, Ms *Run, Rabbit Run* 82/14/1 IWM; 'The beer flowed . . .' Alfred Baldwin INT; Dropped the prefix Herr, Diary of Maj. W G Blaxland 83/46/1 IWM; Deploring his own failure, Lord Avon *The Reckoning* p. 62; 'My audience thinned out . . .' Maj. Gen. Sir Edward Spears, *Assignment to Catastrophe (Vol. I)* p. 25; Churchill and the air raid, Churchill *op. cit.* Vol. I p. 363–4; The false alarm, John Slessor *The Central Blue* p. 234; 'Some 250 people . . .' Shirer *op. cit.* pp. 161–2; Nazi leaders stunned, Nicholas Bethell *The War Hitler Won* p. 84; 'I clung to the thought . . .' Henry J. Greenwall *When France Fell* p. 50.

CHAPTER 3: The Cardboard Army
'As well, if not better, equipped . . .' Collier *op. cit.* p. 14; 'British Army totally unfit . . .' Field Marshal Bernard Montgomery *Memoirs* p. 49; Far less ready than 1914, Bryant *op. cit.* p. 47; 'Not to be used in action', Lt. Col. M. Henniker, 'Prelude to battle', *Blackwood's Magazine* Sept. 1947; Lengths of gas piping, A J Barker, *Dunkirk: The Great Escape* p. 13; 'They were using collapsible boats . . .' Ronnie Noble INT; 'The British Army was geared . . .' Maj. R C Taylor letter to author; 'The countryside of France . . .' Montgomery *op. cit.* p. 50; Wrong to be conscripted, Diary of L W Cannon 79/27/1 IWM; Joining up by bus, Frank Southall, *The First Year*, 84/36/1 IWM; 'We looked like convicts, A R Gaskin diary 87/44/1 IWM; 'At least you'll know . . .' Len Wilson INT; 'Like a school examination', Alfred Baldwin INT; 'Right, you'll be a driver', Laurie Whitmarsh INT; 'It was ideal', Baldwin INT; Gort's appointment, Alistair Horne *To Lose a Battle* pp. 434-6; 'Isn't it grand . . .' Gregory Blaxland *Destination Dunkirk* p. 14; 'But I had no confidence . . .' Bryant *op. cit.* p. 79; 'Job was above his ceiling', Montgomery *op. cit.* p. 52; 'A simple, straightforward . . .' Spears, *op. cit.* p. 34; 'Nothing can save the Poles', R. McLeod and Denis Kelly, *The Ironside Diaries*; 'A stew they'll choke on', Agar *op. cit.* p. 16; 'Many were gulping . . .' Gaskin diary IWM; 'None of the Noel Coward stuff . . .' H C F Harwood, Ms *Oh Threat of Hell* IWM; 'But cold stew . . .' Robert Holding, *Since I Bore Arms* p. 12; The Army chaplains, Gray *op. cit.* p. 13; 'We hope he is right', Eric J. Manley diary P. 284 IWM; 'The lads were all singing', Tom Willy INT; 'My first shock of the war . . .' *Manchester Evening News* 11 March 1980; 'Watched by a solitary . . .' Brodie memoirs IWM; 'Without the enthusiasm of 1914 . . .' Denis Barlone *A French Officer's Diary* pp. 3–4; 'Most unpleasant apprehensions' Bryant *op. cit.* p. 70; 'Clumsy, still beladen . . .' Blaxland *op. cit.* p. 27; 'A wasted day . . .' Bryant *op. cit.* p. 70; French Army pay,

Horne *op. cit.* pp. 29, 90; The Maginot Line, Vivian Rowe, *The Great Wall of France* pp. 17–41, 56, Horne *op. cit.* pp. 24–29; 'A veritable Rock of Ages', Anthony Rhodes, *Sword of Bone* p. 97; 'Whoever is the first . . .' Collier, *op. cit.* p. 5; Gamelin and Vincennes, Horne *op. cit.* pp. 100–102; 'Instead of defending . . .' Bethell *op. cit.* p. 6; 'A small, dapper man', McLeod and Kelly *op. cit.* p. 101; 'Nice old gentleman', Slessor *op. cit.* p. 243; 'My little Gamelin . . .' Günther Blumentritt, *Von Rundstedt: The Soldier and the Man* p. 64; Germany's re-armament, Horne *op. cit.* pp. 38–41, Blaxland *op. cit.* pp. 28–33; 'Bent on innovation', Kenneth Macksey *Guderian, Panzer General* p. 39; 'In the country of the blind . . .' Heinz Guderian *Panzer Leader* p. 20; 'We must burn our boats', Alan Bullock *Hitler: A Study in Tyranny* p. 510; 'We've crossed the border!' Wilhelm Prüller *Diary of a German Soldier* p. 13.

CHAPTER 4: 'Queer Kind of War'

'We waited patiently . . .' Montgomery *op. cit.* p. 58; The Seigfried Line Blumentritt *op. cit.* p. 56, Bethell *op. cit.* p. 171; 'The risks which . . .' Rowe *op. cit.* p. 103; 'Western Powers did not desire war', Spears *op. cit.* p. 35; Bombing the Black Forest, Leopold Amery, *My Political Life Vol. III, Unforgiving Years* p. 330; Leaflet attack, Bethell *op. cit.* pp. 205, 208; 'I was not proud . . .' Avon *op. cit.* p. 77; The German pamphlet, Maj. R C Taylor INT; 'Soldiers of the Northern Provinces . . .' Spears *op. cit.* p. 69; 'Coming up the Rhine . . .' Shirer *op. cit.* p. 188; 'We settled down . . .' Rhodes *op. cit.* p. 74; 'Some of the ditches . . .' Green Howards series, *Scarborough Evening News* Jan–May 1950; 'When we arrived . . .' Rhodes *op. cit.* p. 82; 'I selected a piece . . .' Bristow IWM; 'As had been proved . . .' Hewitt INT; 'Plenty of warm straw . . .' The *Times* 2 October 1939; 'A dreadful place . . .' Bristow IWM; Billeted in pig-pens, Ramsdale IWM; The sugar beet factory, Nettle *op. cit.* p. 134; 'We stepped back a hundred years', Memoirs of A F Johnson 80/42/1 IWM; 'If there was a barn . . .' Baldwin INT; 'The days passed pleasantly', Harwood IWM; 'I was in clover', Diary of Maj. E. Booth IWM; 'Very poor, very badly cooked', Baldwin INT; The BEF diet, Cannon IWM; 'You did very well, lad', Hammond INT; 'A great shock . . .' Hewitt INT; 'Those awful mess tins', Arnold Johnson IWM; 'He had obviously been primed', Brodie IWM; Marmite soup and fish cakes, Graham Brooks *Grand Party* p. 47; 'Despite an interior . . .' Arnold Johnson IWM; 'It was cheap living . . .' Willy INT; 'Compared with the French . . .' Hewitt INT; 'When I read of football hooligans . . .' Willy INT; 'Quite a bit to drink . . .' Len Wilson INT; 'For obscure reasons . . .' Brodie IWM; 'At least 20 were blind drunk . . .' Brooks *op. cit.* p. 55; 'Most of the lads . . .' L B Shorrock Ms *Guest of the Führer* IWM; 'I was considered a snob' Cyril King memoirs IWM; Monty and the VD cases, Montgomery *op. cit.* pp. 59–60; 'We asked a policeman', Taylor INT; 'Half the unit were down . . .' Dennis INT; 'Too damn cold for me', Bill Gardner letter, IWM; 'By the middle of January . . .' Brodie IWM; 'I fell off six times', Willy INT; 'Icy roads and studded boots . . .' Alex Turner (ed.) *My Dunkirk* p. 11; 'The roads are like glass', Diary of Col. J R McDonald 72/54/1 IWM; The frozen beer, Eric Rankin memoirs IWM; 'Driver had to take it in turn . . .' D F Parry memoirs 86/82/1 IWM; 'Boots frozen to my feet', Bill Edwards INT; 'All the officers played . . .' Alan Johnson Ms *Double Survivor* 87/6/1 IWM; 'Good fortune to see Will Hay . . .' Cannon IWM; SECRET AND URGENT Blaxland *op. cit.* p. 46; The film show, Rankin IWM; 'We went by car' Booth IWM; 'A grand little fighting force', Basil Bartlett, *My First War* p. 22.

CHAPTER 5: Through the Forest

Hitler's invasion plans, Wilhelm Keitel *Memoirs* pp. 103–4, B H Liddell Hart *The Other Side of the Hill* pp. 144–7, Macksey *op. cit.* pp. 92–3, Bethell *op. cit.* pp. 405–7; 'Hitler decided to wait' Keitel *op. cit.* p. 70; Plan Yellow, Tom Schachtman *The Phony War* pp. 130–1, Collier *op. cit.* pp. 8–10; The Manstein Plan, Liddell Hart *op. cit.* pp. 94–5, 156; 'Hitler owed his success . . .' Bullock *op. cit.* p. 583; 'The BEF wasn't really . . .' Taylor INT; 'What might have happened . . .' Bryant *op. cit.* p. 66; 'Many of the men . . .' Col. L H M Westropp memoirs 75/25/1 IWM; 'The powers-that-be . . .' Major R M S Neave memoirs 87/35/1 IWM; 'Our hearts bled . . .' Brodie IWM; 'Only one weapon capable . . .' *Scarborough E. News* series 1950; The cardboard folder, Peter Hadley *Third Class to Dunkirk* p. 34; 'The marquees are soaking . . .' J R McDonald IWM; 'The soldiers will know . . .' Chalfont *op. cit.* p. 109; 'I did this because . . .' Alan Johnson IWM; 'From my lowly position . . .' Baldwin INT; 'These were open to examination . . .' Dairy of Maj. W G Blaxland 83/46/1 IWM; Spy scares, War Office file 167/794 PRO; 'More Bakers for the BEF', Gray *op. cit.* p. 21; The King's visit, *ibid* pp. 36–8; Gort and his HQ, Richard Collier *Sands of Dunkirk* pp. 18–19, Andre Maurois *The Battle of France* p. 30; The Hitler chamberpot, Longmate *op. cit.* p. 118; The terracotta dogs, Alexander Werth *The Last Days of Paris* p. 15; 'We don't even hate the Huns', *ibid* p. 83; 'Deep down I knew . . .' Josephine Pearce memoirs 83/52/1 IWM; 'The city had never been . . .' Rhodes *op. cit.* pp. 122, 124; 'One could sense the hostility . . .' Greenwall *op. cit.* p. 62; 'Part of my job . . .' Bartlett *op. cit.* p. 12; Daladier and his government, Horne *op. cit.* pp. 149–50, Schachtman *op. cit.* p. 162; Reynaud takes over, Horne *op. cit.* pp. 150–152; 'It would be criminal . . .' Agar *op. cit.* p. 44; 'An unassailable belief . . .' Dr David Wrench, *RUSI Journal* March 1980 p. 56; 'His all-pervading hope . . .' Churchill *op. cit.* Vol. I p. 198; 'We knew he was trying . . .' Bristow IWM; 'In the name of God, go', Spears *op. cit.* pp. 119–120; 'Would arouse the indignation . . .' Barlone *op. cit.* p. 33; 'A lovely summer day . . .' Manley IWM; 'I was particularly struck . . .' Hadley *op. cit.* p. 8; 'Responsible officers of the BEF . . .' Gray *op. cit.* p. 47; 'The Englishmen's washing . . .' Bethell *op. cit.* p. 403; 'The usual trivialities . . .' Lt. Col. R L Clarke, 'Three Weeks to La Panne, *Royal Engineers Journal* March 1977; 'So on with the Whitsun holiday . . .' *Daily Mirror* 10 May 1940; 'In one village . . .' Shirer *op. cit.* p. 254; Hitler's headquarters, Walter Warlimont *Inside Hitler's Headquarters* p. 101; 'Soldiers of the West Front!', Horne *op. cit.* p. 198.

CHAPTER 6: The Balloon Goes Up

'I looked through the opening . . .' Hurrell IWM; 'A terrific anti-aircraft barrage . . .' Brodie IWM; 'In the very clear sky . . .' S L Rhodda memoirs 85/34/1 IWM; 'There were bombers about . . .' Hewitt INT; 'When my batman . . .' R L Clarke *op. cit.*; 'I told you so, sir' Bartlett *op. cit.* p. 47; 'I was still drunk . . .' Jack Toomey letter IWM; 'I found most of the other . . .' Rhodes *op. cit.* p. 135; 'I then got up . . .' Lt. S J L Hill diary IWM; Langley's posting, Lt. Col. J M Langley *Fight Another Day* pp. 30–31; 'After all the weeks . . .' Vollans IWM; 'The sword had now fallen . . .' Bryant *op. cit.* p. 91; 'I was now going to do . . .' Bristow IWM; Gamelin's Order of the Day, Rowe *op. cit.* p. 140; Belgium's neutrality, Horne *op. cit.* p. 36, Blaxland *op. cit.* pp. 42, 60, Liddell Hart *op. cit.* p. 143; 'Their plight is lamentable . . .' Collier *1940* p. 12; 'If British and French . . .' Churchill *op. cit.* Vol, I pp. 423–424; Plan D, Horne *op. cit.* pp. 108–109, 110–113, Blaxland *op. cit.* pp. 42–45; 'We thought it foolish . . .' Peck INT; 'The infantry were . . .' Matthew

Source Notes

memoirs/IWM; 'I sat on a chair . . .' Blaxland Ms, IWM; Rifle practice, Ramsdale IWM; 'We were mobbed . . .' S J L Hill IWM; The Battling Bootlace, Bristow IWM; 'Gort's Advance Thunders . . .' *Daily Express*, 11 May 1940; 'The British move . . .' The *Times* 12 May 1940; 'With flowers, beer and cheers . . .' *Daily Mirror* 11 May 1940; 'One long celebration . . .' Patterson IWM; The elderly man, Holding *op. cit.* p. 34; 'We were told that . . .' Matthew IWM; 'We congregated . . .' Rhodes *op. cit.* p. 138; 'I could have wept . . .' Schachtman *op. cit.* p. 199; Luftwaffe's strength, John Terraine *Right of the Line* pp. 31, 124; 'not merely gratifying . . .' *ibid* p. 125; Invasion of Holland and Belgium, Horne *op. cit.* pp. 185–190, Schachtman *op. cit.* pp. 195–196; '*Klotzen, nicht kleckern*', Guderian *op. cit.* p. 105; Rommel's letters home, Erwin Rommel *The Rommel Papers* (ed. B H Liddell Hart) pp. 6–7; 'A typical Sunday', Shirer *op. cit.* p. 265; 'The windows began to rattle . . .' Allingham *op. cit.* p. 173; 'The workers of Britain . . .' The *Times* 11 May 1940; Churchill installed, Churchill *op. cit.* Vol. I p. 596.

CHAPTER 7: Nuns by Parachute

'One didn't notice . . .' Gray *op. cit.* p. 55; Air losses, Terraine *op. cit.* pp. 125–126; 'I must impress on you . . .' *ibid* p. 129; 'You British are mad . . .' Robert Jackson *Air War Over France* p. 56; 'A pilot of the last war . . .' Spears *op. cit.* p. 17; 'Many were without boots . . .' WO 167/124 PRO; The horse-drawn columns, A J Hooker diary IWM, Ramsdale IWM, Boyce INT; Night clash with Belgians, Hewitt INT; Belgian phone system, WO 197/119 PRO; The Royal Palace cables, Taylor INT; 'The BBC may prevent . . .' Gray *op. cit.* p. 56; Montgomery's solution, Lord *op. cit.* p. 15; 'It would be a hard-hearted . . .' Papers of Brig. G W Sutton 72/59/4 IWM; 'The last few days . . .' Maj. P R Hill letter 85/40/1 IWM; 'As they filed past . . .' Bristow IWM; 'Oh God, it is dreadful . . .' Diary of Capt. A M Bell Macdonald IWM; 'Nice and shrapnel-proof', Hooker IWM; 'Cyclists in their thousands . . .' Maurois *op. cit.* pp. 179–180; 'Pots with withered plants . . .' Rhodes *op. cit.* pp. 150–151; 'Two carts were produced . . .' Blaxland Ms IWM; 'A touch of the Marie Celeste . . .' Patterson IWM; 'Everywhere traffic-blocks!', Barlone *op. cit.* p. 48; The red blankets, Hooker IWM, Holding *op. cit.* p. 54; The Fifth Column, Horne *op. cit.* p. 74; The poisoned sweets, Werth *op. cit.* p. 68; Washerwoman shot, Ellingworth INT; Like a doctor's surgery, *Scarborough E. News* series; The Embassy refugee, R L Clarke *op. cit.*; 'At the entrance . . .' Matthew IWM; Golf pros shot, Ronnie Noble *Shoot First* p. 23; 'I saw a pigeon . . .' Rhodda IWM; 'Since a nun is not . . .' Allingham *op. cit.* p. 175; The Dundee parachutist, *Daily Mirror* 16 May 1940; Pillboxes locked, Blaxland *op. cit.* p. 80; 'All day he was out . . .' Chalfont *op. cit.* p. 112; 'It is a curious feeling . . .' Brooks *op. cit.* pp. 70–71; Annand's VC, *London Gazette* 20 August 1940; 'At once all the troops . . .' Rev. F J Brabyn diary 87/59/1 IWM; 'A sort of sinister fascination . . .' *Scarborough E. News* series; 'The radio operators . . .' Rhodda IWM; 'I found a scene of horror . . .' Gordon Beckles *Dunkirk and After* p. 56; 'The pilot was badly wounded . . .' Hooker IWM; 'Literally torn to pieces . . .' WO 197/119 PRO; 'Dutch Govt. Flees' *Daily Mirror* 15 May 1940; 'Serious but not critical', *Daily Mirror* 16 May 1940; 'The Germans have not yet . . .' The *Times* 15 May 1940; 'We have been defeated', Churchill *op. cit.* Vol. II p. 38.

CHAPTER 8: 'Run, Run Like Hell!'

Entice the Germans forward, Foster memoirs IWM; 'Our spirits were lightened', Brodie IWM; 'To leave this magnificent . . .' Brooks *op. cit.* p. 5; 'I was getting a bit fed up . . .' Arnold Johnson IWM; Explaining to the troops, Horrocks *op. cit.* pp.

79–81; 'There were no cheering people . . .' Rhodes *op. cit.* p. 164; 'The brigadier did his nut . . .' Ellingworth INT; 'No one felt sorry . . .' Blaxland Ms IWM; 'They didn't seem to mind what happened . . .' Diary of Rev. J E G Quinn P. 247 IWM; 'Like blowing Westminster Bridge . . .' Taylor INT; Guards go wrong way, Blaxland *op. cit.* p. 95; 'There is no doubt that . . .' WO 197/120 PRO; 'Only leaders who drive in front . . .' Macksey *op. cit.* p. 66; Guderian–Von Kleist row, Guderian Ms AL1022 IWM; 'To the last drop of petrol', Horne *op. cit.* p. 351; 'A most unfortunate day', Warlimont *op. cit.* p. 95; Guderian resigns, Guderian *op. cit.* pp. 109–110; 'He rages and shouts . . .' Warlimont *op. cit.* p. 96; 'Hideous, fatal scythes' Churchill *op. cit.* Vol. II p. 53; De Gaulle's attack, Don Cook *Charles de Gaulle* pp. 57–58; 'Nous vaincrons . . .' Werth *op. cit.* p. 64; '*Vous êtes Anglais?*' Desmond Young *Rommel* p. 68; Charles Lamb captured, Taylor INT; Churchill in Paris, Churchill *op. cit.* Vol. II pp. 40–43; Weygand appointed, Jacques Weygand *The Role of Gen. Weygand: Conversations With His Son* p. 39, Collier *1940* p. 65, Barber *op. cit.* p. 29, Spears *op. cit.* pp. 183–184; 'Do for the best', Rowe *op. cit.* p. 158; 'He appeared relieved . . .' Weygand *op. cit.* p. 46; 'Poor old boy', Werth *op. cit.* p. 61; 'Constant harassment . . .' Shorrock IWM; 'When Corps HQ is in front . . .' Brodie IWM; 'It was a time of confusion', Foster IWM; 'We pulled into a field . . .' Ellingworth INT; 'Old carts, wardrobes . . .' Rhodda IWM; 'I looked at the dim forms,' Bristow IWM; 'I was shocked to find . . .' Blaxland Ms IWM; 'One of the officers . . .' Rhodda IWM; 'He was desperately tired, WO 167/124 PRO; 'I took some bromide . . .' Patterson IWM; The nightingales, Hooker IWM; The golden oriole, S J L Hill IWM; 'The hideous lowing . . .' Cannon IWM; Civilians, in their panic . . .' Brooks *op. cit.* pp. 71–72; 'Agonising humanity . . .' Bryant *op. cit.* p. 116; 'Rather shamefacedly observed . . .' Palmer Cook IWM; 'The people were sitting . . .' Lt. Col. J C A Birch memoirs IWM; The Belgian tea lady, Noble INT; 'Through the view-finder . . .' Noble *op. cit.* pp. 22–23; The half-haircut, Brodie IWM; 'Every one that came down . . .' Baldwin IWM; 'Never look a dive-bomber in the face', Toomey IWM; 'High up in the sky . . .' Bristow IWM; Despatch riders chased, Willy, Ellingworth INT; 'I found myself staring . . .' Blaxland Ms IWM; 'There were three boys . . .' Reg Phillips INT; 'The decision to release . . .' Sutton IWM; 'The men want to know . . .' Barlone *op. cit.* p. 50; The Loyals' march, Blaxland *op. cit.* pp. 105–106; 'This old lady came out . . .' Willy INT; The burgomeister's surrender, Blaxland *op. cit.* p. 106; Lord Sysonby's letter, Blaxland Ms IWM; 'One was from the Income Tax . . .' Phillips INT; 'A curiously inadequate ditch, 'Bartlett *op. cit.* p. 74; 'Either through treachery . . .' Sutton IWM; 'The greatest difficulty . . .' Matthew IWM; Sleeping on the march, Taylor INT; 'We were getting nervous' Bristow IWM; 'The picture was now . . .' Churchill *op. cit.* Vol. II p. 48; 'A last alternative', Horne *op. cit.* p. 418.

CHAPTER 9: Battle at Arras

'This remarkable day', Macksey *op. cit.* p. 1; 'Beside himself with joy', *ibid* p. 2; 'We had the feeling . . .' *ibid* p. 115; 'The most sweeping victory . . .' Liddell Hart *op. cit.* p. 181; Giraud's capture, Horne *op. cit.* pp. 392–393, Liddell Hart *op. cit.* p. 183; The Royal Sussex decimated, Basil Karslake *The Last Act*; 'One of the sights . . .' Shirer *op. cit.* p. 297–298; 'They were a sad sight', *ibid* pp. 289–290; 'The right and indeed . . .' CAB 44/60 PRO; 'Gort did not agree', Horne *op. cit.* p. 433; 'An excellent man . . .' Slessor *op. cit.* p. 240; 'Just jelly . . .' CAB 44/60 PRO; Seized by his tunic buttons, Horne *op. cit.* p. 437; 'God help the BEF', *ibid* p. 437; The Frankforce attack, Marshall Cavendish *Hitler's Panzers*, Blaxland *op. cit.* pp.

139–148; 'The only indication . . .' Nicholas Harman *Dunkirk: The Necessary Myth* p. 96; 'Jamming up the roads . . .' Rommel *op. cit.* p. 32; 'A glorious swipe . . .' Blaxland *op. cit.* p. 148; Weygand's trip north, Weygand *op. cit.* pp. 54–57; 'We had to punch holes . . .' CAB 44/60 PRO; Billotte's death, Rowe *op. cit.* p. 189; 'Marked taste for photographers', Barlone *op. cit.* p. 28; 'Staring at a blank wall', Bryant *op. cit.* p. 119; 'Brisk, buoyant and incisive', Roger Keyes *Outrageous Fortune* p. 290; 'The man's mad', *ibid* p. 292; Weygand's Operations Order, Lord *op. cit.* p. 21; 'French Drive Nazis Back', *Daily Mirror* 21 May 1940; 'This turned irritation into annoyance', Petre report CAB 44/60 PRO; Elderly depot personnel, Maj. L F Ellis *Welsh Guards at War* p. 89; Griffin and the calendar, Griffin INT; German infiltration tactics, CAB 44/60 PRO; 'He had thick glasses . . .' Griffin INT; Rooting out infiltrators, 1st Bn. Welsh Guards War Diary; 'A born thief', Ellis *op. cit.* p. 91; 'He was embarrassed . . .' *Scarborough E. News* series; French attack of 22 May, Horne *op. cit.* p. 460; 'Much of Arras was burning', CAB 44/60 PRO; 'Wake up, get up, pack up', Ellis *op. cit.* p. 93; 'I'm riding into battle . . .' 1st Bn. Welsh Guards War Diary; 'He was a good officer . . .' Tom Griffiths INT; 'Permanently mischievous look', Gray *op. cit.* p. 30; The Bren gun-carrier action, Griffin INT, Griffiths INT; Ellis *op. cit.* pp. 93–95; 'Where is the RAF?', Eric J. Manley diary IWM; 'Thus concluded the defence . . .' Ellis *op. cit.* p. 11; 'Absolutely contrary to our wishes', Blaxland *op. cit.* p. 184; 'Nothing but a miracle . . .' Bryant *op. cit.* p. 117.

CHAPTER 10: Cointreau and Cigars

'News from the south . . .' Blaxland *op. cit.* p. 155; 'Suddenly two huge German planes . . .' Brodie IWM; 'They walked all over the place . . .' Lt. Col. J E Wright *The Last 18 Days* 85/20/1 IWM; The German Wally, Hewitt INT; Two more VCs, *London Gazette* 26 July, 20 August 1940; 'They were mortaring us', James Stevenson INT; 'One bottle whisky, one of brandy', Patterson IWM; 'I entered the hotel . . .' Sgt. E R Knight article 83/7/1 IWM; 'The British have established . . .' Blaxland *op. cit.* p. 169; 'These Very lights . . .' Hadley *op. cit.* p. 82; 'Flying about unmolested . . .' Bristow IWM; Rev. Quinn's arrest, Quinn IWM: 'Our orders are to shoot . . .' Barlone *op. ci.t* p. 53; 'So now we have . . .' Bartlett *op. cit.* p. 72; 'I have nowhere to detain . . .' *ibid* p. 83; 'Hitler had provocation . . .' *ibid* p. 77; 'A farmer and his family . . .' *ibid* p. 103; War correspondents at risk, Horne *op. cit.* p. 399; 'Belgian Army also . . .' CAB 44/61 PRO; 'I was mainly ferrying petrol . . .' Stan Smith INT; Bill Edwards's rum, Edwards INT; 'Very much an innocent . . .' John Carpenter INT; 'Our method of living . . .' Macdonald IWM; 'Living like kings . . .' Hooker IWM; The wine and cheese party, Bristow IWM; 'The pungent aroma of cigars . . .' Brooks *op. cit.* pp. 76, 84; Raiding the NAAFI, *ibid* pp. 89–90; 'We were surrounded . . .' Brodie IWM; 'You can't eat *them* . . .' John Farrer diary IWM; 'It was bleedin' beetroot', Dennis INT; 'From leaving Rumacourt . . .' S L Wright Ms 84/26/1 IWM; 'Complete lack of effort', Blaxland *op. cit.* p. 164; 'I was stupefied . . .' Bartlett *op. cit.* p. 89; 'When we limbered up . . .' Baldwin IWM; 'Grimy, bloodstained . . .' Hadley *op. cit.* p. 62; 'Clearly in no mood to halt . . .' Blaxland Ms IWM; The gas alarm, Rhodda IWM; 'Here we go again', Macdonald IWM; 'I couldn't help comparing . . .' Sutton IWM; 'Nazis Lose Their Cattle', *Daily Mirror* 23 May 1940; Panzers turn north, Rommel *op. cit.* p. 34; Lord *op. cit.* p. 26; 'The enemy air force . . .' Rowe *op. cit.* p. 191; 'Give this victory . . .' Blaxland *op. cit.* p. 210; Golf at Le Touquet, Gray *op. cit.* pp. 111–112; 'The last man and the last round', Ellis *op. cit.* p. 97; 'Many of them were drunk . . .' Harman *op. cit.* p. 113; Battle for Calais, Blaxland *op. cit.* pp. 227–244; 'Are you sure . . . ?' Churchill *op. cit.* Vol. II p. 72; 'The eyes of the Empire . . .' *ibid* p. 73; 'Defence of Calais had no effect . . .' Liddell Hart *op. cit.* p. 199; 'Very likely the enemy tanks . . .' Churchill *op. cit.* Vol. II p. 80; The halt order, Liddell Hart *op. cit.* pp. 185–189; 'Unjustly credited . . .' Keitel *op. cit.* p. 114; 'Raised an immediate protest', Blumentritt *op. cit.* p. 75; 'Absolutely speechless', Macksey *op. cit.* p. 118; 'By my estimate . . .' Rommel *op. cit.* p. 34; 'To help the British', Blumentritt *op. cit.* p. 78; 'German military circles . . .' Shirer *op. cit.* p. 298; The King's broadcast, Beckles *op. cit.* pp. 98–99; 'I could feel the pent up . . .' Churchill *op. cit.* Vol. II p. 87; 'It was not until we heard . . .' Ramsdale IWM.

CHAPTER 11: The Useless Mouths

'The leaflets were in bad English . . .' Alan Johnson IWM; 'There is no blinking . . .' CAB 44/61 PRO; 'No course open to you . . .' *ibid*; British generals make for harbours, Spears *op. cit.* p. 178; 'A very hazardous enterprise . . .' Bryant *op. cit.* p. 134; 'If the British had not . . .' Spears *op. cit.* Vol. II p. 24; Col. Whitfeld's report, WO 197/119 PRO; 'Often we would load . . .' Eddie Barry INT; 'A sort of French Merseyside', *Dunkirk, the Story Behind the Legend* BBC TV 3 June 1980; 'With the greatest vigour', Adm. Ramsay report *The Evacuation of the Allied Armies from Dunkirk*, supplement to *London Gazette* 15 July 1947 p. 3299; 'It was like being told . . .' David Woodward *Ramsay at War* p. 27; 'A large number of small vessels . . .' Churchill *op. cit.* Vol II p. 52; 'The emergency evacuation . . .' Ramsay report p. 3299; 'I could see that the nerves . . .' David Divine *The Nine Days of Dunkirk* pp. 88–89; 'Presume troops know . . .' CAB 44/61 PRO; The tanks at Merville, Eric Loveluck letter to author; Brinckman's attack, Capt. R N Brinckman letter 86/61/1 IWM; 'Tired, unwashed and unshaven . . .' Brodie IWM; 'Suddenly the small daughter . . .' Les Boyce INT; Langley's walking stick, Langley *op. cit.* p. 33; Norman Dixon's capture, Dixon INT; Cyril King's capture, King IWM; Lt. Harwood's capture, Lt. H C F Harwood memoirs 84/33/1 IWM; Jack Toomey's escape, Toomey IWM; J O Jones's escape, Jones Ms, IWM; Edmund Booth's capture, Maj. E. Booth diary IWM; 'On the night of the 27th . . .' Baldwin INT; 'At each halt . . .' Holding *op. cit.* p. 105; 'I had a vision . . .' Hewitt INT; 'We're busy encircling . . .' Rommel *op. cit.* p. 39; Monty's night move, Montgomery *op. cit.* p. 61, Chalfont *op. cit.* p. 114; 'I have never felt more naked', Horrocks *op. cit.* p. 83; 'A little masterpiece', Chalfont *op. cit.* p. 114; 'Imagine my astonishment . . .' Montgomery *op. cit.* p. 61.

CHAPTER 12: 'A Regal Judas'

'Unless they saw aircraft . . .' Belgian General Staff report, WO 193/120 PRO; Belgian collapse and surrender, Keyes *op. cit.* pp. 323–361; 'The news fell on us . . .' Weygand *op. cit.* p. 75; 'Never such a betrayal . . .' Spears *op. cit.* p. 248; The Paris demonstration, *Brighton Evening Argus* 29 May 1940; 'God, I always thought . . .' Werth *op. cit.* p. 97; 'To us the British were . . .' Rowe *op. cit.* p. 208; 'Hard and heavy tidings', Churchill *op. cit.* Vol. II p. 87; 'I Shall Betray', *Daily Mirror* 29 May 1940; 'The Face That Every Woman . . .' *ibid* 30 May 1940; 'A relief they've packed up', Bartlett *op. cit.* p. 79; 'From the upper windows . . .' Vollans IWM; 'He might have been pole-axed', Horrocks *op. cit.* p. 84; 'My eyes are wet for joy . . .' Prüller *op. cit.* p. 52; 'Like a soldier . . .' Shirer *op. cit.* p. 299; 'Most of them seemed . . .' Liddell Hart *op. cit.* p. 169; 'Under a clear blue sky . . .' Bartlett *op. cit.* p. 112; 'A horrible sight . . .' Horrocks *op. cit.* p. 85; 'It was now clear to everyone . . .' Westropp IWM; 'A bitter moment for us all', Brooks *op. cit.* pp. 96–97; The gunner who wept, Capt. J S Walsham diary 80/18/1 IWM; 'This was a curious weapon', Carpenter INT; 'They were shooting the horses . . .' Blaxland Ms IWM; 'Many were obscenely drunk . . .' Frank Farley Ms *Home Via La Panne and Dunkirk*; 'Like vultures', Birch IWM; Monty's lunch box, Montgomery *op. cit.* p. 62; 'No thought of retreat', Barker *op. cit.* p. 69; 'French road discipline was nil', Matthew IWM; 'No power on earth . . .' Sutton IWM; 'One panic-stricken major . . .' Brooks *op. cit.* p. 102; 'A whole battalion lay . . .' Loveluck letter; 'The transport column . . .' J B Wright IWM; The Belgian scouts, Langley *op. cit.* pp. 43–44; 'We got through . . .' *Scarborough E. News* series; 'German planes came over . . .' Blaxland Ms IWM; 'Take them high like a pheasant', Langley *op. cit.* p. 44; 'Retreating, upwards and backwards . . .' Whitmarsh INT; 'No matter which way . . .' Hewitt INT; 'It was of interest to find . . .' Blaxland Ms IWM; 'We saluted our fellow-Londoners', Brodie IWM; 'When you get home . . .' Edwards INT; 'My job was to crawl along . . .' Patterson IWM.

CHAPTER 13: Massacre at Le Paradis

Luftwaffe destroy Dunkirk, Cajus Bekker *The Luftwaffe War Diaries* pp. 127–128; 'He must have been sufficiently . . .' Albert Kesselring *Memoirs* p. 59; 'What lorries were there . . .' Adam report WO 197/118 PRO; Tennant sails in, Ramsay report p. 3300; 'The sights of Dunkirk . . .' Woodward *op. cit.* p. 24; 'Please send every available craft . . .' Ramsay report p. 3300; *Queen of the Channel* sunk, Lord *op. cit.* p. 98; The Royal Norfolks massacre, Cyril Jolly *The Vengeance of Private Pooley*; The Royal Warwicks massacre, Rev. Leslie Aitken *Massacre on the Road to Dunkirk*; Sepp Dietrich's generosity, Barker *op. cit.* p. 65; Arthur Baxter's story, Baxter letter; Tom Peck's story, Peck INT; John Hammond's story, Hammond letter; Hurrell's leg injury, Hurrell IWM; Paddy Boyd and the horse, Baldwin INT; 'Stench and filth and gore', McDonald IWM; Firing smoke shells at tanks, Baldwin INT; 'You had to admire their shooting', Dennis INT; 'We had been so intent . . .' Vollans IWM; I was unable to resist . . .' Southall IWM; 'Slept badly . . .' Werth *op. cit.* p. 96 'So after dark . . .' Dennis INT; Stan Smith and the shampoo, Smith INT; Champagne in an enamel mug, Taylor INT; 'There was a group of soldiers . . .' *Manchester Evening News* 12 March 1980; 'A little pimple . . .' Hadley *op. cit.* p. 119; 'A freak of nature . . .' Blaxland Ms IWM; 'We were a rabble', Catt INT; 'Like going to a football match . . .' John Platt memoirs IWM; 'Into this pancake . . .' Gunbuster' *Return Via Dunkirk* p. 184; 'Daddy's old Army bedroll', Macdonald IWM; 'Most of us changed . . .' Matthew IWM; The German escaper, Southall IWM; 'Make them march properly', Brooks *op. cit.* p. 104; 'In Guardsmanlike fashion . . .' Griffin INT; 'Not a star in the sky . . .' Brodie IWM; 'The centre of the road . . .' Sutton IWM; 'The most devastating picture . . .' Keitel *op. cit.* p. 114.

CHAPTER 14: Y for Danger

'Unlimited numbers falling back . . .' ADM 188/788A PRO; 'The red blaze . . .' Woodward *op. cit.* p. 32; 'Keep on sending any ships', ADM 188/788A PRO; 'It took us some time . . .' Capt. T. Kerr letter 75/99/2 IWM; 'An untidy group . . .' Arnold Johnson IWM; 'There appeared to be . . .' Harman *op. cit.* p. 145; 'As far as the eye could see . . .' Hadley *op. cit.* p. 137; 'Thousands and thousands . . .' Horrocks *op. cit.* p. 89; 'My heart, already in . . .' Macdonald IWM; 'I saw all these chaps . . .' Griffin INT; 'The wonderful queues', Baldwin INT; 'The touching thing . . .' *Guardian* 4 June 1980; 'To see them out there . . .' Baldwin INT; 'Extremely good, no panic', Carpenter INT; At that moment . . .' *Dunkirk* BBC TV

3 June 1980; 'But they took no notice', Nettle *op. cit.* pp. 26–27; 'You're not one of my lot . . .' *Manchester Evening News* 12 March 1980; 'Just as it would . . .' Shorrock IWM; 'While we were there . . .' Boyce INT; 'A Maltese steward . . .' Bartlett *op. cit.* p. 119; Sinking of *Wakeful*, ADM 199/792 PRO; Sinking of *Grafton*, ADM 199/786 PRO; 'Can you pull an oar?', Boyce INT; 'Whole ship was trembling . . .' Bartlett *op. cit.* pp. 120–121; 'Everybody started singing . . .' Boyce INT; 'They were mostly unwilling . . .' Lt. R. Bill report ADM 199/787 PRO; 'I personally noticed . . .' ADM 199/787 PRO; Sinking of *Crested Eagle*, ibid; Cdr. Cordeaux's bravery, Papers of Edward Cordeaux IWM; Sinking of *Gracie Fields* ADM 199/787 PRO; 'The Admiralty want men . . .' *Dunkirk* BBC TV 3 June 1980; 'Oh, the terror . . .' Macdonald IWM; 'With hope in their hearts . . .' Walsham IWM; George Hill lies flat, Richard Collier *Sands of Dunkirk* p. 129; 'It was dipping its wings . . .' Vollans IWM; 'I hated Dunkirk', Barker *op. cit.* p. 108; 'A solitary plane . . .' Bristow IWM; 'They gave these helpless chaps . . .' Nettle *op. cit.* p. 50; 'A desperate, frantic cry . . .' Blaxland Ms IWM; 'A feeling of ultimate disaster', Shorrock IWM; 'I was lying on deck . . .' Stevenson INT; 'I was about to make . . .' Hurrell IWM; 'I said to my mate . . .' BBC TV 3 June 1980; 'We couldn't get the bike . . .' Baldwin INT; 'According to our regimental . . .' Catt INT; 'I had a drink of *vin blanc* . . .' Toomey IWM; 'I was in a queue . . .' Smith INT; The tin of apricots, S L Wright Ms 84/26/1 IWM; The tin of sardines, Hooker IWM; 'A milling crowd . . .' Brodie IWM; 'Some of the tins . . .' Bill Richardson INT; 'A French Army captain . . .' Harold J. Dibbens diary 80/30/1 IWM; 'The French staff at Dunkirk . . .' ADM 188/788A PRO.

CHAPTER 15: The Cracked Alliance

Gen. Tesseire's complaint, Harman *op. cit.* pp. 157–158; 'So we waited a bit . . .' BBC TV 3 June 1980; 'As they came nearer . . .' Westropp IWM; The defence of Nieuport, WO 197/119 PRO; 'Under continuous shelling', Hewitt INT; 'Machine-gunners advanced . . .' WO 197/119 PRO: 'There was this column . . .' Dennis INT; Langley's fortress, Langley *op. cit.* pp. 47–48; 'Dunkirk, it must regretfully . . .' Weygand, *op. cit.* p. 79; 'For the first time I sensed . . .' Spears *op. cit.* p. 250; 'Increasingly bad relations . . .' Weygand *op. cit.* p. 76; 'My instructions are . . .' ADM 199/792 PRO; Gen. Champon stranded, Lord *op. cit.* pp. 175–176; Wake-Walker goes to Dunkirk, Rear Adm. W F Wake-Walker *A Personal Record* IWM; 'It would be a needless triumph . . .' Blaxland *op. cit.* p. 329; 'This surprised me', Montgomery *op. cit.* p. 63; Dinner with Gort, Wake-Walker IWM; The Paris meeting of 31 May, Spears *op. cit.* pp. 295–308, Churchill *op. cit.* Vol. II p. 97; 'Now I know where I am', WO 167/124 PRO; 'I stayed behind . . .' Montgomery *op. cit.* p. 64; 'Alex, go over there . . .' Papers of Brig. Cyrus Greenslade IWM; Alexander-Abrial meeting, Harman *op. cit.* pp. 190–192, Lord *op. cit.* pp. 182–183, Nigel Nicolson *Alex* pp. 104–105; 'To think I brought you . . .' Greenslade IWM; 'I had not realized the anxiety . . .' Wake-Walker IWM; 'Bravery, Endurance, Fortitude', *Daily Mirror* 31 May 1940; 'You should withdraw your forces . . .' Lord *op. cit.* p. 183; 'The men were happy . . .' Rowe *op. cit.* p. 215; 'There is an impression here . . .' Lord *op. cit.* p. 209; 'We do not want to find . . .' *ibid*; 'It was an unforgettable sight', Birch IWM; 'I was occasionally nodding off . . .' Taylor INT; 'Like hitting a brick wall', Dennis INT; 'Away we went . . .' Hewitt INT; 'Men promptly sallied forth . . .' Farley Ms; Ervine-Andrews's VC, *London Gazette* 26 July 1940; Will Lacy's walking stick, *Scarborough E. News* series; 'There was a most frightful crash . . .' Langley *op. cit.* pp. 54–55.

Source Notes

CHAPTER 16: Little Ships, Few Planes
The Little Ships, ADM 199/788 PRO; Tough Bros. collect the boats, History of Tough Bros. of Teddington, Misc. 68, Item 1047 IWM; 'We rather shrank . . .' *London Evening News* 5 June 1940; 'It was like Piccadilly Circus . . .' BBC TV 3 June 1980; 'We had no charts . . .' ADM 199/787 PRO; 'Beautiful yachting weather', ADM 199/788 PRO; '*Ou est l'armée britannique?*' Lord *op. cit.* p. 161; Peter Bennett's story, ADM 199/788A PRO; Robert Irving's story, ADM 199/787 PRO; 'Being deaf . . .' *ibid*; 'We had our work cut out . . .' ADM 199/788A PRO; Charles Lightoller's story, Lord *op. cit.* pp. 225–227, Nettle *op. cit.* pp. 115–116; C W Read's report, ADM 199/788 PRO; Owners' complaints, Tough Bros. history IWM; Refusals to sail, ADM 199/786, 788 and 788A PRO; The lifeboats row, Charles Vince *Storm on the Waters* pp. 21–44; Griggs brothers dismissed, *Folkestone Express* 29 June 1940; 'I hailed these conditions . . .' Wake-Walker IWM; Sinking of *Keith*, ADM 199/792 PRO; 'I remember having read . . .' Greenslade IWM; 'Why so friendly?', Barker *op. cit.* p. 184; 'Where's your bloody aeroplane?', W G Murdoch letter to author; Dowding's battle, Terraine *op. cit.* pp. 150–153; 'Atmosphere of devastating strain', Agar *op. cit.* p. 71; Pilots lost to little avail, A E Havercroft letter to author; 'Every time a Hurricane . . .' George Banham INT; 'Our ships nearly always . . .' Wake-Walker IWM; Shooting down a Blenheim, Brodie IWM; 'What bloody poor shots', John Harris *Dunkirk: The Storms of War* p. 108; Dill's memo, Greenslade IWM; 'To lie helpless . . .' Hadley *op. cit.* p. 80.

CHAPTER 17: 'Allez Bloody Vite'
'Tomorrow we'll either . . .' Wake-Walker IWM; 'I don't think . . .' Willy INT; 'One was always expecting . . .' Woodward *op. cit.* p. 41; 'It looked quite smart', *ibid* p. 51; 'To our bitter disappointment', ADM 199/787 PRO; 'Not a Tommy to be had', *ibid*; 'Much to my fury . . .' S J L Hill IWM; '*Allez bloody vite*', W G Hewett *A Jotting from Dunkirk Beaches* IWM; 'I summoned my limited store . . .' ADM 199/788 PRO; 'They naturally considered . . .' *ibid*; French troops were either demoralized . . .' ADM 199/792 PRO; *Kestrel* and *Grouse* ADM 199/787 PRO; 'They held a meeting', Nettle *op. cit.* p. 114; 'The pier was stiff . . .' ADM 199/786 PRO; 'I saw the French . . .' Bill Richardson INT; Barlone's escape, Barlone *op. cit.* pp. 59–63; 'Which I had stuck to . . .' J B Wright IWM; 'Our officer was a big bloke', Rhodda IWM; 'I was careful to transfer . . .' Farley Ms; 'I knew I could reach it', Foster IWM; Smith and *Yorkshire Lass*, Rob Smith INT; 'We saw no beachmaster', Arnold Johnson IWM; 'We saw the top of a head', Catt INT; 'One of the great tragedies . . .' Richardson INT; 'We sat out there wallowing', Ellingworth INT; 'Rather like John Snagge', Hadley *op. cit.* p. 141; David Strangeways' escape, Rev. Canon David Strangeways letter, 21 August 1978 IWM; The lorry jetties, Lord *op. cit.* pp. 164–166, Barker *op. cit.* p. 189; 'Some 15 lorries were driven . . .' Henry J. Cornwell 82/33/1 IWM; 'Someone handed us a sandbag', Rhodda IWM; McClelland's report, ADM 199/788 PRO; 'I could only just hobble', J E Wright IWM; 'Remember your pals, boys', ADM 199/788A PRO; 'It was no more than . . .' Bristow IWM; 'Somehow we kept going . . .' Vollans IWM.

CHAPTER 18: 'Is Anyone There?'
'Thanks largely to the gallant stand . . .' Keitel *op. cit.* p. 115; 'We did not altogether like . . .' *Scarborough E. News* series; 'The British troops were not . . .' Nicolson *op. cit.* p. 112; 'They'll get you, Wells', *ibid*; 'Weary, hungry and scared', Macdonald IWM; 'That musty, military smell', Rhodes *op. cit.* pp. 213–214; Toby

Taylor's story, Taylor letter to author; 'I went down below . . .' J E Wright IWM; 'The final stupidity', Sutton IWM; 'The wardroom presented . . .' ADM 199/786 PRO; 'Greeted kindly . . .' Brabyn diary IWM; 'The wounded seem to need . . .' Manley IWM; 'Anyone down there . . . ?' Bristow IWM; 'There was this flaming great hole', Catt INT; 'I was given hot cocoa', Southall IWM; 'The bullet hit the ground . . .' Edwards INT; 'A soldier was playing about . . .' Westropp IWM; The Chapeau Rouge, Len Wilson INT; 'This will see you home', Lord *op. cit.* p. 262; 'Most of them collapsed', ADM 199/786 PRO; Langley meets the enemy, Langley *op. cit.* pp. 56, 59; 'The whole floor was covered . . .' Shorrock IWM; Hospital ships bombed, Ramsay's report; The rescue armada, *ibid*; 'French still maintain . . .' *ibid*; 'I used to dread it', Willy INT; 'BEF evacuated', Lord *op. cit.* p. 247; 'Is anyone there?', Nicolson *op. cit.* p. 113; Oelhaven's escape, Bekker *op. cit.* p. 130; 'Plenty of ships', Ramsay's report; 'A most disappointing night', Wake-Walker IWM; 'It was all silent', D C Holder letter to author; 'We opened a tin of bacon . . .' Banham INT; 'We are coming back . . .' Lord *op. cit.* p. 252; 'I hoped and believed . . .' *ibid* pp. 252–253; 'Each night had been thought . . .' Wake-Walker IWM; 'The whole scene was filled . . .' Lord *op. cit.* p. 261.

CHAPTER 19: The Last Act

'The French Army had ceased . . .' Blaxland *op. cit.* p. 378; 'The newspaper have . . .' Churchill *op. cit.* Vol. II p. 172; 'Senility, pessimism and ambition', Collier *1940* p. 107; The armistice signing, Horne *op. cit.* pp. 507–508; 'Now Thank We all Our God', Keitel *op. cit.* p. 114; 'We still dispose . . .' Rowe *op. cit.* p. 287; Casualty figures, Horne *op. cit.* p. 510; Air losses, Terraine *op. cit.* pp. 162–164; Shipping losses, War Museum, Dunkirk; 'He was hooted down', Farley letter to author; 'I just couldn't help it', Toomey IWM; 'It was just as if . . .' Catt INT; 'Noise like a German bomber', Bartlett *op. cit.* p. 125; Three to a cell, Phillips INT; 'All the pinpricks . . .' Brodie IWM; 'Gradually our sense of values . . .' Hadley *op. cit.* pp. 144–145; 'England's neck will be wrung . . .' Barber *op. cit.* p. 281; 'The most important thing . . .' Collier *1940* p. 135; 'My duty to appeal . . .' Bullock *op. cit.* pp. 592–593; 'In those weeks . . .' Allingham *op. cit.* p. 163; 'Dunkirk is more than . . .' BBC TV 3 June 1980.

Bibliography

BOOKS

Agar, Herbert, *Britain Alone* (London 1972)
Aitken, Leslie, *Massacre on the Road to Dunkirk* (London 1988)
Allingham, Margery, *The Oaken Heart* (London 1941)
Amery, Leopold, *My Political Life, Vol. III, Unforgiving Years 1929–1940 (London 1955)*
Avon, Earl of, *The Reckoning*, (London 1965)
Barber, Noel, *The Week France Fell*, (London 1976)
Barker, A J, *Dunkirk – The Great Escape* (London 1977)
Barlone, Denis, *A French Officer's Diary* (trans. A V Cass) (London 1942)
Bartlett, Sir Basil, *My First War* (London 1940)
Beckles, Gordon, *Dunkirk and After* (London 1940)
Bekker, Cajus, *The Luftwaffe War Diaries*, (London 1966)
Benoist-Méchin, J. *Sixty Days That Shook the West* (London 1963)
Bethell, Nicholas, *The War Hitler Won* (London 1972)
Blanckaert, Serge, *Dunkerque 1939–1945* (Dunkirk 1984)
Blaxland, Gregory, *Destination Dunkirk* (London 1973)
Blumentritt, Günther, *Von Rundstedt: The Soldier and the Man* (London 1952)
Bond, Brian, *France and Belgium, 1939–1940* (London 1975)
Boothe, Clare, *European Spring* (London 1941)
Brooks, Graham, *Grand Party*, (London 1941)
Bryant, Sir Arthur, *The Turn of the Tide 1939–1943: The Diaries of Viscount Alanbrooke* (London 1957)
Bullock, Alan, *Hitler: A Study in Tyranny* (London 1965)
Butler, Lt. Col. Ewan, *Keep the Memory Green: The Story of Dunkirk* (London 1955)
Chalfont, Alun, *Montgomery of Alamein* (London 1976)
Churchill, Winston S., *The Second World War: Vol I The Gathering Storm* (London 1948)
—— *Vol II Their Finest Hour* (London 1949)
Clay, Ewart, *The Path of the 50th* (London 1950)
Collier, Richard, *The Sands of Dunkirk* (London 1961)
—— *1940, The World in Flames* (London 1979)
Cook, Don, *Charles de Gaulle* (London 1984)
Deighton, Len, *Blitzkrieg* (London 1979)
Divine, David, *The Nine Days of Dunkirk* (London 1959)
Ellis, Maj. L F, *Welsh Guards at War* (London 1946)

—— *The War in France and Flanders 1939–1940* (London 1953)
Feiling, Keith, *The Life of Neville Chamberlain* (London 1946)
Glover, Michael, *The Fight for the Channel Ports* (London 1985)
Gray, Bernard, *War Reporter* (London 1942)
Greenwall, Harry J., *When France Fell* (London 1958)
Grossmith, Frederick, *Dunkirk: A Miracle of Deliverance* (London 1979)
Guderian, Heinz, *Panzer Leader* (London 1952)
'Gunbuster', *Return Via Dunkirk* (London 1940)
Habe, Hans, *A Thousand Shall Fall* (London 1942)
Halder, Franz, *War Diary (ed. Hans-Adolf Jacobsen)* (Stuttgart 1962)
—— *Hitler As War Lord* (London 1950)
Hadley, Peter, *Third Class to Dunkirk* (London 1944)
Harris, John, *Dunkirk: The Storms of War* (Newton Abbot 1980)
Harrison, Tom, and Madge, Charles, *War Begins at Home* (London 1940)
Harman, Nicholas, *Dunkirk: The Necessary Myth* (London 1980)
Hart, B H Liddell, *The Other Side of the Hill* (London 1951)
Hay, Ian, *The Battle of Flanders* (London 1941)
Holding, Robert, *Since I Bore Arms* (privately pub. 1987)
Horne, Alastair, *To Lose a Battle* (London 1969)
—— *The French Army and Politics 1870–1970* (London 1984)
Horrocks, Lt. Gen. Sir Brian, *A Full Life* (London 1960)
Jackson, Robert, *The Fall of France* (London 1975)
—— *Air War over France May–June 1940* (London 1979)
—— *Dunkirk: The Disaster and the Magnificence* (London 1978)
Jolly, Cyril, *The Vengeance of Private Pooley* (London 1956)
Karslake, Basil, *The Last Act* (London 1979)
Keitel, Wilhelm, *Memoirs* (London 1965)
Kesselring, Albert, *Memoirs* (London 1953)
Langer, William L., *The Undeclared War* (New York 1953)
Langley, Lt. Col. J M, *Fight Another day* (London 1974)
Liss, Ulrich, *Westfront* (Neckergemund 1959)
Longmate, Norman, *How We Lived Then* (London 1971)
Lord, Walter, *The Miracle of Dunkirk* (London 1983)
Lyall, Gavin, *The War in the Air 1939–1945* (London 1968)
Macksey, Kenneth, *Guderian, Panzer General* (London 1975)
Macleod, Iain, *Neville Chamberlain* (London 1961)
Macleod R., and Kelly, Denis, *The Ironside Diaries* (London 1962)
Masefield, John, *The Nine Days' Wonder* (London 1941)
Maurois, André, *The Battle of France* (London 1940)
Minns, Raynes, *Bombers and Mash* (London 1980)
Montgomery, Field Marshal Bernard, *Memoirs* (London 1958)
Moss, Arthur, and Kirby, Elizabeth, *Animals Were There* (London 1945)
Murrow, Edward R., *This Is London* (London 1961)
Nettle, Cdr. Stanley, *Dunkirk: Old Men Remember* (Frome, 1988)
Nicolson, Nigel, *Alex* (London 1973)
Noble, Ronnie, *Shoot First* (London 1955)
Prüller, Wilhelm, *Diary of a German Soldier* (London 1963)
Rankin, Eric, *A Chaplain's Diary* (privately pub.)
Retallack, John, *The Welsh Guards* (London 1981)
Rhodes, Anthony, *Sword of Bone* (London 1942)

Bibliography

Rommel, Erwin, *The Rommel Papers (ed. B.H. Liddell Hart)* (London 1953)
Rowe, Vivian, *The Great Wall of France* (London 1959)
Ruge, Vice-Adm. Friedrich, *Sea Warfare* (London 1957)
Schachtman, Tom, *The Phony War 1939–1940* (New York 1982)
Schmidt, Paul, *Hitler's Interpreter* (London 1951)
Shirer, William L., *Berlin Diary* (London 1941)
Slessor, John, *The Central Blue* (London 1956)
Spears, Maj-Gen. Sir Edward, *Assignment to Catastrophe (Vols I and II)* (London 1954)
Terraine, John, *The Right of the Line: The Royal Air Force in the European War 1939–1945* (London 1985)
Toland, John, *Adolf Hitler* (London 1977)
Trevor-Roper, H R (ed.), *Hitler's War Directives 1939–1945* (London 1964)
Trials of Major War Criminals Before the International Military Tribunal (Nuremberg)
Warlimont, Walter, *Inside Hitler's Headquarters* (London 1964)
Werth, Alexander, *The Last Days of Paris* (London 1940)
Weygand, Commandant Jacques, *The Role of Gen. Weygand: Conversations With His Son* (London 1948)
Woodward, David, *Ramsay at War* (London 1957)
Young, Desmond, *Rommel* (London 1950)

NEWSPAPERS

Bournemouth Times
Brighton Evening Argus
Daily Express
Daily Mail
Daily Mirror
Daily Telegraph
Dover Express
East Kent Times
Folkestone Express

Folkestone and Dist. Herald
Isle of Thanet Gazette
Kentish Gazette and Canterbury Express
London Evening News
Manchester Evening News
News Chronicle
Scarborough Evening News
Sheerness Times and Guardian
The Times

Index

Index

Cassandra of *Daily Mirror* 64, 141
Catt, Joe 7, 14, 17–18, 179, 213, 223, 235
Caven, Lt. John 128–9
Chamberlain, Neville 13, 16, 29, 49, 50–1, 63
Champon, General 139, 186
Chandler, Mowbray 173, 174
Charlesworth, Captain Barney 187
Chichester-Constable, Maj. Claude 152
Churchill, Winston 10–11, 14, 50, 52, 57, 63; on French 22, 23; and Panzer breakthrough 75, 81, 98–9; and Weygand Plan 94–5, 100, 105; and Calais 118, 119; and Belgian surrender 140, 141; and evacuation 121, 122, 123, 127, 128, 149, (French share) 186, 188–9, 190, 208, (Gort's) 9, 187; and rearguard 189, 229; rebuilds BEF 232; and *Lancastria* 232–3; defiance 236
Clarke, Dennis 73
Clarke, Lt. Col. R. L. 52, 54, 70–1
Clifton, Brig. Arthur 183, 184
Clouston, Cdr. Jack 166, 169, 173
Codrington, HMS 228
Coldstream Guards 82, 108; *see also* Langley
Cole, June 8
Cole, Ray 11
Collins, Tom, RA 7–8
Collis, Les 176
Comfort 171
Constant Nymph 201
Cook, Colonel Palmer 14, 86
Corap, General André-Georges 58, 75, 92
Cordeaux, Edward 173–4
Cornwell, Henry 215
Count Dracula 197
Crested Eagle 172, 173
Cullingford, Rev. C. H. D. 102

Dabner, Tom 136
Daladier, Edouard 49–50
Davey, George 38
Davidge, Roy 4
Davidson, Brigadier Francis 56
Davy, Lt. Col. George 140
Dean, Captain Brian 226
Deere, Alan 205
Dennis, Harry 13, 37, 76, 114, 158, 159, 184, 193–4, 231
Dibbens, Harold 180, 214
Diesing (Luftwaffe meteorologist) 42, 53
Dietrich, Gen. Josef 'Sepp' 152–3
Dill, Gen. Sir John 19, 122, 185, 188, 189, 190, 206
Dixon, Norman, RE 45, 132–3
Dowding, ACM Sir Hugh 12, 65, 205–6
Driver, Harry and Arthur 213
Duchess of Fife 210
Duggan, R. 128
Duke of Wellington's Regt. 214
Durham Light Inf. 73, 96, 97, 136, 151–2

East Lancashire Regt., 1st Bn. 195
East Surrey Regt. 4, 13, 80–1, 176, 220–2; *see also*: Dennis; Taylor
Eden, Anthony 14, 29, 190, 192, 234

Edwards, Bill 38, 112, 147, 224
Ellingworth, Don 13–14, 70, 77, 83, 88, 91, 213–14
Emmington, Sgt. Bob 89
Endeavour 197
Ervine-Andrews, Capt. Harold, VC 195
Essex Regt. 224
Everett, Captain Bob 182
Express, HMS 173, 230

Farley, Frank 139, 143–4, 194–5, 211–12, 234
Farrer, John 107, 114
Fenella, HMS 172, 173
Fisher, Cdr. Ralph 170–2
Fisher, Gerry 6
Fitzalan-Howard, Lt. Miles 90
Foremost 102 201
Foster, WO Harold 3, 76, 82–3, 212
Fox-Pitt, Brig. William 117
Franklyn, Maj. Gen. Harold 95–6
Furness, Hon. Christopher, VC 101, 103–4

Galatea 201
Gallagher, O. D. 59
Gamelin, Gen. Maurice 24–5, 29, 50, 56, 57, 62; replaced 81, 82
Gardner, Bill 37
Garland, Flying Offr. Donald, VC 65
Gaskin, Albert 18, 20
Gaulle, Gen. Charles de 24, 80
George VI 9, 12, 47–8, 63, 120, 192
Georges, Gen. Alphonse 75, 81–2, 186
Giblett, Maj. W. C. 68
Gilbert, Capt. Alan 2
Giraud, Gen. Henri 57, 92–3
Glen Gower 222
Gloucester, Duke of 48, 82
Gloucestershire Regt., 2nd Bn. 89
Golden Eagle 173–4, 200, 206, 229
Göring, Hermann 13, 15, 53, 61, 164; and Halt Order 120, 149–50
Gort, 6th Viscount 19, 30–1, 37; 48, 58, 82; and Weygand 98, 99; and Arras 95, 102, 105, 115; Escaut line 91, 94, 107, 112, 115; retreat 119, 120, 122–3, 144, 181, 185–6, 187–8; evacuated 9, 187, 189–90, 191–2; further career 235
Gossamer, HMS 166, 171, 216
Gracie Fields 174
Grafton, HMS 169–70, 171–2
Gray, Bernard 20, 47, 48, 51–2, 59, 64, 103, 117
Gray, Sergeant Thomas, VC 65
Green Howards 73, 196; 5th Bn. 45, 70, 100–1, 102, 146, 219; 6th Bn. 114
Greenslade, Brig. Cyrus 190, 191, 204
Greenwall, Henry 15, 49
Grenade, HMS 172–3
Grenadier Guards 3, 77–8, 89, 108–9, 111, 129–31, 158; *see also* Foster
Greyhound, HMS 213
Griffin, George 2, 8, 101, 103–4, 167
Griffiths, Guardsman Tom 103, 104
Griffiths, Sgt. D. H. 101–2
Griggs, 'Buller' and Richard 203–4

253

Index

Maurois, André 48, 69
Middlesex Regt. 76–7, 138, 139, 146
Military Police 2, 88, 124, 215
Mohnke, Wilhelm 153
Mona's Queen 128, 174
Montgomery, Gen. Bernard Law 10, 19, 28, 67, 144, 235; on state of BEF 16, 17; leadership 36–7, 45, 72, 137–8; to 2 Corps 187; and Gort's successor 189–90
Montrose, HMS 169
Mordal, Jacques 181
Morel, Mme Madeleine 5
Morris, Frank 132
Mosquito, HMS 201
MTB 107 230
Munster, Captain the Earl of 120, 187
Murdoch, Bill 204

Neave, Lt. Robert 44
Nettle, Lt. Stanley, RNVR 168–9
New Prince of Wales 200
Newman, Maj. Philip 225
Nicholls, L/Col. Harry, VC 108–9
Nicholson, Brig. Claude 118–19
Noble, Ronnie 16, 71, 86–7
Noël, Marcel 112
Nolan, Tom 173, 174
Noon, Frederick 146
Normanby, Lord 70
Normania 174
Northumberland, Lt. the Duke of 108
Northumberland Fusiliers 100, 103

O'Callaghan, William 152
Oelhaven, First Lt. von 228
O'Shea, Father Cockie 225
Olivier, G. D. 209
Oxfordshire and Bucks Light Infantry 89

Paris 155, 227
Parry, Dave 38
Pascholl, HMS 209
Patterson, Capt. Joe 5, 10, 59–60, 69–70, 84–5, 109, 110, 147–8, 211
Pearce, Lt. Frank 102
Pearce, Josephine 48–9
Peck, Pte. Tom 6, 17, 58, 155–6, 167
Persia (tug) 223
Pétain, Marshal H. P. 23, 82, 233
Petre, Maj. Gen. Richard 93, 100–5
Philby, Kim 59, 117
Philip, Percy 112
Phillips, Irene 8
Phillips, Col. Reg. 88–9, 90, 235
Podmore, Rev. Reginald 153
Polly Johnson, SS 172
Pooley, Albert 152
Pound, Admiral Sir Dudley 186
Pownall, Lt. Gen. Henry 95, 100, 187
Priestley, J. B. 197
Princess Elizabeth 215
Pring, Peter 3–4
Prioux, General 144

Prudential 203
Prüller, Wilhelm 27, 54, 142

Queen of the Channel 151
Quinn, Rev. Gough 77, 110–11

Rackham, Lt. Col. B. B. 146
Ramsay, Admiral Sir Bertram 126–7, 174, 205, 229, 235
Ramsdale, Derek 17, 26, 58–9, 66, 120–1
Rankin, Eric 38, 39
Rayner, Major Ralph 67, 74
Read, Lt. C. W. RNR 202
Reinberger, Major Helmut 42–3
Reinhardt, Gen. Georg Hans 117
Reynaud, Paul 40, 50, 75, 81, 82, 233; and Weygand Plan 100, 105; and British retreat 118, 123, 189, 232
Rhodda, S. L. 54, 71, 73–4, 83, 84, 115–16, 211, 215–16
Rhodes, Anthony 23, 30–1, 48, 49, 55, 60, 69, 77, 144, 220
Richardson, Bill 179–80, 213
Richardson, Cdr. Hector 164–5
Richthofen, General the Baron von 150
Robinson, Cdr. Charles 170, 171
Rommel, Gen. Erwin 62–3, 78, 79, 80, 97, 120, 137, 231
Roosevelt, Franklin Delano 233
Rothband, Geoffrey 21
Royal Artillery Regiments; 2nd Medium 143; 30th Field 52; 32nd Field *see* Macdonald; 53rd Anti-Tank 153–5; 53rd Field 146; 53rd Medium 183; 59th Medium 184; 65th Field 30, 46–7, 52 (*see also* Baldwin); 91st Field *see*: Shorrock; Whitmarsh; 92nd Field 36, 133 (*see also* Manley); *see also*: Canon; Collins
Royal Air Force Squadrons: (12 Battle) 65; (54) 204; (92) 205; (114) 64
Royal Army Medical Corps: 45, 125, 225–6; *see also*: McDonald, J.; Patterson; Wilson
Royal Army Ordnance Corps *see*: Cardy; Hurrell
Royal Army Service Corps *see*: Boyce; Edwards; Johnson, Arnold; Matthew
Royal Berkshire Regt. 152
Royal Daffodil 178
Royal Eagle 179–80, 210–11
Royal East Kent Regt. *see*: Blaxland; Harwood
Royal Engineers 113; 250 Field Co. 215; Territorial *see* Cook; *see also*: Booth; Dixon; Hooker; Johnson, Alan; Sedgwick
Royal Horse Artillery 14, 18; *see also* Rhodes, Anthony
Royal Lancers, 12th 59, 72, 183
Royal National Lifeboat Institution 204
Royal Norfolk Regt. 6, 47, 108, 152; *see also* Peck
Royal Northumberland Fusiliers 100, 103
Royal Scots Fusiliers 47, 72, 88, 152
Royal Signals 35; *see also*: Brodie; Fisher; Nolan; Rayner; Rhodda; Vollans
Royal Sussex Regt. 93; *see also*: Catt; Holding
Royal Tank Regt., 3rd 118
Royal Warwickshire Regt., 2nd Bn. 152